YOUR BABY BIBLE

The ULTIMATE GUIDE to Having a BABY

your baby club

FOREWORD

As the UK's #1 Baby Club, it's important to us that all you hopeful parents and parents-to-be are provided with the most up to date, reliable and factual information in order to help guide you through conception, pregnancy, parenthood and everything in between. From family planning and what to expect in each trimester of pregnancy, to knowing what's normal for your baby, weaning recipes and how to support their development, we've brought you the best experts, specialists, and medical practitioners to bring you: *Your Baby Bible: The Ultimate Guide to Having a Baby.*

With the help from our Official Midwife, Louise Broadbridge of *Let's Talk Birth and Baby* and our other resident experts, our Head of Content & Social, Jasmine Gurney and her team have been able to put this guide together to ensure you're prepared for every eventuality and every scenario you may face along the road to parenthood. This guide is intended to cut through that airy-fairy, rose-tinted-glasses view on pregnancy and parenthood and give you an idea of what it's really like; what to expect *(mucus and all)* and how to do all those things parents struggle with most, ensuring both you and baby are happy, healthy, and prepared for every scenario or poo-nami. Whether you're going it alone, with your partner or doing a combination of the two, you can read this guide as often as you'd like - before conception, throughout pregnancy and beyond, it's here to help you every step of the way.

For those of you who have just peed a positive and have no idea what to do next, you've pretty much hit the jackpot with this guide. We'll be there to hold your hand through thick and thin, from your first GP appointment, to waving a tearful goodbye on your toddler's first day at nursery. For the more seasoned of parents, this will be a great refresher, and you may even find additional information you've not seen before or learn a new way of doing things. Whatever your experience, grab a cuppa and get reading, enjoy every minute of it. Believe us when we say, '*You've got this!*'

Tell us your story. If you have a story to tell, an experience, anecdote, or tips for other parents, why not share your journey with us on Facebook and Instagram *(@yourbabyclubuk)* or email us your experience on bloggers@yourbabyclub.co.uk along with a short bio about yourself.

your baby club

CONTENTS

CONTENTS

CONTENTS

WHO ARE WE?

Your Baby Club began in 2013 when our co-founders wanted to change how the baby industry marketed to parents. We wanted to take out the spam, the incessant phone calls and mailers and put the industry's best parent and baby offers, promotions, discounts, and competitions in front of parents and parents-to-be, all in one place. Members can choose exactly what offers they like and who they want to hear from - putting them in control.

Since then, we have amassed over 3 million members in the UK alone, making us the fastest growing network of mums, dads, carers, guardians, and foster parents in the UK.

YourBabyClub.co.uk has also become the go-to place, not only for the hottest offers, but for information from our team of experts, as well as anecdotes, tips, and stories - written for parents, by parents, stripping down topics to unfiltered and unapologetic discussions, confessions, and advice.

Whether you're struggling with conception, wanting to prepare for labour mentally and physically, having trouble getting your baby to sleep, feed or toilet train, whether you have a picky eater or are just wanting to pull your hair out whilst your once angelic child's hit the terrible twos, our community of real parents, parent bloggers and experts are with you through it all.

DISCLAIMER

The information in this book should not be treated as a substitute or equivalent for advice from qualified medical professionals. Do consult your midwife or GP if any concerns or issues arise throughout your pregnancy and beyond. The authors, nor the publisher can be held responsible for any loss, consequence or claim arising out of the use, or misuse, of the suggestions made in this book, or the failure to follow independently sourced medical advice.

The advice and examples given in this book are based on real experiences, practices and have been written or checked by medical professionals, however, may not be suitable or relevant to your specific needs. Every pregnancy and every woman is different. Should you need further advice, do not hesitate to contact your GP, midwife, health visitor or paediatrician for more tailored assistance.

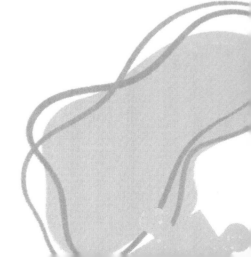

OUR EXPERTS

Throughout the global pandemic, we quickly recognised the importance of giving parents the resources they needed, knowing that they had been cut off from accessing them during lockdown. This made us determined to provide as much support as possible by teaming up with hand-picked experts from around the UK. We ran live Q&As every day and were able to provide valuable insight and expert advice to parents with the help of these specialists. It's this same expert panel, alongside some others we've brought on board, that have enabled us to bring you this resource-packed book.

Before we get into all the useful information, here's our team of experts, their links, and social handles in case you want to get further services from them.

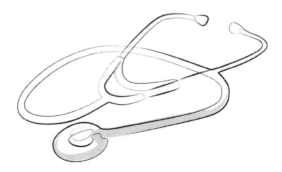

YOUR BABY CLUB OFFICIAL MIDWIFE

Louise Broadbridge RM, BSc, MW, DipHb - Let's Talk Birth and Baby Limited.

Louise is a senior registered midwife, founder of *Let's Talk Birth and Baby*, wife, and mum of two. She strives for honesty surrounding the transition from young and carefree, to pregnancy, early parenthood and beyond. Louise is a strong advocate for both breast and formula feeding and feels it's important that whatever method is chosen by parents, that it is well supported.

Instagram: @thehonestmidwife | www.letstalkbirthandbaby.co.uk
Louise@letstalkbirthandbaby.co.uk

NHS CONSULTANT PAEDIATRICIAN, AUTHOR AND PROFESSOR

Dr. Carly Fertleman (Dr. Carly) MD, FRCPCH, MSc, MB BChir, BA (Hons) Cantab, SFHEA, FAcadMEd - Caroline Fertleman

Dr Carly is a consultant paediatrician and professor of Paediatrics at University College London *(UCL)* Great Ormond Street Institute of Child Health, with over 30 years' experience. She is the co-author of award-winning parenting book, *'Your Baby Week by Week'* which has sold over a quarter of a million copies.

Instagram: @drcarlyfertleman | www.carolinefertleman.co.uk
Twitter: @drcarlyf | Book: bit.ly/drcarly

PAEDIATRIC SLEEP CONSULTANT

Carla Berlin - Snooze Tots

Carla set up Snooze Tots to not only help babies learn to sleep but get parents their much-needed Zzz's! She works with children of all ages experiencing sleep issues and does not believe in just shutting the door until the morning and letting a baby cry it out. It is about finding an approach that suits the baby's age and temperament as well as what suits the parents.

Instagram: @snooze_tots | www.snoozetots.com
Carla@snoozetots.com

EMPLOYMENT LAW SOLICITOR & WOMEN'S RIGHTS SPECIALIST

Emma-Jane Taylor-Moran - Rebel Law Ltd

Emma-Jane is a mum of four *(aged 7 to 30)* and grandmother. Like most women, she juggles work and career with domestic and family life. She enjoys her job as a self-employed Consultant Lawyer, specialising in women's rights in the workplace and discrimination law. She is an ardent supporter of flexible working, modern working practices and new technology.

Twitter: @rebellawltd | www.rebel-law.co.uk
Emma-Jane@rebel-law.co.uk

OSTEOPATH AND LECTURER

Andy Mansfield BSc (Hons). DO, PGDip. - Andy Mansfield Osteopathy

Andy graduated from the European School of Osteopathy *(ESO)* in 2003 and has practices in both Hitchin and St James's, London. He uses a classical approach to osteopathy to release tension and return balance to the body systems and improve natural fluid motion and vitality. He also treats pregnant, postnatal, and hopeful mums-to-be, as well as small babies, infants and children.

Twitter: @andymanosteo | www.andymansfield.com
Andymansfieldosteo@gmail.com

DEVELOPMENTAL BABY MASSAGE PRACTITIONER

Amy Tribe - Let's Talk Birth and Baby

Amy is a classically trained opera singer, which enables her to bring intricate knowledge of the body's breathing and muscular systems to combine with the practice of developmental baby massage. She works with babies across the UK, both in group formats and on a 1:1 consulting basis. She works alongside our midwife and offers the *'Baby Buddha'* series through *Let's Talk Birth and Baby.*

www.letstalkbirthandbaby.co.uk

PRE & POSTNATAL PILATES INSTRUCTOR

Georgia Knott - Gilates Pilates

Georgia is a qualified Pilates instructor, teaching mat, reformer and equipment Pilates based in Peckham, London. She offers online mat classes, pre & postnatal classes, HIIT classes, small group classes, 1:1 sessions and corporate sessions. She also holds weekly free pregnancy Pilates classes on a Wednesday over on our Instagram page.

@gilatespilates | www.gilatespilates.com

HG CAMPAIGNER, PRODUCER AND WOMEN'S HEALTH ACTIVIST

Charlotte Howden - The Sick Film

Charlotte is the co-producer and presenter of the world's first documentary about hyperemesis gravidarum - Sick. She now dedicates her time to raising awareness of this condition and trying to enact change within the medical community to ensure that no women are left to suffer. As an *'HG'* expert and women's health activist, Charlotte has appeared in numerous blogs, podcasts, and TV news shows highlighting the issues that modern mothers face today with their health, particularly during pregnancy.

Instagram: @the_sick_film | Facebook: @thesickfilmHG
Twitter: @film_sick

BABY & CANINE RELATIONSHIP SPECIALIST

Fiona Bird - Let's Talk Birth and Baby

Fiona is a Kennel Club registered dog trainer *(KCAI)* with many years of experience. Ensuring that dogs and babies get along is something she feels is very important for everyone's peace of mind and a harmonious household. She has worked with many breeds of dogs over the years all with their own characteristics and qualities. She even runs *'Barkers and Babies'* workshops through *Let's Talk Birth and Baby* to help with the smooth introduction of pooch to baby!

www.letstalkbirthandbaby.co.uk

Fiona@letstalkbirthandbaby.co.uk

SPECIALIST WOMEN'S PHYSIOTHERAPIST

Nikki Kelham - Let's Talk Birth and Baby

Nikki is a chartered physiotherapist specialising in ante and postnatal care for over 15-years. She is a qualified *'Mummy MOT'* practitioner, a certified APPI Pilates Instructor and an Advanced Pregnancy Practitioner. She loves to empower ladies with knowledge and offer them practical help and specialised treatment programs.

Instagram: @completepilatesmcr |
www.letstalkbirthandbaby.co.uk |
completepilatesmcr@gmail.com

MENTAL HEALTH CAMPAIGNER

Mark Williams - Let's Talk Birth and Baby

Mark is an author, an international campaigner, and a keynote speaker. Mark is the founder of *International Fathers Mental Health Day* and the campaign *#Howareyoudad*, to ensure both mums and dads were getting the support they need. As an Ambassador for the *'Mothers for Mothers Charity'*, he campaigned for a Welsh mother and baby unit to reopen and works to change policies for parents.

Instagram: @fathers_mentalhealth |
www.letstalkbirthandbaby.co.uk

TRYING TO CONCEIVE

So, you're thinking of trying for a baby - how exciting! We've pulled together some tips to help you become healthier, have more fun, and ultimately, feel more prepared to begin your conception journey.

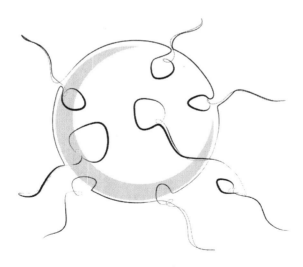

1. DITCH THE PILL

First and foremost, ditch the contraceptives! Whether you are on a hormonal or non-hormonal method of contraception, it's time to get them removed, stop taking or stop using them. It's time to make a baby! Many hormonal contraceptives may take a few months to get out of your system, so bear this in mind if you're wanting to conceive immediately. Non-hormonal methods like the copper coil and condoms, however, do not affect your fertility, and you may be able to fall pregnant immediately after removal/non-use. That's not to say that once you stop taking the hormonal pill you can't fall pregnant, just don't be worried if it doesn't happen straight away. Once you stop using contraceptives, you can better understand your natural menstrual cycle, learn when your ovulation days occur, and measure your body's hormone levels, to know when is best to conceive during your cycle.

2. VISIT YOUR GP

Before taking the step/lunge into parenthood, it is important to talk to your doctor at least 3 months before you start trying. Speak to them regarding any existing health issues, underlying conditions, and

discuss family history *(genetic testing)* on both sides, which may cause complications further down the line, or be potential barriers to you conceiving as quickly. You also want to make sure you're up to date on vaccinations and get tested for heart health issues like high blood pressure and irregular cholesterol levels, as well as any other conditions such as diabetes, asthma or thyroid problems which should be identified sooner rather than later.

3. DON'T FORGET THE DENTIST!

Getting your teeth and gums checked before you start trying to conceive would be a good idea too, as women with unchecked gum disease are typically more prone to miscarriages, preterm births and pre-eclampsia[1]. Once you're pregnant, getting X-rays won't be possible, so it's best to get them checked beforehand.

4. PUT AWAY THE VINO AND PACK OF SMOKES

Sad, we know, but this is a necessary step in helping you conceive, as well as reducing the risk of birth defects, miscarriages, preterm labour, and other associated risks once you fall pregnant. Smoking and drinking during pregnancy are of course a big no-no, but many are unaware that you should start scaling back or stopping altogether whilst you're actively trying to conceive too. If you're certain you're not pregnant, you can indulge in the occasional Friday night drink, but do drink in moderation, so it may be time to swap your cocktails for hot cocoa. That goes for your partner too! Excess alcohol intake, as well as smoking, has been known to interfere with your fertility and the father's sperm.

Remember, no level of smoke exposure is safe, with more notable problems occurring whilst trying to conceive after inhaling second-hand smoke, over direct smoking. Quitting smoking or your proclivity for indulging in a few shots on the weekend, is an incredible achievement, so make sure you remember that when you're kicking addiction's butt! You go mumma!

5. LIMIT THE COFFEE BREAKS

We know, it's asking a lot. A morning coffee, afternoon frappe, cuppa tea or even a shiny can of cola are a *must* at the moment to help us get through the day, but if you're thinking of trying for a baby, limiting your caffeine intake can reduce the risk of miscarriage[2] and prevent those horrid withdrawal symptoms once you fall pregnant. Most doctors recommend a daily intake of no more than 200 milligrams when trying to conceive *(a small cup of coffee is about 100mg)*, though some suggest going cold turkey, especially during conception and in the first trimester. This limit includes all sources of caffeine, including soda, tea, energy drinks, chocolate, coffee and pain medication. It's time to start reading the labels and knowing what you're putting into your body to maximise your chances of falling pregnant and having a happy, healthy baby!

6. GET HEALTHY

While we're not here to tell you to change your lifestyle, getting your body healthy and fit for pregnancy can only increase your chances of falling pregnant. Pregnancy pushes the body in many ways, so a good diet and exercise is encouraged to help your baby develop well and grow. No need for a special diet, but a balanced one with a variety of foods, packed with vitamins and minerals is essential to get the right nutrients that your body and your baby need. Your diet before pregnancy is equally important, and cutting out saturated fats and sugar before, as well as during pregnancy can reduce the risk of your baby developing high blood pressure and weight gain later in life.

7. START SAVING

The reality is, babies are expensive. There's no tiptoeing around that and with statutory maternity pay being very constricting, surviving maternity leave with a newborn isn't easy for many families. If you're thinking about starting a family, it'll make things a lot easier for you if you start saving now. Even if you are putting just £20-£100 aside each month, it'll soon mount up by the time you conceive, and right up to the birth. Of course, the more you save, the more money you'll have to maintain your current lifestyle, throughout maternity leave until you're

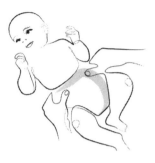

able to go back to work - if you choose to go back at all.

8. VITAMIN SUPPLEMENTS

If you've done any research into pregnancy, or spoken to your GP or gynecologist, you'll know already how important folic acid is during the first trimester. Hopeful mums should aim to take 400 micrograms (ug) of folic acid per day, until at least 13-weeks. Taking folic acid preconception, as well as throughout pregnancy, can vastly reduce the risk of neural tube defects such as spina bifida.

Vitamin D is required to keep our bones, teeth and muscles healthy, and we produce it when our skin is exposed to sunlight, therefore, it is recommended that during the winter months from September to March, women take 10ug of vitamin D every day.

Pregnancy can result in some women becoming deficient in iron. You will be routinely tested for this, however, if you experience fatigue or shortness of breath, speak to your midwife, who will arrange a blood test and prescribe iron supplements if required.

Maintaining a healthy level of vitamins and minerals can also be done through a balanced, varied diet where possible.

CONCEPTION ACRONYMS

If you're tracking your cycle on an app, or have a look at any forums during this time, a lot of OPK, BBT, DPO and hCG letters may come up, and not give you the slightest idea as to what on earth they mean. So here are all the main ones you'll come across, so you can walk the walk, and talk the talk!

AF - Aunt flow *(period)*

BBT - Basal body temperature

BC - Birth control

BT - Blood test

CD - Cycle day

CF - Cervical fluid

CM - Cervical mucus

CP - Cervical position

CY - Cycle

DI - Donor insemination

DPO - Days past ovulation

EWCM - Egg white cervical mucus *(consistency)*

HCG - Human chorionic gonadotropin *(pregnancy hormone)*

HPT - Home pregnancy test

IF - Infertility

IUI - Intrauterine insemination

LH - Luteinising hormone

LMP - Last menstrual period

LP - Luteal phase

OPK - Ovulation prediction kit

POAS - Pee on a stick *(pregnancy test)*

PG - Pregnancy

SA - Sperm analysis

TTC - Trying to conceive

CONCEPTION Q&A

Trying to conceive can take as little as one month. However, it can take others a lot longer. Every individual is different, and fertility can be affected by countless external factors, such as age, weight, caffeine, smoking, alcohol, medicines, and drugs and existing medical conditions[3] - many of which are reversible, changeable, and solvable in order to give you the best chance possible at conceiving.

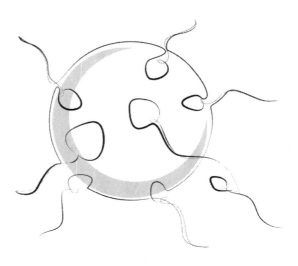

HOW LONG WILL IT TAKE?

A health professional's standard response to this question is always *"up to one year"*. If you visit your GP with worries about your fertility, they won't prescribe anything to assist with conception or refer you for further investigation until you have been trying to conceive for at least 1 year. This time frame also applies if you have a diagnosis that affects your fertility.

After this time, your GP will look at fertility to see if there are any issues and to give you a better idea of why you are struggling to conceive.

When trying to conceive, many things are taken into consideration: sperm quality, egg quality, intercourse timing, ovulation levels, and, of course, general health and age. It's well known that women become less fertile as they age.

CAN I PREDICT AND TRACK OVULATION?

It is generally thought that ovulation is around day 14 of a standard 28-day cycle. We work from day one of your cycle, being the first day of your period, and it's assumed that you will ovulate roughly 14 days later.

However, many women don't have a standard cycle, so ovulation can be later or earlier than 14 days, which can make it difficult to predict.

In the first few months of trying, it's best to try and go with the flow and see what happens.

If you're six months down the line, you may want to start trying to work out your cycle and your ovulation date to be more precise with your timing. You can buy ovulation kits and a BBT thermometer, available online or from your local chemist. It can also be helpful to keep a diary of your cycle noting down the first and last days of your cycle, BBT, ovulation kit results, and any days you have intercourse.

Having sex around ovulation, or your *'fertile window'* will be your best bet at conception. Up to 5 days before ovulations and 1 day after is known to be the *'magic window'*.

WHAT'S THE BEST POSITION TO GET PREGNANT?

Positions that allow for deep penetration are recommended for getting pregnant, as the sperm is deposited close to the cervix during ejaculation.

The missionary position is also recommended as it allows you to lay in the same place afterwards allowing sperm time to swim further towards your cervix.

It's also advised to elevate your hips and legs after intercourse to let gravity work its magic.

Most importantly, try to enjoy yourself and don't let the process become a chore.

GENDER SWAYING – WANT TO CONCEIVE A BOY OR GIRL?

Gender selection during IVF, is the *'choosing'* of a girl or boy embryo, are the only true guarantee of selecting a baby's gender. This method is illegal in the UK and several other countries, meaning you've got luck of the draw; a 50:50 chance of having either.

However, it is suggested by many books, websites, and experts out there, that there are natural ways in which you can try to conceive one or the other. This is known as *'gender swaying'.* There are diets, positions, timings, and all sorts promising varying levels of success.

The most talked about are the Shettles[4] and Whelan[5] methods. These methods promote 57-90% success and are similar in that they both say it's more likely you'll conceive a boy by having sex the day before, or on your day of ovulation. The theory being that the boy sperm *(Y chromosome)* swims fast, is strong, but doesn't live long, so needs to be deposited when the egg is released for maximum chances.

In contrast, it is thought that to conceive a girl, you should have sex 2-4 days before ovulation as the girl sperm *(X chromosome)* isn't as strong, doesn't swim as fast, but can live longer on its journey to meet the egg, and therefore will be waiting around for the egg to release, while the boy sperm have likely died off.

This method isn't scientifically proven or guaranteed to give you the outcome you may want, but your chances of conceiving a baby of either sex greatly increases the closer to ovulation you have intercourse, that much is known.

INFERTILITY AND RELATIONSHIPS

Relationships can be strained if conception is taking a long time, and we all react to this in different ways. One of us may be obsessed with the process, whilst the other may keep their feelings inside. We may therefore think the other person isn't as committed to the process of conceiving when it isn't the case. A lack of understanding of one another's frustrations and emotions can cause arguments which can make you feel lonely and distant.

Make sure you spend time together. Talk about the situation, but make sure it's not *all* you talk about. Remember why you fell in love, and why you wanted to start a family together, the rest will come.

STRESS AND FERTILITY

It's thought that there is a relationship between stress and getting pregnant[6], but it's easier said than done to relax when you are going through fertility issues.

Some of the ways to help you to relax include:

- Acknowledging that you and your partner may be reacting differently to the situation.

- Considering feelings of sadness and grief that may be present when you aren't successful.

- Not giving up on your interests and *'normal'* life.

- Taking a break from trying to conceive.

- Looking at hypnotherapy, yoga, and meditation to focus your mind.

- Keep talking to one other and get support if needed.

CHALLENGES TO FERTILITY

Sometimes getting pregnant isn't as easy as ditching your contraceptives and having lots of sex. For some, it can happen by accident, sometimes, it happens with a little trying, and for a few, it sadly might not happen for a while, or at all. For 1 in 7 couples[7], fertility can be a huge obstacle in the way of your hopes and dreams of having children. It can affect both men and women and can be a very isolating time.

If you have any doubts about yours or your partner's fertility after you've been trying for a year, you are both able to make an appointment with your GP to discuss fertility and put your mind at ease or give you the help you need. This gives you a clearer picture of the road ahead, and the confidence you need to overcome any obstacles in your way, together.

Here are some of the main physical conditions that can impact female fertility:

PELVIC INFLAMMATORY DISEASE (PID)

Any infection affecting the pelvic organs is referred to as PID. It most commonly affects the fallopian tubes; however, it can also affect the uterus and the ovaries. Its most common triggers are sexually transmitted diseases (STDs) such as gonorrhoea and chlamydia that have gone untreated for a prolonged period.

Symptoms can include pelvic pain, unusual vaginal discharge, excessive bleeding during your period, chills, fever, pain when urinating, backache, sickness, and nausea. PID, unfortunately can quite often go undiagnosed, as the symptoms are so generic to many other issues.

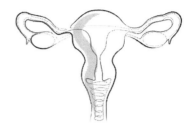

NHS studies have found that 1 in 10 women[8] who suffer from PID experience fertility issues, as it can be left untreated for so long that it can cause scarring to the fallopian tubes. This makes it difficult for the egg and sperm to travel up or down to reach each other. If they do meet, and the egg is fertilised, the scarring can also prevent it from travelling to the uterus and increases the risk of an ectopic pregnancy.

To prevent PID from developing, regularly test for STDs, follow safe sex practices, and treat any contracted infections/diseases immediately. To treat PID once diagnosed, your GP can give you antibiotics to fight off the infection and protect your fertility, however, once the tubes are damaged, this sadly cannot be reversed.

You can, however, have surgery to remove or repair your fallopian tubes, or you can undergo IVF to ensure the fertilised egg bypasses the tubes and implants directly into the uterus.

FIBROIDS

Fibroids within the uterus are non-cancerous (benign) tumours. They can grow in clusters and can be super small or as big as your head. 1 in 3 women[9] in the UK suffer from fibroids, 33% of these experience symptoms such as long, heavy, painful periods, pressure in the pelvic region, and constipation[9], though many women do not experience any symptoms at all. The cause of fibroids is unknown but are more common among women who are overweight. Afro-Caribbean women are also more likely to develop them than Caucasian women[9]. You can also be at a higher risk of developing fibroids if your mother had them.

Fibroids don't always affect fertility and, in fact, can just be left alone, however, in some cases, when they develop within the uterus, they can get in the way of conception by blocking an egg from being fertilised and preventing a fertilised egg from implanting. It's important to note that their size and position ultimately determines whether they will impact your fertility.

It is possible to remove them in a procedure called a 'myomectomy', where a large fibroid or cluster of them can be removed from the uterus and can either be done in an inpatient or outpatient situation.

ENDOMETRIOSIS

Around 10% of females of reproductive age suffer from endometriosis globally[10]. It occurs when tissue from the uterine lining starts growing on another part of the pelvic area, such as the fallopian tubes, bladder, appendix, ovaries, or even the intestines. As it is the same tissue as found in your uterus, it will build up and shed in the absence of pregnancy each month, causing scarring and inflammation. Symptoms include extreme pelvic pain, severe cramps, lower back pain during sex, nausea, and vomiting.

The cause is thought to be a combination of factors. It's thought the immune system malfunctioned and rather than flowing out with your period, the backup of uterine tissue instead headed the wrong way back into the abdominal cavity. It's also thought that genetics play a role in determining whether you will develop it.

In most cases, fertility is not affected, however, there are a few cases where women who suffer from endometriosis have fewer viable eggs due to the condition, or the surgery to fix it caused internal scarring of the ovaries. There is no cure, however, there are several treatments that can help with possible fertility issues. These include surgery to remove the endometrial lesions, fertility medications in conjunction with IUI, and finally, IVF, which offers the best chances.

POLYCYSTIC OVARIAN SYNDROME (PCOS)

Up to 10% of women suffer from PCOS and is the most severe cause of infertility. Polycystic ovarian syndrome occurs when your body produces too much luteinising hormone *(LH)* and the ovaries begin producing mass amounts of testosterone, or the body becomes too sensitive to normal levels of testosterone. This then prevents the ovaries from releasing eggs, which, of course, means the egg cannot be fertilised. PCOS typically occurs in women who are carrying a bit of extra weight or are pre-diabetic, typically have irregular periods or no periods at all, or may experience excessive hair growth and acne on the face.

It's thought that PCOS has a genetic component, meaning if you have a close female relative that suffers, you may be at higher risk yourself. It could also have something to do with your body's insulin levels, and whether it's used properly.

Women can reverse the effects of PCOS through weight management to regulate and restore normal ovulation and periods. Otherwise, your doctor can prescribe medication to aid ovulation, and IVF is always possible to help make pregnancy a reality.

OVARIAN CYST

Fluid-filled sacs can grow in the ovary and are known as ovarian cysts. These blister-like growths can come and go for many women and can be completely harmless. For some, however, these cysts can hang around, double in size, and start causing problems. Most common symptoms include pain localised in the lower abdomen, and irregular periods.

If too many cysts form or grow too large, eggs could struggle to develop or release and prevent ovulation. Some cysts, called 'endometriomas', can even destroy the tissue in your ovaries and decrease the number of eggs you carry. Often however, cysts can sort themselves out, but if they persist or grow, you may need surgery to remove them.

IRREGULAR MENSTRUAL PERIODS

Cycles lasting more than 35-40 days, no periods at all, or abnormal bleeding constitute as 'irregular periods' or 'anovulation' and can all point to the possibility you may not be ovulating at all, and thus are unable to fall pregnant. It is responsible for up to 30% of all cases of infertility[11]. This can be caused by several factors, including stress, eating disorders, being extremely under/overweight, illness, and/or a hormonal imbalance.

Once it has been confirmed by your doctor that you aren't ovulating, they will look at your health and lifestyle to spot any contributing factors to your anovulation. Reducing stress and getting your weight closer to a 'healthy' level can regulate your cycles, however, any extreme weight gain or loss can throw your cycles off balance further. Aim to lose no more than 1-2lbs per week to lose weight safely. If this doesn't work, there are fertility

treatments and further tests that can be done to see if there is a deeper root cause.

Male infertility also makes up 30% of all UK infertility cases[12], so be sure to get your partner checked out too for low sperm count, low sperm mobility, chlamydia, or any other potential causes.

MISCARRIAGE/ BABY LOSS

Most instances of baby loss occur within the first 3 months of pregnancy, but any pregnancy loss before 24 weeks of gestation is classed as a *'miscarriage'*. After this, they will be considered a *'still birth'*. In most cases, the first sign of miscarriage is bleeding, however, this is not always the case and the news that your pregnancy has

ended may not come until you have an ultrasound scan at 12 or 20 weeks.

Not all bleeding in early pregnancy is the sign of a miscarriage, and can often be what is known as implantation bleeding. However, it is important to contact your GP if you do experience any vaginal bleeding at any time during your pregnancy. Miscarriage-associated bleeding is often followed by strong cramps and pain in your lower tummy. Once you have contacted your GP, you will likely be referred to your local early pregnancy unit for further investigation.

CAUSES OF MISCARRIAGE

In many cases, the true cause of your miscarriage will remain undetermined, leaving you wondering what on earth went wrong.

The first thing to note, is that it is highly unlikely that there would have been anything you could have done differently. It is thought that most miscarriages are a result of a chromosomal abnormalities and your behaviour would not have impacted this in the slightest.

Sadly, sometimes they just happen for no reason.

WHAT HAPPENS WHEN YOU ARE EXPERIENCING A MISCARRIAGE

Experiencing a miscarriage can be scary and overwhelming, so it is important that you have your friends or family close by to support you. Once a miscarriage has been confirmed by scan, you will be supported by a specialist nurse or doctor who will explain your options. If your miscarriage has started naturally, you will likely be advised to let nature take its course, and for the pregnancy tissues to come away naturally. In some cases, especially if you are more than 12 weeks along, medication may be prescribed, or minor surgery recommended.

Every woman is different, and physical recovery can range from a few days to a few weeks. Some women feel quite run down and tired, whilst other women soon feel back to normal and the absence of pregnancy symptoms, such as nausea or vomiting can bring some relief during this time.

Your first period will usually start 4 to 6 weeks after the miscarriage bleeding has stopped but can take longer to get back into a regular pattern.

MOVING FORWARD

It is important that you don't underestimate both the physical and emotional toll that losing a pregnancy can have on both you and your partner. You are both likely to be feeling a whole host of emotions, from anger to confusion, and you may both deal with your loss in different ways. If either of you find you are really struggling to navigate your feelings, speak with your GP to find out what mental health support is available in your area.

When you are both ready, you may want to think about trying for another baby. Just because you have had one miscarriage, it doesn't mean you are more likely to have another one. Most women do go on to have a healthy pregnancy and baby following a pregnancy loss.

There is no fixed rule as to when the right time is to try for another baby. Make sure both you and your partner feel emotionally ready. It is advised to wait until your bleeding has stopped but even then, unless your doctor has advised against trying straight away, you are good to go. Lots of baby dust being sent your way!

WHAT CAN I DO TO REDUCE THE CHANCES OF HAVING ANOTHER MISCARRIAGE?

There isn't anything you can do to prevent another miscarriage sadly, as most miscarriages don't have an explanation. However, there are lots of things that you can do to get yourself into the best possible place - physically and emotionally. Try to get yourself physically in a good exercise and diet routine - eating lots of fruit, vegetables, and protein - with a little bit of a treat now and again! Do not underestimate the need to look after yourself mentally and emotionally too - seek help, if needed, from your GP or a fertility clinic. Do something to help you relax such as yoga, massage, or acupuncture. All these things can also help fertility.

FERTILITY TREATMENTS

Around 14% of couples[13] have trouble conceiving and require outside help to make their dream of a baby a reality. Conception isn't always a two-person job either, and sometimes needs the help of some medication, surgery, or even assistance from an embryologist to get that fetus growing. You'll find a summary of the main treatments on the next few pages that you can discuss with your doctor or fertility clinic. Ensure you speak to them about all the risks, concerns and ask them any questions you may have about any of the mentioned options.

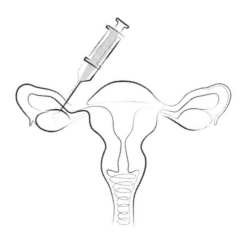

MEDICATION

Some issues with fertility can be aided with the use of medication, some can help almost instantly, and some may take a while to get your fertility up and running again.

Common medications doctors recommend for fertility include:

- Clomifene - which helps aid the monthly release of eggs in those who do not ovulate regularly.

- Tamoxifen - an alternative to the above.

- Metformin - used in women who suffer from PCOS.

- Gonadotrophins - helps stimulate ovulation and can also help male fertility too.

Some of these medications cause side effects including nausea, vomiting and headaches. Make sure you discuss these medications in-depth with your GP.

SURGERIES

When medications don't help, or your fertility complication requires a bit more intervention, surgery may be the answer.

Common surgeries include:

- Fallopian tube surgery - if your tubes are scarred,

you may need to get them repaired. Success depends on the extent of damage they had in the first place.

- Endometriosis, fibroid and PCOS surgeries - laparoscopic surgery is used to treat endometriosis to remove any cysts or to treat fibroids. For PCOS, laparoscopic ovarian drilling *(heat or laser)* can be used to destroy the affected part of the ovary if medication is unsuccessful.

- For the males, any blockages to the epididymis can be surgically corrected to ensure sperm can be ejaculated properly and sperm is extracted, quality tested and frozen for later use.

ARTIFICIAL INSEMINATION (AI)

Artificial insemination isn't always an option when female

infertility is an issue, but due to its high success rate, it can cut out the months of trying to conceive naturally. It consists of taking your partner's *(or a donor's)* sperm and placing it inside your fallopian tube whilst you're ovulating, allowing conception to happen naturally whilst boosting your chances of successful fertilisation.

It is usually performed when sperm count or sperm mobility is low, for single mothers, or for same-sex couples to start their journey to becoming parents.

INTRAUTERINE INSEMINATION (IUI)

IUI is another method that gives sperm a little helping hand to get where they need to go, by bypassing the usual barriers - the vagina and the cervix. If infertility is unexplained, or the male has mild fertility problems, IUI is the go-to method. In conjunction with medication, at the time of ovulation, 'washed' sperm *(that has had the chemical-filled, bacteria-ridden, seminal fluid separated from the sperm and motile/non-motile sperm are segregated, purified, and prepared for fertilisation)* is injected via a flexible catheter directly into the uterus next

to a fallopian tube. This cuts the amount of swimming the sperm needs to do and greatly improves the chances of fertilisation. IUI can either be done with frozen or fresh sperm. To improve sperm quality, men will be asked to abstain from ejaculating 48-hours prior to producing a sample which will be taken up to 2-hours before the insemination procedure. If IUI is unsuccessful after 3-4 rounds, you will be advised to try IVF.

IUI is not recommended for women who have significant blockages, scarring or conditions that affect the fallopian tubes, a history of pelvic infections, or advanced endometriosis. It is also not typically attempted in women over 40, if your male partner has a very low sperm count, or significant issues with sperm mobility and morphology, as IUI is unlikely to succeed.

IN VITRO-FERTILISATION (IVF)

Sometimes fertilisation doesn't happen on its own, or with the assistance that IUI and AI offers. Sometimes, sperm and eggs need fertilising in a lab, and once successfully fertilised, are injected directly into the uterus. Ovulation suppressants are sometimes taken initially to control the timing of your ovulation, and you are then injected with hormones to stimulate egg release on-demand.

Most women can expect daily injections of LH and gonadotrophins. You will need to go to the fertility clinic every few days during this stimulation phase so a doctor can check, via an ultrasound, how many follicles are growing, and check on their development, as well as the thickness of the uterine lining. You will also be given a blood test to check your hormone levels. Once it is concluded that your follicles are mature, egg retrieval can begin.

You'll receive an hCG injection to conclude the maturing process and begin ovulation. During this phase, you'll be told to abstain from unprotected sex (use a condom) to avoid extra embryos being fertilised on their own - you won't want 6 babies at once! 9-14 days after stimulation, and within a day and a half of your hCG trigger, your doctor will retrieve up to 15 eggs through a 20-40-minute ultrasound-guided needle procedure.

Next comes the sperm sample - fresh or frozen. The sperm is washed and popped in a

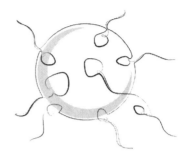

petri dish with your eggs and allowed to explore on their own or, through ICSI, whereby a single sperm is injected directly into an egg, allowing immediate fertilisation. This is how couples in some countries can choose if they want a boy or girl (in the UK, this selection is only granted if there is a genuine medical reason why either sex must/ mustn't be conceived). They are then left to incubate for 12-24 hours.

An embryologist will then monitor each embryo for the next week, assessing their growth and development. By day 6, there should be a healthy blastocyst. Only 30-50% of embryos[14] make it to this stage. If there is a worry of any genetic problems, some couples prefer their embryos to be screened (preimplantation genetic diagnosis testing (PGD/PGS) to eliminate any risk of the genetic disorder passing down to the child.

Within 1-2 days of fertilisation, women will receive a progesterone supplement to prepare their body for pregnancy - optimising their uterus lining prior to transfer and implantation. 3-5 days after successful fertilisation and possible screening, the embryos are carefully transported into the uterus through an ultrasound-guided flexible catheter. Depending on your age, multiple embryos can be transferred. There is a high chance of multiple babies/twins through IVF when multiple fertilised embryos are implanted, so be sure to have in-depth discussions with your doctor about all the pros and cons of IVF and your chances of success.

Within a few days, you may feel cramping and get some spotting, bleeding, or discharge *(but this is rarely a cause for alarm)*. This could be a sign of implantation and is a normal occurrence in early pregnancy. Around 9-12 days after transfer, you'll have a blood test to confirm your pregnancy. But don't be tempted to take an HPT before your blood test, as these can give false negatives.

If your blood test comes back positive, you'll be told to stop taking progesterone and they'll perform another check of your hCG levels to ensure your pregnancy is progressing. You will then get an ultrasound within 2-3 weeks. If negative, you and your partner will be told the next steps for subsequent cycles. Remember, not all IVF treatments are successful first time around.

IVF is typically the option for same-sex couples and couples who have fertility issues too severe for things to happen naturally. The main downside can be the cost. IVF can be extremely costly outside of NHS help. Women under 40 can be offered 3 rounds of IVF on the NHS if she's been unable to conceive after 2 years of trying, or after 12 rounds of failed AI/ IUI, depending on region and services available. Stricter criteria are in place for women aged 40-42 who are only offered 1 round of IVF on the NHS. Check the NHS website for more information about how to qualify for free IVF. Going down the private route can cost up to £5000[15] per cycle in the UK *(as of 2021)*.

EGG/SPERM DONATION

If either you or your partner suffers from infertility, you

may be able to use an egg/ sperm donor. This is typically done through IVF and can be done under the NHS, although waiting lists can be extremely long.

It is worth noting that anyone who registers to donate after 2005 can no longer claim anonymity and must provide information about their identity, medical history, and background. Children born because of egg/sperm donation have the legal right to find out the identity of the donor once they turn 18.

If going privately for any of the above treatments, the cost is certainly something to consider, as well as the clinic's success rate, waiting lists, range of treatments offered and clinic location. Be sure to ask for a fully costed plan, personalised to you, find out exactly what is and isn't included *(medication, scans, fees)* before committing to anything. You can ask your GP for advice and recommendations, as well as checking out the list of *HFEA licensed clinics in the UK online.*

We wish you the very best of luck and copious sprinkles of baby dust in your journey to becoming a parent!

SURROGACY AND ADOPTION

If a biological baby is all you've dreamed of, but you cannot conceive or carry a pregnancy yourself, surrogacy or adoption may be an option for you. In the next couple pages, we will be looking at the differences between the types of surrogacies, as well as the different ways to go about adopting a child.

SURROGACY

A surrogate is a woman who is willing and able to go through the pregnancy with your biological baby - so your egg and partner's sperm/your partner's sperm and a donor egg/your egg and donor sperm. The main downside to this is the complex legal issues, and possible emotional aspect of a surrogate pregnancy. In the UK, the surrogate woman, regardless of who's egg or sperm made the baby, is deemed the legal mother of the baby[16]. Therefore, they can keep the baby if that is what they decide. Surrogacy contracts are not enforced here in the UK, and surrogates will have to sign a parental order after birth, transferring parental rights to you, and a new birth certificate will be issued.

There are three types of surrogacies:No

- Gestational surrogacy

- Traditional surrogacy

- Reciprocal IVF

GESTATIONAL SURROGACY

When a woman carries a baby that is not genetically related to her, is an option if you have viable eggs but cannot carry the pregnancy yourself for any reason. The egg and sperm

are combined in-vitro *(IVF)* and transferred into the gestational carrier's uterus.

TRADITIONAL SURROGACY

This is when the sperm from the male partner of an infertile couple is inseminated into a surrogate, with luck, resulting in a pregnancy. This can also be achieved through IVF. The couple then, through a parental order, become the baby's legal parents once it is born. This is a good option if you don't have any viable eggs or cannot carry the pregnancy yourself, but still want a biological relation to your partner.

RECIPROCAL IVF

This is when eggs are taken from one partner, combined with donor sperm, and transferred into the other partner through IVF, giving both women the knowledge that the baby is theirs, whether biologically, or grown inside them.

Choosing a surrogate can seem daunting, especially if it's a stranger. They'll be between 21 and 45, healthy, have a support bubble around them, and understands the process fully. You can also go through non-profit agencies to find a surrogate in the UK. They can do all the pre-screening for you; help you find specialist lawyers and guide you through everything. If you choose a friend or family member to be your surrogate, rather than finding one through an agency, once all the mental health evaluations are concluded, legal bits are done and you've decided what route you want to go down - IUI/IVF/AI, you'll want to hash out all the costs. The total cost for surrogacy in the UK can range from £20-60,000 and includes surrogate expenses, fertility costs, agency fees and legal fees[17] (2021).

ADOPTION

If surrogacy and fertility treatments are not an option, there are over 78,000 children in England alone in need of a loving family. Almost anyone over the age of 21 can adopt a child, single, married, divorced, same-sex couples, anyone! Provided you have a fixed permanent residence in the UK and have lived here for a minimum of 1 year - meaning you don't have to be a British citizen to adopt.

There are two ways you can adopt a child in the UK - through a council approved agency, or through a voluntary agency. The agencies can help guide you through the whole process, the legalities, and the screening process. During the screening, you will have to undergo several assessments to test your suitability for adoption, a full criminal background check, medical exam, and will need to provide 3 referees who can testify to your character. One of these referees can be a relative. If you pass, the process of finding a suitable child can begin. This process can take around 6 months, after which, a child will be matched with you for adoption. There are children in the system from newborn to aged 17, all longing for a home and family. To make the adoption legally binding, you, or yourself and your partner can apply for an adoption court order, which grants you full parental rights and responsibilities for your adopted child.

ADOPTING STEPCHILDREN

You are also able to adopt a stepchild as your own. You must first inform the local council of your intent, and within 3 months, apply for the court order. Your stepchild must have lived with you for a minimum of 6 months. Like the adoption process, you must first go through an assessment and provide a report from a social worker on your partner, the child and the child's other birth parent. The adoption order then cancels out any other order or arrangement that gives the other birth parent rights or access to the child.

OVERSEAS ADOPTION

Adopting a child from overseas is also possible in the UK and can be done through your local council or through a voluntary adoption agency that specifically deals with overseas adoption. This is only possible if the child is not safe in their country of origin, and there is proof that the adoption would be in their best interests.

You must also be cleared by a UK adoption agency as suitable to adopt a child from overseas. The process is like UK adoption; however, the agency may charge a fee. In addition, your assessment will be sent to the overseas adoption agency. Your adoption application will then be sent to the child's country of origin, and you will have to go and visit them. The agency will guide you through every step of the way.

The Department of Education will also charge a flat fee for case management and processing. There may also be restrictions on adopting from certain countries, so it's worth checking online for the up-to-date list. For adoptions taking place in one of the restricted countries, you will need to apply to the *Inter-country Adoption Team.*

Funding is also available from the *'Adoption Support Fund',* which provides therapy for adoptive children and their adopting families, to help you settle in together, build confidence, and manage behaviours.

EARLY PREGNANCY SYMPTOMS

Maybe your period is just one day overdue, or perhaps you're a few weeks late... or perhaps you're not due on yet, but you've got that gut feeling that something's happening to your body. Maybe you've actively been trying to conceive, or this has come as a surprise. Regardless of the reasons or events that have led you to read this guide, you're likely sitting down asking yourself, *"am I pregnant?"*

Early signs and symptoms of pregnancy can crop up at different times in different women. Some rarely experience any symptoms until several weeks into their pregnancies, and for some, they can show up just a few short weeks after conception, arriving hard and fast.

Below are the most common signs and symptoms that you could have a bun baking in that oven of yours, so read on to find out:

MISSED PERIOD

Missing a period is probably the most common and most obvious sign of pregnancy. Some women can have an unusually short or light 'period' around 12-14 days after conception, around when you'd expect your next period. This is usually implantation bleeding when the fertilised egg buries itself in the lining of your uterus.

FATIGUE

When you fall pregnant, a considerable amount of energy is used growing your little ball of cells and the placenta, which can drain your energy completely and cause fatigue a few days after you conceive.

SMELL SENSITIVITY

You may notice that your sense of smell has skyrocketed if you're pregnant. This is an early pregnancy symptom that can make previously mild odours very offensive.

SICKNESS OR NAUSEA

Nausea and sickness can hit you like a wave at any time of day or night, and it begins for most women when they're about 6-weeks pregnant, though it can be earlier. Increased levels of progesterone (and other hormones like oestrogen and hCG), can cause you to digest more slowly, which ends up making you feel a little seasick/nauseous. If this is severe, it may be a sign of hyperemesis gravidarum which you will need to see your GP about.

BREAST CHANGES

Your breasts may start to feel a little tender and swollen, and your areolas may start darkening and enlarging. The hormones oestrogen and progesterone are responsible for this, however there is a positive to this pain - it's a sign that your body is preparing to produce milk for your baby!

FREQUENT URINATION

You may notice an increased need to pee, due to the increasing levels of hCG in your body. This hormone helps increase blood flow to your kidneys, which will efficiently rid your body of toxins. Your ever-expanding uterus will also start pressing onto your bladder and make you need to wee more often.

FOOD AVERSIONS

Your increased sense of smell can also cause you to go off certain foods during early pregnancy. It can turn your stomach to the point of nausea or worse, make you vomit. You can also experience irregular bloating for the first 8-12 weeks. This will go down and will be replaced by a small bump once baby has grown.

RISING BASAL BODY TEMPERATURE (BBT)

If you've been trying for a while and have been measuring your basal body temperature each morning after waking up, you may see a spike by 1 degree once you've conceived, and it will remain at that elevated temperature throughout your pregnancy.

MOOD SWINGS

You can blame the surge of hormones for your frequent mood swings. Feeling moody, upset, happy, then lonely, and back again is common in the early weeks of pregnancy, as your hormones are all over the place. It's entirely normal, but you may want to warn your other half!

WHEN TO TAKE A TEST

If you're experiencing any of these and still aren't sure whether you're pregnant for certain, it's time to take a test. Many HPTs can identify a positive pregnancy result before you've even missed a period and can be highly accurate. Any positive, no matter how faint, calls for a celebration! If you pee a negative, it doesn't always mean negative. It's best to wait just a few more days and then try again, it may be too soon to call. The day of your expected period is the best day of your cycle to get a more accurate reading. If the result is positive, book yourself onto *Let's Talk Birth and Baby's 'Early Pregnancy'* workshop, so you can find out everything you can expect over the next few weeks and when you'll meet your midwife - congrats!

FIRST TRIMESTER

WELCOME TO PREGNANCY

The first trimester is the first 3 months of pregnancy which is marked by the first day of your last menstrual period, until the end of week 12. You'll likely be halfway through your first trimester before you even know you're pregnant!

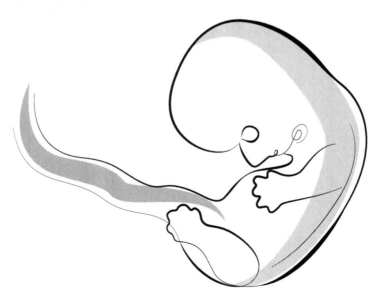

Your baby will do the most rapid growth during these 3 months, growing from a single cell and increasing by 10,000 times its size in the first 7 weeks alone, to 1.6cm in length and around 1 gram in weight at the 7-week mark. Evolving through the stages of zygote, blastocyst, embryo and finally to fetus at the end of the trimester. During this time it develops all of its features, bones, organs, muscles, nervous system, brain, and even a tiny beating heart.

You'll likely feel pregnant before you look it, with your hormones rising, the dreaded early symptoms will pop their heads up - tender breasts, nausea, and fatigue, or maybe you'll feel none of them! Every pregnancy is different, but the week-by-week guides later in this book should help you to understand what's happening inside you, as well as common symptoms and help to guide you through the next steps.

YOU GOT THIS!

CALCULATING YOUR DUE DATE

Working out when you're due sometimes feels like rocket science and can be a bit overwhelming. Is it 9 months from your positive pregnancy test? Is it 40 weeks? Is it from the date of your last period? Is it from the date you had sex? Just sit back, take a deep breath, we'll help you work out when your baby might be entering this world.

So that you have a benchmark in place to measure the growth and development of your baby, pregnancy is said to be 40 weeks long, even if it isn't *(only about 50% of first-time mums give birth in their 40th week[18])*. A full-term baby can be born between 37 and 42-weeks' gestation. Over 41-weeks is classed as overdue but isn't abnormal.

Annoyingly, the day *'X'* from which we start counting 40 weeks isn't from the night you conceived, nor from the day you ovulated. 40 weeks is counted from the first day of your last menstrual period *(LMP)*.

Yep, that means any sign of blood, whether it's spotting or full on *'that time of the month'*, that's your day 1 of pregnancy, even if you don't fall pregnant for another 2 weeks.

So, let's do the maths, say your period started on 4th October, you had sex and conceived on the 19th of that month, and you took your pregnancy test on 30th. Ignore every other date other than when you started your last period and count 40 weeks from that date. Your baby's due date in this scenario, will therefore be around the second week of July the following year *(around 9th-11th depending on your period cycle length)*. You can also calculate it by subtracting 3 months from your LMP and add 7 days. You should arrive on the same date.

Of course, this means by the time the sperm meets the egg and cells start multiplying, you're already in week 2 of pregnancy, and you'll be in week 4 by the time you miss your next period and discover you're pregnant.

We know it doesn't make much sense, but it is what it is.

When you have your first scan between 12-14 weeks, which measures the size of the embryo/fetus, the sonographer might give you a slightly different date, but just remember, the due date is always an estimate. Only 4% of babies are born on their estimated due date[19]. Ultimately, your baby will be the one that tells you they're done cooking, we just must do all we can to prepare for that day.

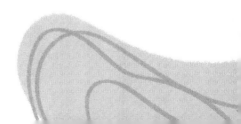

DECIDING ON YOUR BIRTH OPTIONS

When you are still in your first or second trimester, you may have started to think about how you'd like to give birth and already have your hospital/birthing unit chosen and scheduled in. Although hospital births are the most common, there are other options available

and giving birth in a hospital doesn't mean that you must be in a bed either.

Here's our guide to the most popular types of birth to help you with your choice.

HOSPITAL BIRTHS

According to the ONS *(2019)*, 34% of British women gave birth in a hospital unit[20]. Obviously, the main benefit of giving birth in a hospital, is that you have a lot of staff around you, particularly specialist consultants, to support you at every step. You'll also have access to all the pain relief options with an anaesthesiologist on-site.

BIRTH CENTRES

A birth centre is another popular choice that combines some of the medical requirements you may need or want, with a more home-comfort feel. In the same ONS study, 63% of women gave birth in midwife-led units/birth centres[20]. They are less *'medical'* than a hospital but do offer a certain level of care. They are NHS run, usually led by midwives and support staff, and can offer birthing pools, complementary therapies, and sometimes even family accommodation, making your birthing experience a little more comfortable. Talk to your midwife about whether

this option is available to you. Often, high-risk pregnancies need a little extra care on a maternity ward in hospital. Birth centres are also not available everywhere, so you may need to travel a distance to your nearest one. Bear this in mind when you are booking yourself in and make sure that your travel options are available from 36-weeks. A birth centre will not be able to offer a full range of pain relief, or any special assistance with the birth *(such as caesareans or assisted delivery)*. If you do require further medical attention, you would be transferred to the hospital by ambulance. Some birthing centres are located next to hospitals, whereas some will require a little drive. According to hospital stats, you will likely receive more 1 to 1 care in a birth centre than in a hospital, which can be useful after birth, for aspects such as breastfeeding initiation.

HOME BIRTHS

Home births have become more and more popular and are often the first choice for women in their second pregnancy. Home births are suitable for women who have a low-risk pregnancy and no complications expected during childbirth. As with any labour, midwives will monitor your baby and progress throughout, and if they feel concerned at any time, they may ask you to transfer to a hospital via ambulance - so keep a bag packed just in case. Also, something to note, is that no pain relief will be available at home, other than gas and air, as well as pethidine.

Having a planned home birth does not need to be difficult, but you will need to make sure you are prepared, and well in advance of your due date. You may also want to hire or buy a TENS machine for some at-home pain relief. The room you choose to give birth in will need to be big enough for you, the birthing pool *(if you're using one)*, your midwife, and your birthing partner to move around in. It should be a suitable temperature, not too warm or too cold. It's ideal to cover the floor with a rubber mat or old sheets but remember that sheets will not fully protect a carpet underneath. You'll also need easy access to a tap to fill up the pool, and no, you can't use your bath as a pool!

WATER BIRTHS

Water births are much less stressful for your baby when they are born, as they are being born into a similar environment to the amniotic fluid in your womb. For you,

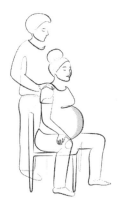

it can reduce the need for pain relief and be a more relaxing experience than in a hospital room. Calming music on, lights dimmed, and the relaxing feeling of being in the warm water makes water births extremely popular these days. Your partner can either assist from outside the pool or get in there with you - if your hospital or birthing unit allows. Many birth centres have pools available for each room, and some hospitals also have these facilities. It is worth noting that pain relief options are limited when using a pool too. Water births are often not advised for high-risk pregnancies or those that will require intervention, but you still may be able to go in the pool before you've reached active labour.

HYPNOBIRTHING

The premise of hypnobirthing is that you will be calmer and less stressed by using hypnosis during your labour and birth. It uses language to refer to the stages of birth, to invoke a more positive attitude about what is to come. Hypnobirthing is supported in all birth settings. Midwives claim that using the techniques can give a shorter length of first stage labour, a reduction in the intensity of pain felt and less fear and anxiety felt after birth.

The techniques include suitable labour and birth positions, methods for self-hypnosis, and deep relaxation and breathing techniques for labour. It can be helpful to involve your birthing partner in your hypnobirthing preparations so that they can act as a prompt for you if needed, to keep you focused and calm. Hypnobirthing is often recommended for women who have previously had a traumatic birth experience or are extremely anxious about their first labour and birth.

OTHER THINGS TO CONSIDER

It may be possible for you to choose a water birth, or to use hypnobirthing to assist your birth. These are available at several hospitals and birth centres, although they cannot guarantee they'll be available for us if there is a high demand for these services when you arrive.

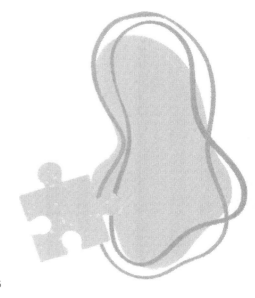

MEDICAL PROFESSIONALS YOU'LL MEET ALONG THE WAY

For most people, pregnancy is full of scans, checkups, antenatal appointments and tests to ensure both mum and baby are happy and healthy throughout their 9-month pregnancy.

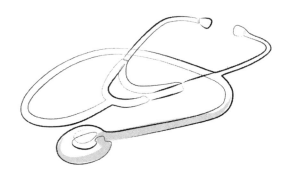

For a handful, the road to pregnancy and beyond is filled with so many more, but the basic appointments most women can expect involve the following medical professionals:

GP

Whether you're thinking about starting a family and need a preconception medical check or you've just found out you're pregnant and need a midwife referral, your GP will always be your first point of call for your health and wellbeing. If you have a home birth, your GP will likely perform the newborn (NIPE) check, rather than a midwife. You will also head to them for your 6-week check post-birth, to check on you and baby, check on any stitches or c-section scar and talk through post-birth contraception.

MIDWIFE

You'll see your midwife several times and may even see a few different midwives throughout your pregnancy. They will look after you during your pregnancy, throughout labour and even after your baby arrives. They'll take care of everything from blood tests, checkups, mental and physical wellbeing discussions, as well as coach you through labour and how to breastfeed. Once they're happy and you're sent home, you'll be passed over to your health visitor.

SONOGRAPHER

The all-important scanner of your uterus! The sonographer appointments, to many women, are the most important and you'll have a minimum of 2 scans throughout your pregnancy. The first ultrasound and nuchal translucency (NT) scan around 12-14 weeks is known as the dating scan to give you a due date. The NT scan also screens for Down's syndrome, Patau's and Edward's syndrome if you want that testing done.

The second scan, between 18 and 24-weeks, is known as your mid-pregnancy anomaly scan and looks for 11 physical conditions in your baby and if you want to know, the sex of your baby.

DIETITIAN/ SPECIALIST DIABETIC MIDWIFE

If you suffer from gestational or normal diabetes, you'll likely be referred to one of the above during your pregnancy. They will look at your current diet and suggest changes to help manage your blood sugar and maintain a healthy diet.

ANAESTHETIST

If you require an epidural during labour, or opt for a c-section, the anaesthetist will be there to offer you pain relief.

NEONATAL NURSES

If your baby needs to go to the neonatal intensive care unit *(NICU)* or requires special care, it will be a specialist neonatal nurse that looks after them.

OBSTETRICIAN

Specialising in complicated pregnancies and childbirth, the obstetrician will be there to conduct some necessary treatments. If your labour requires it, they will be at the other end of the forceps, take charge of a ventouse birth, or lead a caesarean, and will ensure your baby is delivered safely.

PAEDIATRICIAN/ NEONATOLOGIST

These baby and child specialist doctors will be available to you when a birth may be a little less straightforward and will care for your baby in a neonatal unit. You'll also see a paediatrician for any illnesses your child may have whilst growing up, alongside your GP.

HEALTH VISITOR

They will be your post-pregnancy guardian. They'll pay you a visit to your home while you're still pregnant, then once you're home with the baby, your health visitor will pop round after 10 days and keep you on track for a healthy recovery and help with the first few months with the baby. If you'll be caring for this baby on your own or are both struggling with this big change, your health visitor is also able to offer you support.

PHYSIOTHERAPIST OR OSTEOPATH

Joint, muscle, and back pain are common complaints in pregnancy, and if you're really suffering, you will want to head to one of these specialists to alleviate your pain. After birth, pregnancy physiotherapists can help women with their incontinence issues as well. *Let's Talk Birth and Baby* also run a specialist women's *'Pelvic Girdle Pain Workshop'* to teach you how to cope.

YOUR MIDWIFE APPOINTMENTS

So, you have had a positive pregnancy test - now what? Well, you can expect to attend a fair few appointments over the next few weeks. That said, after your initial excitement, it can feel a little bit like an anti-climax as no one really needs to see you until you are at least 10-weeks pregnant.

Here is the schedule you can expect for your maternity care:

FIRST THING'S FIRST

The first thing to do is contact your GP or midwife, just to let them know that you are pregnant. If you haven't been taking it pre-conception, then you should also start to take folic acid supplements which help to prevent birth defects such as spina bifida.

Between 8 and 12 weeks, you will have what is known as your *'booking'* appointment. This lasts up to an hour, as there is lots of information to go through. Your midwife will ask you lots of questions about both you and your partner's medical history. This is to ensure that you get the care that is appropriate for your needs.

In addition, at this appointment, you will be given lots of information that will explain:

- Your baby's development throughout pregnancy

- Nutritional information

- Exercise in pregnancy

- What to expect in your antenatal appointments

- Birthplace choices

- Antenatal classes

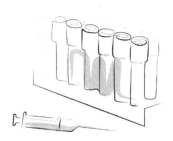

- How you wish to feed your baby.

Many hospitals now use electronic notes but if not, you will be given your handheld notes to keep with you. Remember to take these with you to every appointment and if you go away anywhere - just in case!

During this appointment, your midwife will also:

- Take your blood pressure

- Take blood to ascertain your blood group, cell count, rhesus factor, antibodies and screen for HIV, hepatitis B and syphilis.

- Measure your height, weight, and note your BMI

- Test your urine for any infection or protein

- Check your pulse

- Explain all about the screening tests available

- Book your 12/13-week ultrasound appointment

- Ask you how you are feeling emotionally

Before the end of your 13th week, you will be given an appointment to attend your dating *(nuchal)* scan. Although it's referred to as a dating scan, screening for chromosomal abnormalities such as Down's syndrome are also offered at this scan.

16-WEEKS

At this appointment, you will be given details of your next scan and review your blood tests. You will also have your blood pressure, urine, and pulse checked again. They may also use a doppler to let you listen to the baby's heartbeat.

BETWEEN 18 AND 20-WEEKS

It's scan time! At this scan, the sonographer will assess the development of the baby to ensure that all the internal organs are growing as they should be. Now the baby is that bit bigger, it is easier to look in detail at the bones, heart, spinal cord, brain and other bits and pieces. At this scan, you can also find out the sex of your baby if you wish to do so.

25-WEEKS

If this is your first baby, you will be offered an appointment at this time just to check how you are getting on. As will be the case at every appointment, your midwife will check your blood pressure, pulse, urine, and emotional wellbeing.

28-WEEKS

All pregnant women will see their midwife at this point as you will be offered a blood test to check how your iron levels are doing. Many women become anaemic during pregnancy and can feel particularly tired. If your tests do show that you have a low iron level, you will be prescribed iron tablets to give you a little boost.

Your bump will also be measured at this appointment and the results plotted on a chart. This helps the midwife to monitor your baby's growth and flag up any concerns regarding too rapid or slowing growth. Any such concerns would be referred for an additional scan to have a closer look.

At this appointment, if you haven't organised them already, your midwife should advise you of any antenatal education that is available. However, you can always arrange this for yourself with

our Official Midwife over at
Let's Talk Birth and Baby.

31-WEEKS

Another additional
appointment for first-time
mums. Any recent blood test
results will be reviewed and
your bump, blood pressure
and pulse measured.

34-WEEKS

Another antenatal checkup
to monitor how your blood
pressure is doing, and to
ensure you haven't got any
protein in your urine. Both
assessments are looking
for a condition called pre-
eclampsia which presents
with high blood pressure
and needs to be carefully
monitored.

36-WEEKS

This appointment may be
slightly longer, as you discuss
with your midwife your
plans for delivery. This is an
opportunity for you to chat
about:

- Where you plan to have
  your baby

- Pain relief options

- How you plan to feed your
  baby

- Coping strategies for
  labour & birth

In addition, you may be given
information regarding

- Breastfeeding

- Caring for your newborn

- Vitamin K injection

- Newborn screening
  programme

- Emotional wellbeing

38-WEEKS

Although your due date is still
2 weeks away, if your baby
arrives now, that is fine. At
your 38-week appointment
your midwife will discuss your
options should you go over
your due date. As always, your
blood pressure, urine and
pulse will be monitored at this
visit.

40-WEEKS

Your baby is now officially due
for eviction, and you will see
your midwife at this stage and
be given more information

regarding your choices. Your midwife may also discuss booking you in for a sweep, which is an internal vaginal examination where the cervix is located, and the midwife sweeps her fingers around the inside to encourage the commencement of contractions. You do not have to have this if you don't want it.

41-WEEKS

As per the norm, you will have your blood pressure, urine and pulse checked and your bump measured. You will be offered a membrane sweep at the appointment and induction of labour can be discussed and if you agree, a date booked in.

42-WEEKS

If you have chosen not to be induced, you will have the usual observational checks at this appointment and may also be offered a CTG *(cardiotocograph)* just to keep an eye on the baby's wellbeing whilst we are waiting on their appearance.

BLOOD SCREENINGS & TESTS

Something some of you may be dreading... Needles! During pregnancy, you'll be offered several blood tests that check the health of both you and your bubba. They help you make decisions about your care and the care of your baby, both before and after birth.

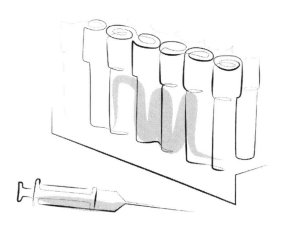

WHEN ARE TESTS DONE?

These tests are undertaken between 10 and 14-weeks, as well as around 28-weeks at your midwife or scan visits.

Blood screenings and other tests that can be conducted during pregnancy include:

- Checking hCG levels

- Rh factor

- Blood sugar levels

- Finding out your blood group

- Checking for blood or genetic disorders, as well as STIs

- Checking for immunity to infectious diseases

- Vitamin D deficiency

- CVS testing for Down's syndrome, Patau & Edward's syndrome, sickle-cell anaemia and other conditions (via samples from the placenta)

- Group B strep (via vaginal swab)

BETWEEN 8 AND 14-WEEKS

Here you will have Rh factor testing, which finds out your blood type, and whether you are rhesus positive or negative. This can help if problems occur and you need a transfusion, or if you show to be Rh negative and your baby is Rh positive. If your baby's blood meets yours during delivery, there can be complications with Rh factors mixing. If you're Rh-negative, you'll be screened for antibodies at 28-weeks, as well as during delivery. You may require an injection of Rh immune globulin following birth if your baby is born Rh-positive.

28-WEEKS

Now your iron levels will be checked again to test whether you have developed iron deficiency (anaemia). If your result is that you do, your doctor will offer iron supplements and folic acid, as a simple way to counteract the issue. Another test they may perform at this stage, will be to find out whether you have developed gestational diabetes if you have certain risk factors like raised BMI or family history.

Aside from a few essential screenings, all tests are completely optional, but it may give you peace of mind getting as much information as possible.

HIGH-RISK PREGNANCIES

Falling pregnant can be an exciting time, but also one that brings about a period of uncertainty and terminology that you may not have expected or understand. Add to that the news that your pregnancy, for whatever reason, has fallen out of the *'low-risk'* category, and you can suddenly feel that the rug has been pulled out from underneath you.

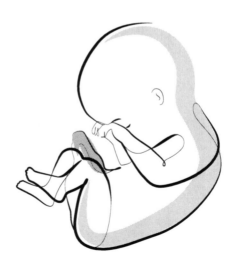

There are lots of tests, observations, and screening programmes that you will be offered throughout pregnancy to check that everything is on track, which we've just covered in the last two sections. However, should you find yourself being told of a certain concern, be it high blood pressure, gestational diabetes or that your baby is on the large side, you can feel confident that you are in safe hands.

If you've been told your pregnancy is at a higher risk from the start during your booking appointment, you will be given a consultant appointment to discuss your ongoing care and assess whether you are high-risk. If you are, you will likely have consultant-led care, meaning you will be monitored a bit more, have a few more scans and tests than normal and there may be some suggested limitations to your birth options. Many of these appointments will be with your consultant obstetrician.

Often, certain conditions can develop during pregnancy, where you will have specialist midwives or doctors that will provide you with specific advice relating to your circumstances, and you will also be offered more frequent monitoring to make

sure things remain on track. The best advice we can give you, is to keep asking those questions. If you are unsure about any answers, just let them know and they will be happy to explain things again. There is no such thing as a silly question and the likelihood is, that it has been asked 1000 times before.

There are several things that could turn your otherwise normal pregnancy into one that's higher risk.

These include, but are not limited to:

- Gestational diabetes
- High blood pressure/pre-eclampsia
- Larger babies
- Rh sensitisation
- Abnormal placental position
- Baby growth under 10th percentile

OTHER FACTORS THAT WOULD MAKE YOU HIGH-RISK:

- Aged under 17 or over 35
- A BMI under 18.5 or over 30
- Any pre-existing conditions/illnesses that could make your pregnancy more difficult/

complex (e.g., epilepsy, blood disorders, asthma, high blood pressure)

- Any difficulties or complications in previous pregnancies

- Twins/triplets etc.

- Family history of pregnancy complications/illnesses

- History of mental health issues (e.g., anxiety, depression)

Of course, when it comes to choosing your birth options, being higher risk can make some decisions more complex, for example, a home birth may present more challenges and as such, it could be advised that this would not be the safest option. Where you have your baby is your decision and it is one that should be supported by your care providers.

WHAT IF IT'S RECOMMENDED YOU CHANGE YOUR PLANS?

Being advised that where you have chosen to have your baby is not recommended, can be disappointing. No one can force you to have your baby anywhere you don't want to. Your decision cannot lawfully be overridden by anyone else unless you lack the mental capacity to make that decision. Remember,

the midwives and doctors looking after you truly do want what is safest for you and your baby. They also want you to make informed decisions based on that desired outcome. Make sure that when you are considering the advice of your team, that you fully understand their recommendations and if you are unsure or don't understand something, don't be worried about asking for things to be explained again.

HAVING MULTIPLES

Can you believe that in the UK, over 9 thousand sets of twins and 132 sets of triplets/quadruplets were born in 2018[28]? The number of multiples births has steadily risen over recent decades. One reason for this is because more women have access to fertility treatments, making birthing multiples more common. Secondly, women are having children later in life, which increases your chances of having twins. You'll need to wait for your 12-week scan to find out if you're having more than one baby.

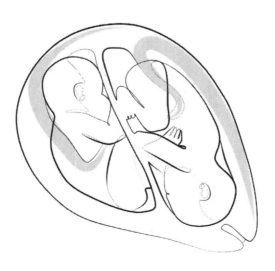

There are two different types of twins - identical and non-identical.

IDENTICAL TWINS

Identical twins will always be the same sex. That is because following the fertilisation of a single egg, it divided, creating identical twins, or a *'monozygote'*, with the same XY mix, as there was just one egg.

NON-IDENTICAL TWINS

More commonly, there are non-identical twins. These little ones can be either sex - a boy and a girl, both girls and both boys. At the point of fertilisation for these tiny people, two eggs and two sperm met and fell in love. Unlike identical twins, who have the same genes, these guys are completely different, as two different eggs were fertilised.

Though only a scan will confirm if you are hosting a small party in there, there'll be a few tell-tale signs that there maybe twice the fun ahead:

- Increased morning sickness & nausea
- Measuring larger for your expected dates
- Higher than normal hCG levels *(pregnancy hormones)*
- Extreme tiredness
- Increased weight gain

Did you know there is an old wives' tale that suggests that if you are tall, you have an increased chance of having twins?

As your pregnancy progresses, you may also find that you seem to experience more pronounced symptoms than your counterparts just housing the one baby. As the babies take up more room, you may find that you become short of breath, and could also suffer from anaemia. Your midwife will keep an eye on your blood tests and may recommend you have some supplements.

If you have just found out you are expecting twins, don't worry if you aren't jumping for joy immediately. The prospect of one baby can be daunting, so it is not surprising that some women finding out this news are a little overwhelmed. Don't be surprised if it takes your partner a little time to get their head around it too.

Not only are there different types of twins in terms of identical and non-identical, the way in which they are housed during pregnancy can also vary:

DICHORIONIC DIAMNIOTIC (DCDA)

These are the most straightforward. They both have their own placenta and own amniotic sac with an inner and outer membrane *(amnion and chorion)*. Think of these guys as having their own house, own drive, a moat, and a fence! These guys have it all.

MONOCHORIONIC DIAMNIOTIC (MCDA)

These bundles of fun have just one placenta, and both have an inner membrane, but only a single outer membrane. A bit like living in a house made into two flats!

MONOCHORIONIC MONOAMNIOTIC (MCMA)

One placenta and sharing the membranes. This type of twin pregnancy is rare, and you will be very closely monitored.

Once you have had your scan, your consultant will explain everything and what care you should expect to receive throughout your pregnancy. Most multiple pregnancies result in healthy babies in mum's arms, and are overall uneventful. However, carrying two or more babies does carry more risks.

There is an increased chance of maternal anaemia, pre-eclampsia, and gestational diabetes when expecting more than one baby. Your midwife will look out for these things though, so don't worry too much. There is also an increased chance of premature birth, and in fact, most multiples are born before 40-weeks. Depending on the type of multiples you are having, you will be offered a planned birth from 32-weeks with MCMA twins and 37-weeks with DCDA twins.

Another reason that you may need regular scans, is to ensure that your babies aren't showing signs of twin-to-twin transfusion syndrome *(TTTS)*. This is caused by abnormal connections between blood vessels, and can result in an imbalance of blood flow, which in turn sees one twin thriving over the other. If this occurs, your care plan will be individualised to meet your circumstances.

PREGNANCY PAST 35

Over the past few decades, the age at which women are starting their families has got progressively later. Current research is unclear regarding if it is just 1st-time mothers, or all mothers that are at increased risk of complications, therefore, if you are over the age of 35, you will be offered a little extra monitoring to ensure everything is staying on track. These types of pregnancies are given the somewhat unkind medical term *'geriatric pregnancy',* though there are many campaigns to get this terminology changed.

The midwife looking after you is well trained to pick up on any changes in pregnancy that could be a cause for concern and will refer you to a consultant should the need arise.

Pregnancies later in life carry a slightly increased risk of:

- Developing gestational diabetes

- C-section birth

- Down's syndrome

- Stillbirth

Overall, stillbirth rates are low, however, they do increase slightly in older women, that's why having extra monitoring is so important. You will usually be offered an induction of labour at 40-weeks to minimise the increased risk. There are many people that would suggest this is over-medicalising the birth, but make sure you are guided by your circumstances. Asking your consultant to assess placental function and baby's overall wellbeing is a sensible route before declining induction for any reason.

It is worth noting that these risk increases for stillbirth are minimal and should not be something that causes you anxiety throughout pregnancy. That is why your midwife will look after you and refer if needed.

As is the case with all pregnant women, you will be offered pregnancy scans and blood tests which can screen for chromosomal abnormalities such as Down's syndrome. On average, women under the age of 30 will have a 1 in 1250 chance of having a baby that develops Down's syndrome in the womb. The risk then increases to 1 in 640 for women between 30 and 35. For women over 42, this increases further to an average of 1 in 41[21]. Should your screening show a raised risk result, you will be offered further diagnostic testing which will give you a more definitive answer.

It all sounds glum but remember many older mums have healthy pregnancies with healthy babies to cuddle at the end.

PREGNANCY COMPLICATIONS

So, you've had your booking appointment and may even have had your scan results back confirming everything is sailing along nicely. For most women, that continues to be the case, but sometimes you can be thrown a curveball. There are certain conditions that can develop in pregnancy that may mean that you need a little extra monitoring to keep you and your baby safe and well. This could be anything from pre-eclampsia to obstetric cholestasis.

Your midwife will monitor you throughout pregnancy and should anything develop, they will refer you to a consultant obstetrician to discuss the plan moving forwards.

GESTATIONAL DIABETES (GD)

GD doesn't always carry symptoms and is only detected when blood sugar levels are tested during screening.

Gestational diabetes is caused by insulin resistance, like type 2 diabetes, but disappears after birth and most women give birth to healthy babies.

Gestational diabetes is treated through diet changes and monitoring of blood sugar levels, and in some cases, with medication.

HIGH BLOOD PRESSURE (HYPERTENSION)

If you take medication for high blood pressure or hypertension, you will need to tell your midwife so they can monitor you more closely.

To reduce high blood pressure and keep it within the normal range, you should stay as active as possible during pregnancy.

Keeping your salt intake low and eating a well-balanced diet can also help to reduce your blood pressure.

PRE-ECLAMPSIA

Pre-eclampsia usually *(but not always)* develops later in pregnancy. In some cases, pre-eclampsia can cause severe complications for both mother and baby. Although in most cases, it does not affect the baby's health.

Symptoms can include swelling of the hands and face, severe headaches, nausea, vomiting, dizziness, blurred vision, pain below the ribs, and sudden weight gain not attributed to baby's growth.

The only action that will fully resolve pre-eclampsia is the delivery of your baby. However, if you are still a few weeks away from delivery, you may be given medication to control the symptoms until it is safe for baby to be born.

LOW-LYING PLACENTA (PLACENTA PRAEVIA)

Placenta praevia, or low-lying placenta, is where the placenta attaches to the bottom of a woman's uterus, partially or entirely covering the cervix.

Placenta praevia is a condition that needs to be monitored, and the placenta usually moves to the correct position without intervention.

If the placenta hasn't moved by the time your baby is due to arrive, your baby will need to be born by caesarean section.

OBSTETRIC CHOLESTASIS

Itching is common in pregnancy, and usually caused by raised levels of hormones in the blood.

Your bump may also feel itchy while your skin stretches to accommodate your growing bump but itching during pregnancy can also be a symptom of a liver condition called obstetric cholestasis. If your itching is particularly bad at night and especially on your hands and feet, it is important that you let your midwife know, so you can be checked. Obstetric cholestasis carries a higher risk of stillbirth, meaning you should be monitored more closely.

A simple blood test will diagnose this, and you will have regular liver function tests so your doctor can monitor the condition.

PRETERM LABOUR

Babies born before 37 weeks of gestation are referred to as *'preterm'* or *'premature'*. Roughly 8 in 100 babies were born premature in the UK in 2019[19].

If you go into premature labour, your midwife or doctor may offer medication to help slow down or stop your delivery.

If your labour starts before 36-weeks, you may be offered steroids to help your baby's lungs mature. After this point, your little one's lungs should have developed enough to be able to breathe on their own without this medication being given.

If you are between 24 and 29-weeks pregnant and in premature labour, you will be offered magnesium sulphate to protect the baby's brain development as well as steroids to help your baby's lungs mature.

NUCHAL CORD

When the umbilical cord gets wrapped around your baby's neck before birth, it is referred to as a *'nuchal cord'* and is surprisingly common but unlikely to cause any complications. Surrounding the vessels supporting your baby, is a substance called *'Wharton's jelly'*, which provides protection to your baby's lifeline.

BREECH BABY

If your baby is bottom or feet first, this is known as breech position.

If baby is still in breech position at 36-weeks, you might be offered, an *'external cephalic version' (ECV)* where your obstetrician will try to turn the baby by applying pressure on your abdomen.

It can be uncomfortable, but around 50% of breech babies are turned with this method[22]. If ECV doesn't work *(and babies can sometimes move back to breech)*, your options for delivery will be discussed with you.

ECTOPIC PREGNANCY

A fertilised egg can get stuck and implant itself in the fallopian tube during its journey to the womb. 1 in every 90 pregnancies are ectopic. If left to develop, there is a high risk of the tube rupturing, causing major internal bleeding. The pregnancy is considered too risky and will need to be ended through medicaton or via keyhole surgery.

Symptoms include normal pregnancy signs, tummy pain down one side, vaginal bleeding, pain in your shoulder and discomfort going to the toilet. If you experience any of these before 12-weeks, seek medical help.

GROUP B STREP

Group B Streptococcus *(GBS)* is a transient *(comes and goes)* bacterium commonly found in the body and usually causes no harm to you - which is why it is not routinely tested for in pregnancy in the UK. On rare occasions, it can be passed onto baby during labour, and even more rarely, can cause more serious infections such as meningitis, sepsis, and pneumonia in baby. If you test positive for GBS following a urine test, you will be given antibiotics. You will also be administered antibiotics during labour to protect baby and prevent any risk *(small)* of the infection passing onto them. If baby shows signs of developing GBS after birth, they too will be treated with antibiotics.

Remember, knowledge is power. Knowing about various complications and things that could arise during pregnancy and labour can greatly improve your mental ability to adapt and stay calm when met with diagnosis, complex terminology, and changes to your treatment/care.

MORNING SICKNESS

You'll be pleased to know that not everyone gets morning sickness. About 70-80% of women do experience some level of nausea and/or vomiting[23], but not all. Fingers crossed you're in the other 20-30%! Nausea is a spectrum too, where some may feel only mildly queasy at the sight of food, others could be full-on gagging at the most random of smells, and some never vomit, but do feel a bit nauseous. It can be occasional, or it can be constant, and can hit at any time of day or night. It can hit early on in your pregnancy and typically lasts until 12-14-weeks, though some women suffer much longer. Every woman and every pregnancy is different, so let's help you understand what's causing it, and how to relieve it.

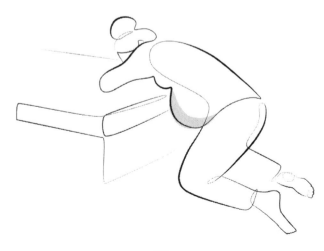

Morning sickness *(nausea and vomiting in pregnancy - NVP)* typically kicks in around the 6-weeks mark, when your hCG and estrogen levels are elevated in your first trimester. Combined with gastroesophageal reflux, *(due to the relaxation of your digestive tract tissue)*, and the super heightened sense of smell pregnant ladies develop, morning sickness can be one of the most dreaded early symptoms.

It is a common worry amongst first-time mums, that not being able to keep food down is stopping your baby from growing, but this is rarely the case. If you are throwing up lots and subsequently losing weight yourself, this can be a cause for concern as it can indicate excessive sickness. If this is the case for you, speak to your doctor, as you may be suffering from what Kate Middleton had; hyperemesis gravidarum *(HG)*.

Although we don't really know the exact cause of NVP, some theories on morning sickness speculates a few factors.

POTENTIAL CAUSES

- If you are carrying multiple fetuses, or those with higher-than-average hormone levels can experience sickness more often, whilst those with low hormonal levels may suffer occasionally or even not at all.

- Some women are neurologically more sensitive than others meaning they're more likely to respond to irregular hormonal changes and other triggers during pregnancy. If you get carsick or seasick quite a lot, you're also more likely to have severe morning sickness and nausea.

- Stress can also be a factor. Emotional stress is a known aggressor of your digestive system. So, try and stay as relaxed as possible in those early stages and you may find your NVP doesn't hit as hard.

- Fatigue - both mental and physical, can aggravate symptoms of nausea and vomiting, which in turn increases your level of fatigue - what a horrible cycle!

- Morning sickness also tends to be a lot more common and severe in first pregnancies, as your body is new to the rapidly changing hormones, as well as the mental element of increased anxiety when you're going through this all for the first time.

- Some women also swear that you'll have worse NVP if you're expecting a girl, though there is no scientific evidence to support this.

Although there's no cure, here's some tips on how to relieve those horrid feelings of nausea:

- Nausea is more likely to hit when you have an empty stomach, so try and eat as early as you can, so that you're not chucking up stomach acid. Similarly, try and have a snack *(high in protein and complex carbs)* before bed so that your stomach isn't too empty while you sleep. Keep something like a rice cake, crackers, or nuts and seeds on your bedside table so that you can snack on them throughout the night for when you get up for your midnight toilet runs.

- Don't stuff yourself like a Christmas turkey. An over-full stomach is just as nausea-inducing as an empty one. Eat little and often and those bouts of queasiness may subside.

- Getting food in your stomach and keeping it down should be your main priority but try to eat as healthy as you can. A balanced diet, high

in protein and calcium for those baby-making nutrients, as well as complex carbs, can be the difference between throwing up all day and feeling a little nauseous in the morning.

- Be sure to increase your fluid intake if you're throwing up a lot. Not only is it much more pleasant *(if that's possible)* to upchuck liquid than re-experience your dinner, but also, your body needs hydration more than it needs food. So, try and pack some nutrients and vitamins into a smoothie or juice. Electrolytes and coconut waters are also great for nauseous mums to be. If you find that your sickness is becoming debilitating, it is important that you contact your GP, as it may be necessary for you to have a short stay in hospital to rehydrate you and ensure you are not becoming deficient in certain nutrients.

- The best old wives' tale - stock up on ginger! Use ginger in your cooking, whether you're making soup, stir fry or baking a cake, ginger is a home remedy we can all get behind. Ginger biscuits, gingerbread and even hot water with ginger can get you feeling better.

- Some swear by anti-sickness bands, like the type you'd wear when on a boat or in a plane. They lay across pressure points, which in Chinese medicine, is said to help relieve sickness. You can also try acupuncture for this too.

- Brush your teeth or gargle with mouthwash *(that is free from alcohol)* after throwing up. This can stop you from feeling sick and freshens your vomit-scented breath.

- Finally, rest up. Get as much sleep as you can! You're less likely to feel nauseous when you're asleep than when you're awake, so here's an excuse to take those midday naps you're likely in desperate need of.

If all else fails, speak to your GP, as they will be able to prescribe you with some anti-sickness medication suitable for pregnancy. Again, if you are concerned about the severity or frequency of your morning sickness and think you may have HG, consult your doctor who will be able to help.

HYPEREMESIS GRAVIDARUM

CHARLOTTE HOWDEN

HG CAMPAIGNER, PRODUCER AND WOMEN'S HEALTH ACTIVIST

Hyperemesis gravidarum *(HG)* is an extreme form of pregnancy nausea and sickness that affects between 1 to 3 in 100 pregnant women in the UK every year[24]. It is characterised by excessive nausea and vomiting in pregnancy - more than you'd usually expect, that is.

Whether you are pregnant for the first time or the fifth, every pregnancy is different, and it can be hard to tell if something is unusual or not right. The fact is that morning sickness is such an accepted part of pregnancy that it can be easy to pass off more extreme versions of it as just "*really bad*", but, if you are experiencing any of the following, then you might not have normal morning sickness, and could be suffering from HG, for which you will need to see your GP, obstetrician, or midwife to get access to treatment and support.

SYMPTOMS

- Vomiting multiple times throughout the day

- Unrelenting nausea that does not subside

- Unable to keep down food or fluids

- More than 5% weight loss

- Having a heightened sense of smell that exacerbates the nausea

- Experiencing excessive saliva that causes you to constantly spit

- Not being able to pass urine as frequently or at all

- Dehydrated

You may not experience all these symptoms, or you may not think that it isn't "*bad enough*" to warrant help, and so our advice is to ask yourself this question:

"AM I ABLE TO FUNCTION AS A NORMAL HUMAN BEING, AND GO ABOUT THE MAJORITY OF MY DAY AS USUAL, AND MANAGE MY SYMPTOMS ADEQUATELY, WITHOUT NEEDING INTERVENTION?"

If the answer is no, then you should talk to your GP, obstetrician, or midwife.

There is no cure for hyperemesis, but early intervention via medication and re-hydration treatment is key to managing its severity.

Some women do experience being dismissed by their doctors and can be told that what they are experiencing is 'normal', or that there is nothing that can be done to help. Do not be turned away and continue to suffer. It is common for women to have to get second and third opinions, and it can be hard to keep fighting for your own care, so if you can, have someone to advocate for you.

There are numerous anti-sickness medications that can be prescribed to pregnant women, and an informed doctor will be able to start you on the *'lowest rung of the ladder'* of first line medications that could help. If they do not, then they should be proactively monitoring you and moving you up the ladder to second-line medications.

In the UK, we have an incredible charity called *Pregnancy Sickness Support*, that operate a helpline for sufferers, and have lots of information on their website that will be useful. They can also help to advocate for you to advise your doctors on what they *can* do to help you.

Please do not suffer with HG alone. It is incredibly important to have a community around you, as this condition can take its toll on your mental wellbeing too. 49% of women with HG have been found to suffer with antenatal depression, and 29% may suffer postnatally[25], so please do join one of the online HG support groups.

Follow Charlotte Howden on Instagram to find out how she was able to navigate HG, her details can be found in *'Our Experts'* on page 12.

If you can, watch the documentary *'Sick - The Battle Against HG'*, which is now available on Prime Video in the UK.

KEGEL EXERCISES

You've probably heard people refer to kegel exercises during pregnancy, but what are they actually for? When do you need to start them? And how do you do them? Kegels are designed to help strengthen your pelvic floor muscles, which link up to your rectum, uterus, bladder, and small intestine. They can help control incontinence during pregnancy and after birth, as well as get you ready for labour.

As your baby grows, your pelvic floor muscles are really tested. Many pregnant women experience a weak pelvic floor and sometimes may wee a little when laughing, coughing, and sneezing, due to their baby putting pressure on their bladder.

When giving birth and your baby is travelling down the birth canal, your pelvic floor muscles are the ones helping the baby be delivered through your pushing. It's therefore important to strengthen these muscles as early on in your pregnancy as possible and continue your exercises until the end.

HOW DO I EXERCISE THEM?

To contract these muscles, imagine you are holding in some wind and close the back passage. Draw that same feeling forwards and imagine that you are stopping yourself from having a wee. Once you've located these muscles you can start to exercise them.

To do this, tense, and release all at once, individually control them and try to isolate them. Try this in a range of different positions until you have these exercises down to a tee. Try and repeat these exercises of 10-15 repetitions, at least 3 times per day.

The great thing about these exercises, is no one will know you're doing them, meaning you can do them just about anywhere, any time.

LEARN TO RELAX THEM

Learning how to relax these pelvic floor muscles is just as important as strengthening them. An overactive pelvic floor can cause pelvic pain, and activities such as having a wee or penetrative sex may become painful.

Practising abdominal breathing can also help you to learn how to relax the pelvic floor. Put one hand on your tummy. As you take a steady breath in through your nose, feel your tummy gently push into your hand and relax the pelvic floor muscles.

HOW WILL I KNOW THEY'RE WORKING?

In short - you won't wee yourself! You can start feeling results within a few weeks and once labour comes around - you'll be pushing like a pro!

SEX DURING PREGNANCY

Hormones are on the rise, and whilst you're feeling nauseous during the first trimester, sex might be the furthest thing from your mind. For some however, these extra hormones can make women particularly frisky in the bedroom. You might be a bit worried about what intercourse itself or sperm could do to a fetus. We're here to tell you the good news - sex is perfectly safe whilst pregnant!

Getting busy in the bedroom will not harm your baby, at any stage of pregnancy, and your partner cannot penetrate past the cervix, so your baby won't have the faintest clue what's going on.

Whether you're just not feeling it, or you want it more than ever, changes to your sex drive are perfectly normal, and it isn't something to worry about.

The closer you get to D-day, if you're having a normal pregnancy and haven't encountered any complications, having sex and orgasming will not increase your risk of pre-term labour. However, an orgasm or the act of intercourse itself can set off mild contraction-like cramps. During these cramps, you'll feel your womb harden - no need to worry though, the baby's not coming just yet! Just laydown until the contractions pass.

WHEN CAN'T I HAVE SEX?

If you've experienced any heavy blood loss during pregnancy, it's likely your doctor or midwife will advise against having sex, so as not to disrupt a low-lying placenta or possible haematoma.

OTHER REASONS YOU MAY WANT TO AVOID SEX INCLUDE:

- There is a high risk of infection if your waters have broken and you've lost your mucus plug, as your baby will not have protection from bacteria.

- If your cervix has displayed any issues during the pregnancy, such as opening too early or becoming too thin.

- If you're expecting twins or have previously had early labours.

If you are sleeping with multiple partners during pregnancy, be sure a condom is always used for protection against STIs.

HOW CAN WE DO IT COMFORTABLY?

Comfortable positions are rather limited due to your bump, your back, or joints, and of course your tender breasts. Therefore, laying on your sides, either facing each other or the classic spooning position can be great for enjoyable, comfortable sex.

WHAT TO EAT DURING PREGNANCY

One minefield pregnancy can bring, is the issue of what you are able to eat, and more importantly, what you can't. It's important to eat healthily during pregnancy, a balanced diet. Paying close attention to what foods you eat can ensure the avoidance of harmful foods and drinks, which may affect the health or development of your growing baby.

Eating healthily should be a fundamental part of day-to-day life, whether you are pregnant or not, meaning throughout your pregnancy you should continue a healthy, varied, and balanced diet as you would normally. One trap many fall into is *'eating for two'*, as they feel they need to take in more calories to accommodate the baby, however, this is in fact a myth. You only require very few extra calories. You will not need any additional calories in the first trimester, however once your baby has grown, you will only need around 200 calories more[26], depending on how active you are.

FOOD TO INCLUDE IN YOUR DIET:

- Lower fat milk products such as natural yoghurt or semi-skimmed milk

- Fruit and veg

- Whole grains

- Lean meats *(or high protein vegetarian alternatives such as lentils and pulses)*

- Water

FOOD YOU SHOULD AVOID:

- Undercooked, raw, or processed meats

- Raw eggs

- Caffeine *(200mg daily limit)*

- Lots of high mercury fish *(shark, swordfish, king mackerel, tuna)*

- Undercooked or raw fish

- Unpasteurised milk, cheese, and fruit juice.

- Alcohol/drugs

- Unwashed produce

- Junk food

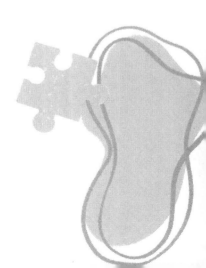

EXERCISE IN PREGNANCY

Pregnancy can be quite demanding on the body. Not just with your bump growing, draining all your energy and smushing your organs out the way, but on your muscles, your bones, and your joints. Despite this, exercise during pregnancy is encouraged, but only do as much as you can manage.

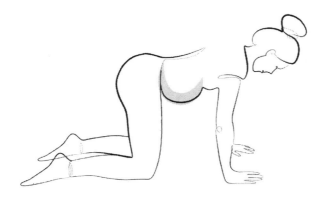

The NHS says,

"THE MORE FIT AND ACTIVE YOU ARE DURING THE PREGNANCY, GENERALLY, THE EASIER YOUR BODY WILL BE ABLE TO CHANGE AND ADAPT TO ITS CHANGING SHAPE AND HELP YOU PREPARE FOR LABOUR TOO".

Whether you go for walks, a light jog, do some calming yoga, or love lifting weights and going to your favourite gym classes - whichever you feel comfortable doing, trying some form of exercise will help you avoid many problems later in the pregnancy and labour, but take it easy.

The NHS's main advice:

"DON'T EXHAUST YOURSELF".

Pregnancy is tiring enough as it is, so only do what you can, when you can, and for as long as you can, nothing more.

Always get a sign off from your doctor or midwife before starting any new regime or continuing your existing heavy routine. If you become breathless, you're going too hard. If you weren't active pre-pregnancy, talk to your midwife about starting up an aerobic exercise and don't go suddenly from 0-100. Take it slow and go from 15 minutes a couple of days a week, working your way up to 30 minutes a session, daily.

TOP TIPS

- Always warm up before and cool down/stretch after each workout.

- Any daily amount is better than nothing but aim for 30 minutes per day.

- Drink plenty of water and fluids whilst exercising and avoid working out in hot weather.

- If you're in a class, make sure the teacher is aware of your pregnancy, how many weeks you are, and is properly trained in adapting exercises for prenatal fitness.

- Swimming is a great exercise, as it will put less strain on your pelvis and spine with the water supporting your new bump weight. Some pools even provide fun aqua-natal classes!

- Any exercises with a risk of falling should be avoided or proceeded with caution (*horse riding, ice hockey, cycling, gymnastics, trampolining etc.*).

EXERCISES TO AVOID

- After 16-weeks, avoid laying on your back for a prolonged period of time[27], as the bump will press on your main blood vessel which lays by your spine, and can leave you feeling faint.

- Avoid any contact sports where there may be at risk of you being struck/hit/knocked, whether that's with a flying tennis ball, or someone's gloved hand.

- Scuba diving is a big no-no. Babies have no protection from decompression sickness or gas embolism.

- Do not partake in sports above an altitude of 2500m above sea level as both you and your baby could suffer from altitude sickness.

RECOMMENDED EXERCISES:

- Core-strengthening exercises

- Jogging

- Pelvic tilt and pelvic floor exercises

- Pilates

- Pregnancy yoga (from 12 weeks)

- Swimming

- Light weightlifting

PRE & POSTNATAL PILATES

GEORGIA KNOTT

PRE & POSTNATAL PILATES INSTRUCTOR

Pilates is a low impact workout *(which is why it is ideal for pre and postnatal women)* that helps to strengthen your body, improve your posture and flexibility, as well as relieve stress and tension. There is a real focus on building core strength, which in turn will help you in day-to-day life *(particularly with the changes your body is going through in pregnancy and after giving birth)*.

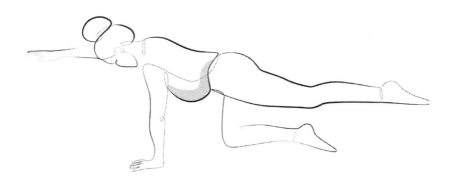

Pilates consists of slow and precise movements that target areas of your body for it to move and work in the most efficient way.

Pilates is extremely beneficial during pregnancy and after giving birth for many reasons- see full list of benefits below.

WHAT ARE THE BENEFITS OF DOING PILATES WHEN PREGNANT?

- Strengthen pelvic floor
- Posture awareness
- Prevent back pain
- Prevent/minimise diastasis recti (or 'divarication' - when your abdominal muscles separate, leaving a gap between them).
- Strengthen core
- Speed up recovery postpartum
- Improve general fitness, health, and wellbeing
- Relieve stress and tension

WHAT ARE THE BENEFITS OF DOING PILATES POST-BIRTH?

- Strengthen pelvic floor
- Regain good posture

- Prevent back pain
- Improve diastasis recti
- Strengthen core
- Restores confidence
- Improve general fitness, health and wellbeing
- Relieve stress and tension.

It is recommended that you don't start Pilates any earlier than 12-weeks, and no earlier than 6 weeks postnatal or 12 weeks if you have had a c-section.

PLEASE NOTE THAT IT'S ADVISED YOU DISCUSS YOUR PLANS TO EXERCISE DURING PREGNANCY WITH YOUR DOCTOR OR MIDWIFE. IT IS ALSO RECOMMENDED THAT YOU DON'T START A NEW FORM OF EXERCISE WHEN PREGNANT – STICK TO WHAT YOU'VE DONE PREVIOUSLY, PROVIDED THEY'RE SUITABLE.

Georgia, is a qualified Pilates Instructor and runs regular Pilates classes, including pre and postnatal small group sessions and 1:1 sessions. Her details can be found in 'Our Experts' on page 12.

TOP 5 PILATES EXERCISES

GEORGIA KNOTT

PRE & POSTNATAL PILATES INSTRUCTOR

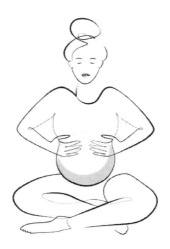

1. BREATHE

In Pilates, there is a specific breathing technique that aids movements and muscle activations for each exercise. The breath pattern is typically to inhale deeply through your nose, filling the rib cage, and exhale through pursed lips. This style of breathing is known as *'lateral breathing'*.

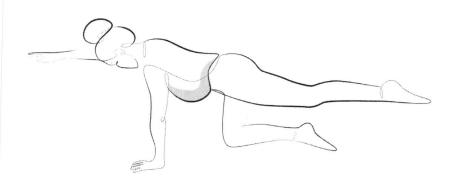

2. SUPERMAN

Start on your hands and knees - hands under shoulders and knees under hips. Whilst exhaling, reach out your opposite arm and opposite leg, and hold the position as you inhale. Breathe, reaching and stretching from fingertips to toes. Exhaling again, return your limbs back to the starting position, whilst keeping your spine neutral and body stable *(neutral spine is keeping your back flat from pelvis to neck, imagining you could rest a glass of water on it, and keep it there for the duration of the exercise!)* Do this 30 times, alternating sides, so 15 on each side.

Benefits: The 'Superman' exercise really tests your stability, core, and back strength, although it looks so simple - when done correctly, you should really feel everything working. This helps to give you stability, control, and proper alignment of the back of your body when moving. All of which is important when pre and postnatal.

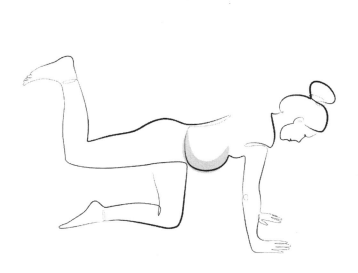

3. DONKEY KICKS

Start again on all fours. Find your neutral spine and raise your leg behind you. Keeping a 90-degree angle on your knee and hinging at the hip, flexing your foot as you do so. The sole of your foot should be facing the ceiling. On an inhale breath, return the leg back to the starting position, and repeat 15 times, then switch to the other leg.

Benefits: These are a great way of targeting your glutes and help to build core stability, strength, and tone. This exercise works your core muscles, hips, and shoulders and if you really focussed on control, it works your balance and aligning your spine

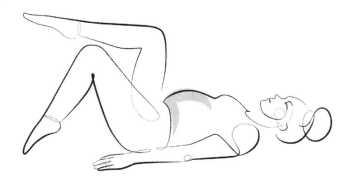

4. TOE TAPS (*POSTNATAL ONLY)

Laying on your back, carefully bring one leg at a time into a tabletop position, with your knees at 90 degrees and your back flat on the mat. Whilst inhaling, slowly hinge your leg down at the hip and *'tap'* one foot down, maintaining the 90-degree angle at the knee. Exhale and return the leg back up to the starting position. Engage your core as you do this. Alternate legs and repeat 15 times, moving slowly. This can also be performed with one leg at a time if you need more stability.

Benefits: The toe taps are a great exercise to work your deep core muscles. It is these exercises that are important to help rebuild core strength post pregnancy/birth.

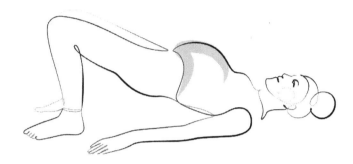

5. BRIDGE (*POSTNATAL ONLY)

Laying on your back with your hands by your side, knees bent *(hip distance apart),* and your feet flat on the floor, breathe out and start to slowly lift your hips up off the ground, moving bit by bit through your spine. Hold at the top on an inhale breath and then slowly make your way back down.

Benefits: This is a great exercise for many reasons; it improves spinal mobility, strengthens core and glutes, and helps to lengthen the front of your body. All of which can help with any back pain you may be experiencing from being pregnant or holding/feeding your baby.

40 THINGS MUMS WON'T TELL YOU ABOUT PREGNANCY

One thing you will notice in pregnancy, is how many women don't actually talk about their pregnancies, not about everything that's for sure. There's a secret club women tend to join when they fall pregnant, to keep all the bloat and ankle swelling, heartburn and discharge a secret from hopeful mums-to-be so we don't *put them off*. At *Your Baby Club*, we're very much about making sure women have all the information possible, so mums-to-be don't feel so surprised or alone when strange things start happening to their bodies - knowledge is power after all.

So, here's a list of things other mums probably won't have told you about what to expect during pregnancy:

- Pregnancy isn't anything like you see on TV or Instagram.

- Pregnancy for you can be completely different to how it was for your sibling/mum/friend.

- Pregnant women are twice as likely to develop thrush.

- Vaginal discharge will increase significantly, particularly in the third trimester

- Your skin sensitivity can change, meaning you may be more prone to sunburn, eczema, acne, dryness, stretch marks and rashes.

- Your hair can grow thicker and quicker and fall out less - though we're sorry to say, post-postpartum hair-loss is also something no one tells you about.

- You may also start growing hair *(or at least the hair there gets darker)* in places you don't want - belly, face, around the nipples being most common.

- Hair can change texture and sometimes even colour.

- Pregnant women are more prone to heartburn, trapped wind, diarrhea, constipation, hemorrhoids, UTIs and varicose veins.

- Your nipples will grow, and areolas will darken. Your breasts may also increase a cup size *(or a few)*, so you'll likely need to invest in some new bras.

- Birthmarks, freckles, and moles can darken, and new ones can appear.

- A line will appear down the centre of your belly *(linea negra)* but should fade after birth.

- Your cute little innie belly button may turn into an outie in the third trimester as your bump grows and skin stretches.

- You will need to pee - a lot. Incontinence is also

- common - get those kegels in ladies.

- You will feel the heat a lot more - time to lose the layers and take cold showers.

- *'Baby brain'* is real - you may forget things you've just been told 5 minutes prior.

- You'll need to learn to shave blind, oh and forget about doing your own pedicure or wearing lace up shoes!

- Your feet might grow a shoe size or two, sometimes permanently!

- You may not look pregnant for a while - particularly if it's your first child.

- You also may start showing early, particularly if a subsequent pregnancy.

- Your ribs can expand and change shape.

- Your joints can loosen, making you less stable and more prone to injury.

- Your bump can look totally different to someone else's at the same gestation.

- You may gain more weight than you thought. Equally, you can also lose weight - everyone is different.

- Your dreams can become more vivid and realistic - sadly, Chris Hemsworth is not really in your house - sorry!

- Pregnant women often struggle to sleep and can develop insomnia, particularly in the second and third trimesters.

- Your sex drive can change and either go completely off sex or go into hyper-drive!

- Your boobs can start leaking - this can happen at any time.

- By the third trimester, you may need help sitting up, getting up, getting out of bed, and even putting on your socks.

- It's okay not to enjoy some or all aspects of pregnancy.

- Kicks for some, can be uncomfortable - it's also okay not to enjoy them either.

- Depression during pregnancy is much more common than you'd think, as are sleep problems, mood swings and changes to your eating habits. If these feelings persist make sure you talk to your GP or midwife.

- *'Eating for two'* is a myth - your appetite can decrease as your stomach gets more and more compressed by your growing uterus. You also only need up to 200 additional calories per day by the final trimester.

- Your sinuses can swell *(pregnancy rhinitis)* and leave you feeling like you've got a cold most mornings.

- Strangers may try and touch your bump - it's okay to say no.

- Don't always expect people to give up their seat on public transport for you.

- It can be hard keeping your pregnancy a secret in the early stages - remember it's completely your choice when and if you tell people.

- It's okay not to love your body during pregnancy and beyond - you'll get there.

- You'll probably cry a lot more than usual, often for no reason at all.

- You'll spend more time shopping for baby stuff than you've ever spent shopping for yourself.

Now you're a bit more clued up on what to expect, hopefully nothing will come as a shock. Of course, this is not an exhaustive list, and is intended to help you feel a little more normal, less alone and more informed. Not everyone experiences the same symptoms, emotions, or physical changes, but if anything does crop up that makes you a little uneasy or you feel isn't normal, do contact your midwife who can give you further guidance.

WEEK 1-3

As we've covered earlier in this book, pregnancy is tracked from the first day of your last period, and there isn't actually any sign of baby until week 3.

Week 1 is your body starting its new menstrual cycle. Day 1 begins on the first day of your period. Your typical period will last between 7 and 8 days, which is shortly followed by your luteal phase.

At around week 2, your uterine lining will thicken, your ovarian follicles will mature, and an egg *(or two)* will be released. This happens around day 14-18 of your cycle, depending on your usual cycle length. Once your egg is released, it makes its way down the fallopian tube, in search of fresh sperm.

Week 3 is when the magic happens -following intercourse, sperm have found your egg and the egg has allowed one lucky swimmer to penetrate its core. This fertilised egg then becomes a *'zygote'*. This once single cell is now multiplying at an astonishing rate, transforming into a little ball of cells called a *'blastocyst'.*

It continues to make its way down the fallopian tubes into the uterus, where it will spend the next 8 and a half months growing into an adorable little baby.

WEEK 4

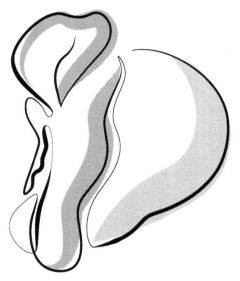

Have you peed on a stick yet? Do you even know you are pregnant? Probably not! You're unlikely to have missed a period yet.

During week 4, implantation occurs. This happens around 6-12 days after conception and may be indicated by a little spotting *(light bleeding)*, as the blastocyst buries itself and attaches to your uterine wall - easy to mistake for the start of your next period.

Depending on the number of days in your monthly cycle, you likely conceived around 2 weeks ago, and your tiny human is currently no bigger than the tip of a needle! Yet, in nine months' time, your gorgeous baby will fill a baby grow - how cool is that!

This little pinhead-sized ball of cells is growing at an unbelievable rate, and the fertilised egg is dividing over. The little embryo also splits in two, half forming your little one, and the other becomes the placenta. Your amniotic sac is beginning to form, as is the little yolk sac your baby will live in during its stay.

Your little blob has three layers, each beginning to grow into different parts of the body. The *'endoderm'*, which is the inner layer, starts to grow your baby's digestive system, as well as their liver and lungs. The middle layer, which is called the *'mesoderm'*, soon becomes the heart, bones, sex organs, kidneys, and muscles. Finally, the *'ectoderm'*, which is the outer layer which starts to transform into your baby's central nervous system, nails, hair, skin, and eyes.

As the baby's blood vessels start to form, their blood is now beginning to circulate and help with the development of their tiny heart. For the next few weeks, your baby is an *'embryo'*, and takes all the nourishment it needs from the yolk sac. Once you are around 12 to 14-weeks pregnant, the placenta will be fully formed and ready to take over all the hard work. This is when you'll start to feel more normal.

How are you feeling? The likelihood is you will feel normal as pregnancy symptoms don't tend to rear their heads for a few weeks yet. But there are certainly some tell-tale signs for many women which we covered in *'Early Pregnancy Symptoms' on page 45*. So, sit back, take a big breath, and relax as your body does all the hard work!

Oh, and congratulations! Stay with us and we will take you step by step through your pregnancy with a weekly update on what your tiny human is up to!

IF YOU'VE NOT BEEN TAKING PRECONCEPTION VITAMINS, IT'S TIME TO STOCK UP ON FOLIC ACID AS THE NEXT FEW WEEKS ARE THE MOST CRUCIAL TO BABY'S DEVELOPMENT.

WEEK 5

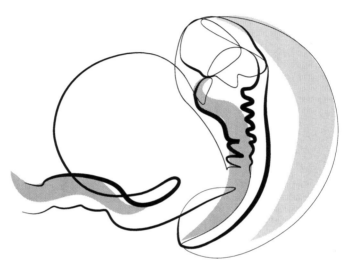

Holy moly! There is some crazy growing going on in there! Imagine all those women out there that have a hive of activity going on, but don't yet know they are pregnant! You can usually take an early home pregnancy test between 7 and 14 days after ovulation, or up to 6 days before your missed period. Once those two lines or a '+' appears, you're pregnant - congratulations mumma!

Your little embryo has progressed from the size of a pinhead last week, to a grain of rice this week. Now, all of this under a microscope looks more like a tadpole than a baby but watch this space - your tadpole will turn into a prince *(or princess)* and not a frog!

A busy week too for your embryo's heart, as it takes its first beats this week following the division of the chambers. How amazing that these beats will now continue for at least the next 80 years!

The forming blood vessels are starting to transport blood, aiding the development of the growing heart and circulatory system.

You may be starting to feel some tenderness in your boobs, which may also be a little bigger. Light period cramps can often occur around this time as everything continues to settle in. Some women do experience some light spotting at this stage, known as implantation bleeding. However, any bleeding that is persistent or heavy should be checked out.

Your diet is just as important now as ever before *(if not more so)*. The temptation to eat for two can be strong but remember you don't need any additional calories for the first trimester, so be mindful that you could end up putting on additional weight.

Keeping up with your normal exercise routine is fine *(assuming you are not bungee jumping),* but if you haven't already, now will be a good time to cut down or stop any bad habits like smoking or drinking alcohol and check out our guide on '*What to Eat During Pregnancy*' on page 89.

If you haven't started taking them yet, you need to start taking folic acid and vitamin D supplements, essential to your baby's steady growth and development, as well as your health. You'll need to take at least 400ug of folic acid per day to prevent the development of neural tube defects in the early stages of development, until at least 13-weeks.

WEEK 6

Oh dear! Have you started hibernating? Growing a tiny human can be extremely tiring, and an emotional roller coaster. Don't be surprised if you find yourself being a teensy bit moody too with all the extra hormones floating around your body. It is important to remember though that if this mood persists, it may be worth a chat with your GP.

No longer a grain of rice, your little one is now a prize... baby SEAHORSE! Don't worry, this change in shape is the transition to getting 1st prize in the baby show by week 40! If you were able to get a good look at your little seahorse, you would be able to see dark spots where the eyes are growing, and small buds where the arms and legs will start to grow.

How amazing that in just a few short weeks, we are starting to see all the signs of a new person emerging.

Also growing this week is your little one's kidneys, liver, and lungs. Their jaw, cheeks, and chin are also developing and little indentations on the side of its head will eventually become ears. The little bump on its face will grow into a cute little button nose in just a few short weeks! Its tiny heart is now beating away at over 110 times per minute and continues to get faster each day until it's double the speed of yours - pumping blood around its teeny tiny body.

Pregnancy hormones are getting high now, so the nausea may have reared its ugly head. Whether you vomit, or just have that horrible feeling in your throat, we're sorry to say, it may be something you need to get used to, as it can linger for a few weeks. You may still have tender breasts and cramping, both of which are completely normal. If your vomiting is constant and you can't keep any food down, see your GP or doctor as it could be HG.

It will also be a few weeks yet until you see a midwife, but it may be a good time to ring up your GP or community midwife and let them know your news, and get you booked in for your booking appointment at 8-weeks. Don't forget, you are now entitled to free prescriptions and dental care, so you will want to get your exemption certificate.

Why not sign up to *Let's Talk Birth and Baby's 'Early Pregnancy Workshop'* to find out all you need to know at this stage, who you'll need to tell, when you'll have appointments and what to expect - or just keep reading!

WEEK 7

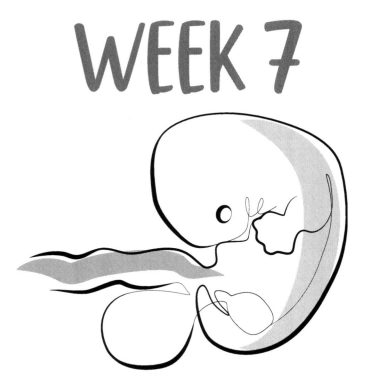

Now 10,000 times bigger than at conception, this single cell is now the size of a Smartie!

Speaking of Smarties, your little smarty pants is concentrating on brain development, with 100 brain cells being produced every minute. Production of all the blood cells is the work of the liver at the moment. This will continue until the bone marrow is in place and ready to take over the task.

Arms and legs are continuing to lengthen and strengthen, and tiny hands and feet will soon be visible. It is not only your baby that is growing, but their accommodation has also had an extension too and is now double the size it was. Despite all this energy you must be using to grow all these things, you may not be feeling too hungry as that famous pregnancy downside, morning sickness is still hanging around.

Morning sickness can also last well past the stick of midday, with some women suffering day and night. Make sure you are eating little and often, and maybe ask your partner to bring you a slice of toast in the morning before you get up.

You may also start to feel like you live in the bathroom, as the steadily increasing fluid volume results in frequent wee trips! Unfortunately, this little symptom of pregnancy is here to stay, as your growing baby will soon start to use your bladder in the same way it will use a trampoline when it is a toddler!

If you haven't already done so, now may be a good time to let your maternity unit know you are pregnant. Asking your doctors surgery how to self-refer is probably the easiest way to get the right contact numbers.

Continue to take your folic acid tablets, as doing so reduces your baby's risk of spina bifida. You should take them until around 13-weeks.

WEEK 8

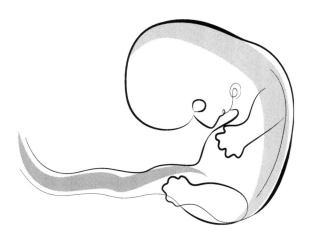

Did you know that there's an old wives' tale that suggests a faster beating heart is a sign you may be having a baby girl? Either way, your baby's heart is beating twice as fast as yours and is currently drumming away at around 140-170 bpm. Later in pregnancy, this will drop to between 110-160bpm. However, at the moment, growing a head, arm and leg buds *(which are developing at a rapid rate)* takes lots of energy. Their tiny heart is working hard to get everything in place.

This week will see the eye colour start to develop, and baby is growing around 1mm per day in size.

Things should be bumbling along just the same for you as your blood volume continues to increase, and your clothes may be feeling a little tighter. You may notice an increase in discharge, which can be blamed on pregnancy hormones and is nothing to worry about.

WEEK 9

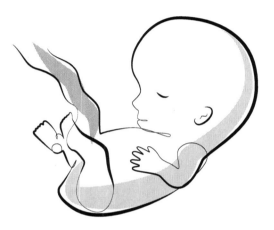

Little Babba has reached the dizzy length of 2.5cm, about the size of a playing die. This week, they're starting to stretch out, to make room for all the internal organs, which are now taking shape. Although you can't feel it yet, the baby is moving around all over the place, and is starting to look more human, as their facial features are settling into the right places.

You may also be noticing some tenderness, as well as some visible changes to your breasts now. The areola *(the dark circle around the nipple)* may have grown larger and darker and the small bumps will have become more defined - which is a normal sign of your body getting ready for breastfeeding.

Though you are under no obligation to tell your employers that you are pregnant just yet, if your job puts you at risk in any way, it may be worth having a risk assessment carried out so that your role can be adapted to keep you and baby safe and well.

WEEK 10

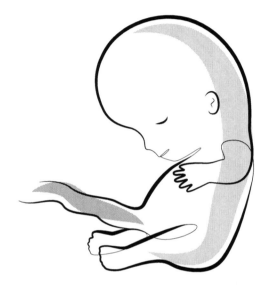

Are you suddenly finding that you are having really vivid dreams? This is not unusual but can be a little startling when you are suddenly talking to the animals and dreaming that you can fly! Don't worry, you're not going mad. There is so much going on at the moment both physically and emotionally, that your brain is working overtime, but it will settle down. You may want to have a notebook and pen handy so that you can record your night-time thoughts to show your little one in the years ahead!

You may also be feeling a little bloated - a sign of your slowing digestive system, but ensure you are continuing to eat a healthy diet, rich in fruit and fibre to keep things moving. Also, as always, it's very important that you keep hydrated.

Despite what you may read online, it is perfectly safe to exercise in pregnancy. If you are used to regular exercise, just continue - you may wish to adapt things if you are playing extreme contact sports, but a little exertion is fine. If you are not a regular mover but want to start, now is a great time to take up some walking, or swimming - something light. Just don't overdo it!

Now the size of a cotton wool ball, your baby has graduated from an embryo to a *'fetus'*! Its eyes are now able to react to light and are still slightly open as the eyelids develop. It's also amazing to know that all their little milk teeth are now in place, and their jawbone is also taking shape. Cartilage and bones continue to form around the body, and small indentations appear on the legs which will develop into the knees and ankles. Your baby's elbows are already working. Its stomach is forming digestive juices, the kidneys are producing urine *(following the ingestion of amniotic fluid)* and finally, if a boy, his testes *(which will begin their decent into the scrotum after birth)* will begin producing testosterone at this stage.

WEEK 11

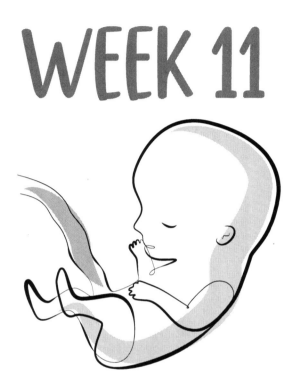

Oh no! Have all those pregnancy symptoms been getting you down? Hang in there, for most people by this point, the end is in sight. By 12 to 13-weeks once the placenta takes over, you will start to feel a whole heap better and finally get some energy back.

Finding yourself eating for two? After all those years of watching what you eat, it can be really tempting to just let rip. However, it is worth keeping in mind that you don't require any additional calories for baby in the first trimester, so go easy on the extra food as this will grow you and not baby. If you have been suffering with morning sickness, you may notice that you have likely lost weight, so it's important to try and replenish those lost nutrients - if you can keep it down, that is!

The amount of weight a woman gains in pregnancy can vary, but the average is between 1st 8lbs and 1st 12lbs *(9.9kg to 11.7kg)*. Most of this weight is down to your growing baby, amniotic fluid, increased blood volume, water, and the placenta, even if your baby only ends up being 7lbs at full term. In preparation for breastfeeding your body is also storing fat ready for milk production, so don't be alarmed when you step on the scales - in fact, feel free to avoid them!

Remember to check out our 'What to Eat During Pregnancy' guide on page 89 if you are unsure about nutrition in pregnancy.

If you are still feeling tired with all this baby growing, try to have an afternoon nap (if work and your body allows), or catch a few Zzz's when you get home. Just make sure your partner wakes you up after an hour or you will likely be up all night!

Your rapidly growing baby is now 4cm in length and weighs in at 7 grams. Still tiny, but so many amazing things make up this tiny human. Taste buds are in place along with the fingers, nails, toes, and hair follicles. Their facial features will also start to take shape this week.

If it's a girl, her ovaries will be forming now. Baby will also have visible nipples, open nasal passages at the end of the nose, and a tongue. Baby is also taking on the recommendation for lots of exercise and is busy kicking and skipping away in there! In a few weeks' time, you will be able to feel all the action!

Baby's skin is still transparent, so if you were able to have a sneaky peak, you would see the little heart beating away at twice the rate of your own. This will slow down over time but for now, there is lots of work to do.

WEEK 12

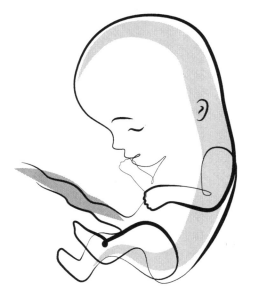

Yay! You have hit the 12-week milestone. One that everyone is pleased to get to at this point, as the risk of miscarriage reduces significantly, and a lot of your worries are rightfully eased. If you have been suffering with nausea and fatigue, you may well find that those symptoms start to ebb away from this point onwards, and likely be replaced with a renewed sense of energy as you make your way into your second trimester.

Remember, it continues to be important to keep hydrated, as your body produces the amniotic fluid surrounding your baby, and your increased blood supply means you must keep taking in a healthy level of water each day, as well as your prenatal vitamins.

Amazingly by this point, all the building work is complete, with all the necessary bits and pieces in place; the stomach, liver, pancreas, and intestines, and is practising using its tiny little lungs. Even though it has doubled in size since week 9, all your baby needs to do now is continue to grow! At the moment, the baby is around 5 cm long and weighs about 18 grams - around the size of a small plum or lime, so plenty more room for packing on some pounds!

You are finally at the end of your first trimester, but sadly, so too is your ability to fit into your regular clothes. A tricky time as you are maybe not big enough for maternity wear, but your usual clothes may be asking for some backup! Time to start shopping maybe. Our essentials include maternity leggings and baggy T-shirts (*go one size up for growing room if non-maternity wear*) and oversized jumpers.

As your little one grows, they are starting to ascend out of the pelvic area, and you may even be able to feel the firmness of your baby in your belly and see a slight bulge side-on. Have you started to take some snapshots of your baby bump?

THAT'S YOUR FIRST TRIMESTER DONE!

SECOND TRIMESTER

BETTER DAYS ARE COMING

For many, the second trimester is saying goodbye to the horrid morning sickness, and hello to a bit more energy and less anxiety as your hormones change. But at least you're out of the uncertain time that is the first trimester. You'll have had your 12-week scan by now, meaning you've finally been able to see your little one on an ultrasound and have circulated the pictures round your friends and family, having them all cooing and excited for another addition to your household. The second trimester includes weeks 13-27 of pregnancy.

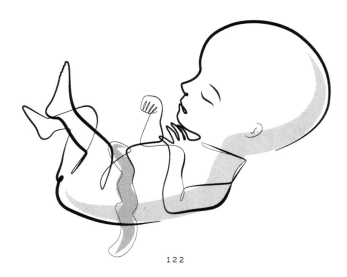

Your frequent visits to the bathroom will have eased off a bit by this point, as baby starts to descend out of the pelvis into its newly expanded living quarters, and your bump is just about to start showing - looking less like bloating and more like a baby growing! In this trimester, a lot of development occurs in the baby's brain and body, as it starts to look more and more human by the day. Its features move into their rightful place, limbs become more proportionate and the little one starts wriggling around, ready to start jabbing you from the inside when they taste something you've eaten via their amniotic fluid. These should start around mid-way through your second trimester if this is your first pregnancy, subsequent pregnancies may feel flutters a little earlier on.

By the end of this trimester, you'll also find out the sex of the baby *(unless you want it to be a surprise)* and be able to start preparing their nursery ready for their arrival in just a few short months.

THIS IS THE TRIMESTER YOU'LL LIKELY ENJOY THE MOST!

MATERNITY LEAVE

EMMA-JANE TAYLOR-MORAN

EMPLOYMENT LAW SOLICITOR & WOMEN'S RIGHTS SPECIALIST

If you're in employment, once you find out you're pregnant you'll likely start thinking about your finances, when you'll tell your employers, and when you want to start and end your maternity leave. We've teamed up with a specialist employment solicitor to answer all your common questions.

WHEN SHOULD I TELL MY EMPLOYER?

Many women want to wait to tell anyone until they get their anomaly scan out of the way and feel more secure in their pregnancy (at 12-weeks). When you decide to tell your employer, is completely up to you.

If you are in a job that poses extra risk to your baby, then you should tell your employer as soon as possible, so that they can do a risk assessment and make sure you are both safe. Sometimes this might mean moving you to a different role temporarily.

You might even be suffering from horrendous sickness very early on and need time off or some understanding from your employer, so it is best to tell them as it gives you some legal protection.

If you want to take maternity leave, you need to tell your employer that you are pregnant at least 15 weeks (around week 25) before the week your baby is due, as well as when you want to your leave to start.

You should always notify them in writing and keep a copy.

CAN I GET TIME OFF FOR ANTENATAL APPOINTMENTS?

Yes, you are entitled to paid time off to attend antenatal appointments, and you will need to request each occasion from your employer, showing proof if you are asked.

You can take as many as you need, as recommended by your midwife, GP, or consultant. This can include parenting classes and alternative therapies. If your employer refuses a particular request, they must have a good reason, and act reasonably.

If you can book any appointments outside of working time, that is usually helpful, but it is not always possible.

HOW MUCH MATERNITY LEAVE CAN I TAKE?

You can take any period from 2 weeks up to 12 months (for factory workers the minimum is 4 weeks). You can start your maternity leave as early as 11 weeks before your due date if you wish, It will start early if your baby comes early, or if you are off sick with a pregnancy related illness in the 4 weeks before your due date.

Your holiday continues to accrue while you are on leave, so lots of women tag their holiday on either at the start or end of maternity leave which gives you a few more weeks with your baby before you go back *(paid at full rate)*.

You should give your employer at least 4 weeks' notice if you wish to change the date you start your maternity leave, if you can.

If you want to share some of your maternity leave with your partner, you can *work out your eligibility online* for what's called *'shared parental leave'*.

WHAT PAY WILL I BE ENTITLED TO?

This depends on your length of service. You may be entitled to statutory maternity pay, maternity allowance, or an enhanced rate of maternity pay set out in your employment contract or staff handbook.

There's a *handy calculator online* to help you work out what leave and pay you can get. You will be taxed at the appropriate rate and your pay should be set out on payslips as usual.

It is always worth asking your HR department for details of any enhanced contractual maternity pay that you might be entitled to.

You can contact *Citizens Advice* for help calculating pay and any top up benefits you might be able to claim *(e.g., child benefit)*.

If you are using shared parental leave, when you swap over with your partner, it is called *'shared parental pay'*, but check your eligibility first to figure out what works best for your family. You can *apply online* and you should both give your employers at least 8 weeks' notice.

WHAT ARE MY RIGHTS WHILE I AM OFF?

You should get the same treatment by your employer *(except for pay)* as you did while you were at work. For example, your employer should carry on paying into your pension while you receive maternity pay, you should continue accruing holiday *(including bank holidays)* and you are entitled to the same pay reviews and bonuses *(pro rata if based on time/work done)*.

Some employers find it easy to forget about you while you are on maternity leave, on an *'out of sight, out of mind'* basis. Whilst you may not want to be bothered too much with work-related contact when looking after a young baby, you probably don't want to be completely out of the loop either. It is a good idea to agree with your employer before you go on leave as to how much contact you would like. For example, will you be logging into your work email account and monitoring communications and how often, or do you want to only be emailed important staff news on your private email?

You can have up to 10 *'keeping in touch'* days *(known as KIT days)*, where you get full pay, even if you do less than a whole day's work each time. This can take different forms, including attending training, working from home, going into the workplace, and attending meetings. You need to arrange these with your employer.

If you are sharing parental leave with your partner, you can each work up to 20 days while you are on leave. These are called *'SPLIT'* days and are on top of the 10 KIT days you can take.

You have special legal protection from being treated unfairly and discriminated against while you are pregnant and while you are on maternity leave. You should not be treated unfavourably just because you are pregnant or on leave or have just had a baby.

If you think you have been treated badly, then first, talk to your manager or HR about it and see if they will put it right. If not, then you can write to them with your complaints *(this is called a 'grievance')* and they should investigate, hold a meeting with you and provide you with a formal response. You can appeal the outcome if you are not happy with it.

If you are in any doubt, or the issue is not resolved, then speak to your union rep *(if you are a member)*, call the Acas helpline on 0300 123 1100, or get advice from a specialist employment law solicitor.

CAN I BE MADE REDUNDANT WHILE I'M ON MATERNITY LEAVE?

Yes, but you also have extra preferential rights to be considered for any available jobs over and above those not on maternity leave - *'first dibs'* if you like.

Your employer must consult with you about a potential redundancy situation to the same extent as they need to with your colleagues. Sometimes they forget to include women on maternity leave in a consultation process, and this is discrimination. It is also discrimination if they choose you to be made redundant just because you are pregnant, on maternity leave, or have just had a baby. If you think this has happened, get some legal advice straight away.

WHAT IF I WISH TO RETURN PART-TIME OR NOT AT ALL?

You might not feel comfortable leaving your baby for long periods, or may not be able to find good childcare, especially if you work full time. Many women want some level of flexibility or part time working once their maternity leave ends. It might be to fit in with childcare, to facilitate ongoing breastfeeding, or just because your priorities have changed. If this is the case, then you need to talk to your employer. You can do this informally or you can make a formal statutory flexible working request if you are eligible. There are *some good tips online* about how to see if you are entitled, and how to do it.

If your employer agrees to change your working hours or pattern, then they often do so on a temporary basis to see how it works out, or they might make it permanent. You shouldn't be treated less favourably just because you work part time. Your pay, benefits, pension, and holiday should then be calculated pro rata.

If you find that your request is refused, depending on the circumstances, this might be discriminatory. You are then faced with the binary choice of returning to a job on full time hours or leaving the job altogether. Your relationship with your employer may also have broken down because of this. You should get legal advice about your rights in this situation, as you may be entitled to claim compensation if you have been discriminated against and/or lost your job because of unfair and unlawful treatment.

If you need any further information or have any issues arise following the announcement of your pregnancy or feel you've been discriminated against, contact Emma-Jane Taylor-Moran. Her contact details can be found in *'Our Experts'* on page 12.

CHOOSING WHERE TO GIVE BIRTH

There are typically three popular birth settings when it comes to choosing where to deliver your baby; in your own home, in the hospital or in a midwife-run birthing unit.

Within a few weeks of discovering you are pregnant, it's worth looking at your nearest birthing options, and weighing up your options. You'll likely be asked, when you inform your GP of your pregnancy, which hospital or unit you'd like all your booking appointment, tests and scans done, alongside your midwife appointments which can be there, or at your GP's surgery. Don't feel panicked if what's most convenient for these appointments isn't where you want to give birth - you can change your mind later and go for a home birth or different unit/hospital - though it is easier having everything in one place if you have the option to. You never know, you might just have to go to whatever is closest when the time comes! The NHS website has a postcode checker online to find your nearest services too.

PERSONAL EXPERIENCES AND STATS

Do you know anyone who's given birth recently? You can ask family and friends about their experiences with different hospitals/units or what it was like giving birth at home to get some first-hand recommendations. It's also a good idea to head to Facebook and look up the hospitals/units you're looking at and search for groups that have 'voices' or 'midwife' or 'maternity' in the name. Within these, you can usually find infographics on their annual birth stats - how many used a pool, mode of delivery, busiest days, recovery rate, stillbirth rates, percentage of breastfeeding initiation and rate of 1-2-1 care - all useful information to consider for choosing your desired hospital or unit. You can also find information on *Which?'s* website where they have a handy comparison tool for you to use.

THINGS TO CONSIDER

Obviously choosing the nearest has the best advantage of being able to get there quickly but depending on the type of birth you want *(See 'Writing a Birth Plan' on page 193)*, your nearest maternity services may not be equipped with the resources or facilities you need/want. You'll also want to look at visiting policies. Some services will only allow one birth partner, some don't allow visitors once you've given birth, and some will let you have whoever you want, where you want.

Consider how you'd like to feed your child too. Looking at the breastfeeding initiation rate will give you a good idea of what support will be available for either method of feeding.

THINGS TO ASK

Here are some good questions to ask your midwife to get the answers you need:

- What equipment is available?

- Can I bring belongings from home?

- Who is allowed to accompany me - can they stay with me throughout my time there?

- Can I move around during labour?

- What are my options for pain relief? Can I have an epidural if I change my mind?

- Are there any restrictions on visitors or limited time my partner can stay?

- When will I be discharged?

- If my baby needs special care, will they remain in the same hospital as me?

- Will my baby be always with me?

Once you've decided where you want to be cared for, you can book in via your GP or midwife. So long as you have a straightforward 'low-risk' pregnancy, you have your choice of where you'd like to go.

If you have any medical requirements (*i.e., had problems in previous pregnancies or a health condition that requires a specialist consultant*), or you are deemed 'high-risk', you may be advised to select somewhere that is equipped with everything you may need, or ensure you are close enough to a hospital should you or your baby need one.

YOUR SONOGRAPHER APPOINTMENTS

These ultrasound scan appointments are a great way to check on your baby's growth and development, as well as check for abnormalities. Here's an overview of when each of your routine scans are and what to expect at each appointment. Under the NHS, you typically only have two scans, but if your pregnancy is deemed high-risk, you may have a few more scans than this for further monitoring. You can also pay to have more scans via a private practice too.

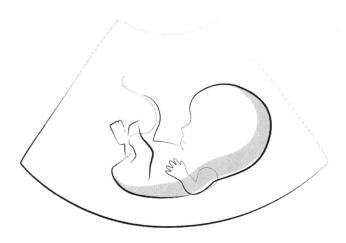

8-12 WEEK SCAN

Your first sneaky peek at your baby is an exciting event and one that makes things seem a little more real - and just a little bit scary! However, your first scan is not just for a preview.

Often referred to as a dating scan, at your first ultrasound, the sonographer will confirm your pregnancy, and give you an estimated date of delivery *(EDD)*. At this appointment, you can also choose to have nuchal translucency screening, which tests for Down's syndrome, Edwards' and Patau's syndrome.

If your wish is to have the screening, a blood test will be done and during the scan, a measurement of the fluid at the back of the baby's neck will be recorded. This information and your age will be combined to ascertain the chances of you having a baby with any of these syndromes.

It is important to understand that the results do not provide a diagnosis but will advise if you have a higher or lower chance of your baby having any of these syndromes. If your results are returned and you are in the higher chance category, you will be offered further diagnostic testing, which your midwife will fully explain to you. Again, you do not have to have further testing if you want to.

20-WEEK SCAN

Your 20-week scan is a lovely time to have a look at everything that has developed in the past couple of months. More importantly, it is offered to check the physical development of your baby. The sonographer will look at the baby's internal organs, as well as the bones and spinal cord. They will have a look at their growth and give you a current approximate weight and size which can be plotted on a growth chart.

You may also decide at this point to find out if you are having a girl or a boy. Do let the sonographer know if you don't want to know, so that they don't give it away, though sometimes it's obvious on the scans!

See *'Understanding your Baby's Growth Chart'* on page 186 for a breakdown of what terms and abbreviations on your scan report mean.

UNDERSTANDING YOUR HOSPITAL NOTES

Navigating pregnancy can seem like a minefield, with appointments, scans, and well-meaning advice from friends, family and even strangers! Just when you think you have a handle on it, you flick through your hospital notes, and you suddenly feel like you need to learn a new language!

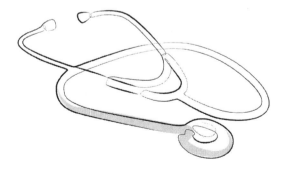

Your maternity notes keep records of your pregnancy journey. They are put together at your first antenatal appointment and are filled in by medical staff at every appointment to keep track of both you and your baby. You will take these away in a folder or book, and you'll need to bring them to every appointment, scan, and test, as well as have them with you when you go into labour so that any nurse, midwife, or doctor can have your comprehensive notes and know all about you and what care you need.

We've put together a list of terms and abbreviations that you may come across in your notes or hear in conversation to decode them and make them easier to read and understand.

WHAT'S IN YOUR NOTES?

- Your details - name, address, contact number, NHS number, next of kin, your partner's details *(if applicable)*.

- Details for your midwife - your GP, antenatal clinic, birth suite, and hospital contact numbers.

- Your medical history, in detail - current/recent illnesses, medications, and mental health.

- Family medical history of diseases and genetic conditions.

- Info on any previous births, pregnancies, or infant loss.

- Dates of appointments and your EDD.

- Blood test results, ultrasound scans and screening test results.

- Blood pressure readings, urine tests, vaccinations, fetal movements, heart rate and baby's position.

- Tracking of your baby's growth in the womb.

- Your birth plan - place of birth, type, pain relief options, birth partner, etc.

ANTENATAL (BEFORE BIRTH)

ABX - Antibiotics

AC - Abdominal circumference - *your baby's tummy will be measured during ultrasound*

AF - Artificially feeding - *both feeding*

A/N - Antenatal - *before baby is born*

ANC - Antenatal clinic

AP - Abdominal palpation - *your midwife feeling your bump*

APH - Antepartum haemorrhage - *bleeding during pregnancy*

BMI - Body mass index

BPM - Beats per minute - *how fast your baby's heart is beating*

CVS - Chorionic villus sampling - *a diagnostic test for fetal abnormalities*

DAU - Day assessment unit

ECV - External cephalic version - *turning a breech baby*

EDD - Estimated date of delivery

EPU - Early pregnancy unit

G - Gravida - *how many times a woman has been pregnant*

GBS - Group B streptococcus

HC - Head circumference

HVS - High vaginal swab

P - Parity - *how many babies a woman has given birth*

SFH - Symphysis fundal height - *the measurement of your bump*

SPD - Symphysis pubis dysfunction AKA pelvic girdle pain

UTI - Urinary tract infection

ANTEPARTUM – DURING LABOUR

ARM - Artificial rupture of membranes - *having your waters broken*

BBA - Born before arrival - *baby not born in hospital as planned*

BP - Blood pressure

CDS - Central delivery suite - *also known as labour ward*

CEFM - Continuous electronic fetal monitoring - *generally by CTG*

CEPH - Cephalic - *baby's head is coming first*

CMV - Cytomegalovirus - *this is also known as herpes virus*

CTG - Cardiotocography - *machine used to monitor baby's heart during labour*

CX - Cervix

EBL - Estimated blood loss

EFM - Electronic fetal monitoring

EL LSCS - Elective lower segment caesarean section

EM LSCS - Emergency lower segment caesarean section

FBS - Fetal blood sampling

FH - Fetal heart

FM - Fetal movements

FMF - Fetal movements felt

FSE - Fetal scalp electrode

GDM - Gestational diabetes

IDDM - Insulin dependent diabetes mellitus

IOL - Induction of labour

IM - Intramuscular - *refers to injection*

IV - Intravenous

IVI - Intravenous infusion

LFT - Liver function test

LSCS - Lower segment caesarean section

NAD - No abnormality detected

NBFD - Neville Barnes forceps delivery

PET - Pre-eclampsia

PPROM - Pre-term pre-labour rupture of membranes

PROM - Pre-labour rupture of membranes - *waters broken but contractions not commenced*

SVD - Spontaneous vaginal delivery

SB - Stillbirth

TENS - Transcutaneous electrical nerve stimulation

BABY'S POSITIONS

LOA - Left occipito anterior

LOP - Left occipito posterior

LOT - Left occipital transverse

OA - Occipito anterior

OT - Occipito transverse

ROA - Right occipito anterior

ROL - Right occipito lateral

ROP - Right occipito posterior

ROT - Right occipito transverse

'Occipito' refers to the back of a baby's head.

POSTNATAL – AFTER BIRTH

BF - Breastfeeding

BNO - Bowels not open - *can refer to yours or your baby's bowel movements*

BO - Bowels open - *can refer to yours or your baby's bowel movements*

BW - Birth weight

CCT - Controlled cord traction - *refers to gentle pulling on the cord to deliver the placenta*

DOB - Date of birth

DVT - Deep vein thrombosis

EBM - Expressed breastmilk

MROP - Manual removal of placenta

NPU - Not passed urine

PN - Postnatal

PPH - Post-partum haemorrhage

BLOOD TESTS, SCREENING & INVESTIGATIONS

AFI - Amniotic fluid index - *this is the measure of amniotic fluid around the baby*

AMNIO - Amniocentesis - *a test to test for certain chromosomal abnormalities*

FBC - Full blood count

GTT - Glucose tolerance test

HB - Haemoglobin

LVS - Lower vaginal swab

MSU - Mid-stream specimen of using

MOEWS - Modified obstetric early warning chart - *where your observations are recorded*

X-MATCH or XM - Cross matching blood - *in preparation for a possible transfusion*

YOUR CARE TEAM

CMW - Community midwife

CONS - Consultant

MCA - Maternity care assistant

MW - Midwife

REGISTRAR - Senior doctor

SHO - Junior doctor

SMW - Senior midwife

SPR - Specialist registrar

STMW - Student midwife

This is not an exhaustive list so if you see something you don't understand just ask!

HOW YOUR PARTNER CAN HELP

Husbands, partners and significant others, gather round! While your special lady is going through the magical *(and painful, stressful, exhausting, and weird)* process of pregnancy, you may be feeling rather useless and irrelevant given the miracle of life happening nearby, but don't worry, here are five simple tips to help you make your other half's life a great deal easier throughout their pregnancy and beyond.

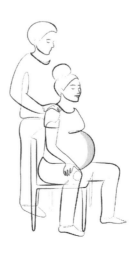

HAVE CONVERSATIONS

Talk to her, listen to her problems, issues, or positives, and support her. Don't be afraid to contribute to the conversation by sharing your own issues, this can create the sense that you're in this together, instead of them being all alone. It may be an idea to do some research surrounding some areas of pregnancy *(or read this whole book)*, so that you aren't left trying to answer questions without any relevant knowledge.

DO THE SMALL THINGS

Do the washing up, get the milk in, give her a massage if she is aching. There are loads of little things you can do across the day which will not only make their life easier but can also give her a boost by adding these little positives. It doesn't have to be big or romantic, just things that will take away unnecessary strain or stress.

PRIORITISE HER

Make sure you always have time for her, and don't become too distanced. Know what she wants at different times throughout the pregnancy, ask her what those needs are and be supportive of her and her decisions. Your relationship will be key to keeping her calm throughout the rough days of the pregnancy, so your support and time will be invaluable.

MAKE SOME MEMORIES

Obviously, the further into the pregnancy you get, the fewer options you will have for this, but cherish these last few weeks where it is just you two. Take the time to spend with your partner, whether that is going out and doing things, or spending nice lazy days at home with them. This is a great way to create some positive memories of pregnancy for her, rather than just memories of morning sickness and uncomfortable waddling!

BE POSITIVE

Tell her how well she is doing, or how beautiful she looks that day, or how strong she is being - make sure she knows how proud you are of her, and how much you care. Your support is crucial and as simple as this is, saying things like this can be a great boost to any pregnant woman's morale.

ANTENATAL CLASSES

How do you learn about all the things you need to know? How do you know if you want to attend antenatal classes? Are you better knowing, or not knowing? In fact, only you know how much you want to know.

Our experience tells us that those that attended good quality antenatal classes, reported a more positive birth experience because there was nothing out there to surprise them, and they felt more in control.

WHEN TO START

We would avoid signing onto classes too early, unless it's an early pregnancy workshop, as you don't want to forget all the information by the time you need it. Once you have had your 20-week scan, you are at a great point in your pregnancy to book onto some classes.

There is a wealth of choice out there and it can be difficult to know which one is the best fit for you.

WHAT YOU'LL WANT TO LEARN

There's so much information on pregnancy, birth and beyond that a new mum can learn, want to know, and can benefit from. Gathering as much knowledge as possible gives you a huge advantage verses going in blind. Knowledge can arm you with the confidence you need to face every eventuality head-on, know what's happening to your body as your baby grows, what your options are during labour, what all the medical jargon being used means, and give you an idea of what to expect once baby arrives, like how to do the basics like change a nappy and breastfeed. These classes can help prepare you, your birth partner and baby's other parent (if different) for the road ahead - the more information you have, the more prepared you can be.

You'll want to look for courses that cover at least the following:

- Natural birth
- Complex birth
- Pain-relief in labour
- Epidural
- Induction
- C-sections
- Instrumental delivery
- Home births
- Hypnobirthing
- Formula feeding
- Breastfeeding

There are also classes out there that cover everything you need to know in early pregnancy too which cover everything you can find up to this point in the book and more - what to do, what to expect, when your appointments are etc.

Additional knowledge you can gain through workshops and classes for once baby is born also include:

- Infant first aid

- Practical parenting - changing nappies, sleep safety etc.

- Developmental baby massage

- Weaning and infant nutrition

- Mental health and wellbeing

MIDWIFE-LED COURSES

The most important questions are *'who is running the course?'* And *'what is their experience of caring for women in labour?'* Ideally, we would recommend attending a midwife-led course. That way you know that all the information will be evidence based and delivered through experience and years of medical training.

Head over to *Let's Talk Birth and Baby*, where you'll find our Official Midwife has all these bases covered. She even offers her first class FREE. Details can be found in *'Our Experts'* on page 12.

OSTEOPATHY DURING PREGNANCY

ANDY MANSFIELD BSC (HONS), DO, PGDIP

OSTEOPATH & LECTURER

Osteopathy is a system of health care developed in the 1870s by Andrew Taylor Still. It puts the person and their history at the centre of the interaction between practitioner and patient. Osteopaths take an in-depth case history before an assessment and build a bespoke treatment plan, suited to your body, your needs, and your musculoskeletal issues.

During pregnancy, your body is going through a process of remarkable change - especially in the last three months. Pre-existing stresses and strains from your history can really come to light as the ligaments soften, and the joints become more mobile. Sciatica, lower back pain, rib pain and pubic pain are all common symptoms throughout pregnancy.

Osteopathy can help reduce these symptoms and manage this process of change through balancing joint mobility and advice on posture and activity.

Pain in pregnancy is common but is NOT normal and should be addressed. Even if you're not suffering musculoskeletal symptoms, we often recommend a check-up every four to six weeks as bump grows to prevent the development of symptoms and enable women to move better, feel more relaxed and most importantly, be more mobile.

MOBILITY IS KEY TO ALLEVIATE HIP AND BACK PAIN

It's important to keep moving during your pregnancy - think mobility rather than activity - and remember, we all have different *'normal'* activity levels. Osteopaths can offer advice on adapting your normal activities to help maintain effective posture, and for you to potentially treat any symptoms yourself.

At the later stage of pregnancy, it's more important for the osteopath to check the balance of the pelvis to optimise the muscle tone and joint mobility prior to labour.

The birth process can be traumatic for mum as well as baby. After the delivery, osteopaths can also help you return to your normal pre-pregnancy activities, by helping release any strains that pregnancy, and labour may have induced.

OSTEOPATHY CAN ALSO BE USED FOR BABIES

Osteopaths have a highly developed sense of touch, being able to feel strain patterns throughout the body. These patterns may be affecting multiple tissues and creating symptoms in seemingly unrelated areas.

The birth process involves a compression as the baby passes through the birth canal. Fortunately, the bones in the baby's head have not developed patent joints at this stage and can overlap to help them fit through.

This is a normal part of the process and helps to stimulate various processes as the baby transitions to life outside the womb. Sometimes this compression can continue after birth because of trauma or less than ideal circumstances. This can lead to discomfort or tightness in muscles and connective tissue.

Stresses and strains like this may lead to colic, sleeplessness, problems latching when feeding, as well as general seemingly unexplained discomfort and other symptoms. Osteopaths use gentle techniques to balance and release any strain or tension patterns and allow freedom of movement throughout the body to help baby become a happy baby.

Parents often report that babies sleep better, and feed easier after treatment, reducing stress for mum and dad too.

For more information on osteopathy, contact Andy Mansfield. His details can be found in *'Our Experts'* on page 12.

PELVIC GIRDLE PAIN

NIKKI KELHAM

SPECIALIST WOMEN'S PHYSIOTHERAPIST

Pain in the lower back, hips and/or groin can be diagnosed as pelvic girdle pain *(PGP)*. It affects 1 in 5 pregnant ladies[32] and is most common in the second and third trimesters.

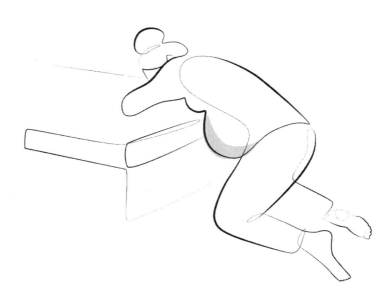

Historically, the pelvis would be described as *'unstable'* in pregnancy. Hormones *(especially one called 'relaxin')* were once blamed for everything related to PGP. We now know that hormones play a fundamental part in helping the ligaments to relax in the pelvis in preparation for labour and birth. This does cause some minimal movement around the joints, but the pain you may be experiencing is most likely to be because of a combination of factors.

We shall look at the reasons why you may be experiencing pain and some tips and advice on how to manage it throughout pregnancy.

As we're sure you have noticed, your body is forever changing throughout the course of your pregnancy. Your waistline is expanding, your centre of gravity is shifting and there is now more weight pushing down on your pelvis. Your body is adapting to these incredible changes and you may have found that your bottom has flattened, the arch in your lower back has increased, and your mid-back feels stiff. All these changes, can contribute to the pain that you are experiencing.

WAYS TO MANAGE YOUR PGP

1. DECREASE STRESS

We know that the more stressed and anxious someone becomes, the more they are in pain. Muscles like the pelvic floor can become overactive when someone is stressed, leading to increased pain.

Taking smaller, shallower breaths can also occur *(especially as the pregnancy progresses),* which in turn increases stress levels. As you can see, it's a bit of a vicious circle, which can be broken with a bit of work.

Learning how to breathe well *(especially in the third trimester when you feel like you have run out of room),* is something that can be a key skill for both during pregnancy and afterwards.

To try this, have a sit down so that you are comfortable. Putting one hand on your bump, take a slow breath in through your nose and feel your bump rise into your hand slightly. Everything should be relaxed including your pelvic floor *(that's important).*

As you breathe out through your mouth, feel your bump sinking away from your hand. We are now going to try this breath out through the mouth, contracting the pelvic floor at the same time as we covered in *'Kegel Exercises'* on page 85. To contract the pelvic floor, we focus on the back passage first. Imagine you are holding in some wind and squeeze the back passage closed. That feeling of closing and lifting is then brought forwards to the front passage. Imagine now that you are stopping yourself from having a wee. Try not to squeeze your bottom cheeks at the same time though.

It can be quite tricky to coordinate this at first but keep practising and it will come. There are so many advantages to this breath work. We want to make sure that the pelvic floor can both relax and contract effectively, and this is a wonderful way to practise this. By breathing slowly into the tummy rather than a shallow breath into the shoulders, tension will be reduced throughout your whole body.

2. FUNCTIONAL MOVEMENTS

Day-to-day movements can be slightly modified to manage your PGP. Many pregnant ladies can reduce their pain considerably by adopting these habits:

- Walking - reducing stride length and not walking past the pain.

- Standing - being aware of how you stand. Try putting an equal amount of weight through both legs and not favouring one side. Trying to tuck your tailbone under slightly *(pelvic tilt)* will take some of the strain out of your lower back and your deep abdominals will support the weight of your bump a bit more.

- Carrying kids/objects - try to keep whatever or whoever you are carrying in front of you rather than on a hip or in one hand to the side.

- Going up stairs - placing one foot firmly on the stair in front, squeeze that bottom cheek as you breathe out and bring the other foot to join it. No breath-holding and no pulling yourself up with the bannister. Yes, it may seem slow and monotonous, but you are re-educating your brain to use your glute muscles effectively.

- Getting in and out of the car - be *'lady-like'* and put your bottom on the seat first and try to bring your legs together and swing round *(use your hands if you need it to)*. It's the reverse getting out of the car.

- Getting out of chair - slide your heels back, lean forwards, use your hands as necessary to push up with. Before you go to stand, breathe out, engage the pelvic floor *(as previously described)* and up you go.

- Getting out of bed - roll onto your side, legs out first, use your hands to push you up into sitting position.

- Putting your knickers/ socks on - it's not best to be single leg standing if you have PGP, have a sit down to put them on.

- Sleeping - try putting a pillow between your knees to sleep, as this keeps the pelvis in a neutral position. If there was ever a time to buy some silk nightwear it may be now. Being able to slide whilst turning in bed may be a game changer!

3. BELT OR NO BELT?

Support belts can be worn to reduce PGP but can sometimes make it worse if the muscles are overactive.

To test this out get a scarf/ towel and wrap it around the outside of the hips *(low under the bump)*. You will know soon if it feels wonderful, or awful! If it feels like it *'holds'* you well, then it is a great idea to wear either a scarf or belt to decrease your pain so that you can then start some muscle strengthening work to manage your PGP throughout the rest of the pregnancy.

4. PAIN RELIEF

- Painkillers - Taking painkillers regularly throughout your pregnancy won't harm you or your baby. Paracetamol can be bought over the counter as the first port of call. Stay away from Ibuprofen, however.

- Heat/ice - Depending where your pain is, you may prefer using a hot water bottle or an ice pack, either is fine.

5. MUSCLE STRENGTHENING AND MOBILITY

Hopefully, once you have consistently done points 1-3, you will find that your PGP reduces, or is at least manageable. It is then time to start strengthening the muscles that have gotten lazy during pregnancy to help support your growing bump.

Most commonly, the glutes *(that flat bottom we talked about)* need some attention. There are 3 muscles that make up the glutes, *'gluteus maximus' (the powerhouse)*, the *'gluteus medius'* and the *'gluteus minimus' (the stabilising duo)*.

Seeking out a pelvic health physiotherapist, pregnancy Pilates class, or working with a pregnancy trained personal trainer can be a great help to strengthen them in a way that doesn't cause you more pain.

Mobility work into the lower and mid-back can really help to ease PGP. Stiffness in the joints and tightness in the muscle can often cause pain.

EXERCISES TO TRY

- Cat/cow posture - In a four-point kneeling position on the floor, breathe in. On your breath out, arch your back up like a cat. Lift

through the pelvic floor, tuck your tailbone under and pull your bump up towards your spine. Breathe in to hold. Breathe out and return to neutral. Repeat this a few times *(e.g., 8-10)*

- Thread the needle - In four-point kneeling position, take a breath in. On the breath out, slide the back of the right hand underneath the left arm as far as you can. Breathe in to hold. On the breath out, engage your pelvic floor and bring the right hand back. Switch sides. Repeat again *(e.g., 5 to each side)*.

6. SEE A PELVIC HEALTH/ WOMEN'S HEALTH PHYSIO

Getting assessed by a specialist physio will give you reassurance as to what exactly is causing your PGP.

They will be able to help release overactive muscles with manual therapy as well

152

as give you a specific home exercise plan to help manage your PGP throughout your entire pregnancy.

Let's Talk Birth and Baby have a specialist women's physiotherapy team that run a regular *'Pelvic Girdle Pain Workshop'* to provide instant relief. Details for Nikki can be found in *'Our Experts'* on page 12.

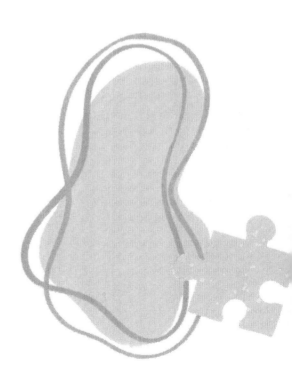

WEEK 13

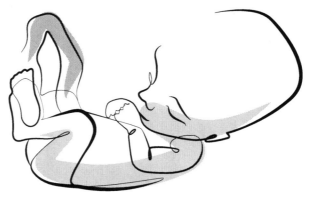

Help is finally here! In the form of your perfectly grown placenta! Now you're in the second trimester, the newly grown placenta takes over the care and maintenance of your baby, as it busily provides your baby with all the nutrients and oxygen it needs. At the same time, the placenta takes away all the waste products that the baby doesn't need.

As a result, some of those pesky pregnancy symptoms may be taking a back seat and you get a little extra spring back in your step! You may be also getting a little extra growth around your waistline and your clothes may be starting to pinch just a little!

Wrapped around little one now, is a bag of protective waters - their amniotic fluid. This 'bag for life' is made up of two layers; the 'amnion' and the 'chorion'. This fluid filled sac provides a cushion for your growing baby.

As you would expect, your baby continues to grow rapidly in size and now has teeth, vocal cords, and even fingerprints!

Now you are feeling a little sprightlier, you may want to be more active, and get back to exercise if you have had a break. Take things slowly as you ease back into things. Things may start to feel a little different from a movement perspective as you get used to your changing sense of balance. As baby peeks above the pubic line, the pelvis is getting a little too cramped now.

Don't forget - eating for two is an old wives' tale to be ignored. You will regret it later down the line if you put on lots of unnecessary weight, as baby only needs a maximum of 200 calories, mainly in the third trimester though, so look after yourself and keep treats to that all too boring minimum!

WEEK 14

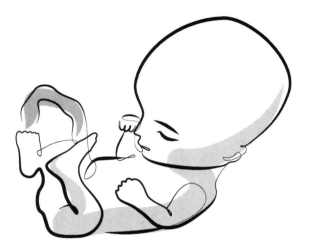

Small, but perfectly formed! Your baby is around the size of a lemon now and is approximately 8.3cm long and weighs 43 grams. Believe it or not, in the first few weeks of pregnancy, all babies are pretty much the same size as each other. It's only the later stages that determines whether your baby will be big, little, or somewhere in between.

Baby is moving around all over the womb and enjoying the ever-decreasing space. Its liver, kidney, and spleen are all working well and functioning as your baby ingests amniotic fluid, which is then excreted in the urine.

Whatever the size now, they are still tiny, so to keep warm, they have developed themselves a little fur coat! Known as *'lanugo'*, this thin layer of tiny hairs will help your baby maintain body temperature and at the same time, protect the skin.

If you have kept your pregnancy under wraps up until now, you may be starting to think about sharing your news as your bump becomes more visible with each passing week. However, don't feel you have to tell anyone, you can stay a secret mum for as long as you are able. It's up to you!

WEEK 15

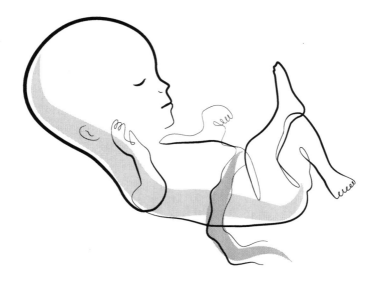

You will be amazed at just how much your baby has grown in just a few short weeks. It's now 10cm in length and about the size of a navel orange. Baby's ears and eyes are in the right place, and finally has the coordination to wiggle their fingers and toes, as well as suck its thumb. They can now suck, swallow, and make breathing movements ready to enter the world in five short months.

You should now be able to feel your growing uterus sneaking up and out of the pelvis, giving you a noticeable bump. It may now be time to change your sleeping position - sleeping on your front may not be particularly comfortable anymore. The recommended sleeping position for pregnancy, is on your left side as this allows for optimal blood flow for both you and baby. After 28 weeks of pregnancy, it is recommended that you avoid sleeping on your back or laying on your back for extended periods of time.

Don't worry if you cannot see or feel your bump yet as baby appears over the pubic bone at different points in pregnancy - it will come!

If you can already see your tummy growing, now may be a good time to start taking some bump pictures for the album!

Baby is practising swallowing and continues to move around in its comfortable mansion - little do they know that before long, this mansion will feel like a tiny one-bedroom flat.

You may be feeling like you are full of energy and may notice an increase in your sex drive - on the other hand, you may feel the complete opposite! As always, everyone is different.

In the UK, dental care is free, as are prescriptions throughout pregnancy and for the first year following your baby's arrival. So now is a good time to register with a dentist, if you aren't already, and book yourself a checkup. Your teeth can take a little bit of a hammering in pregnancy, so it's important to look after your pearly whites - brush and floss regularly! It's also worth noting that bleeding gums and nose bleeds can also occur during pregnancy, which is attributed to the increase in blood volume.

WEEK 16

What is your singing voice like? Do you know that your baby can now hear you when you're singing in the shower? All the noises on the outside world are travelling through, and your baby will be hearing the muffled noises of everyday life.

Don't worry though if your singing voice could scare cats, your baby loves the sound of your voice and of those you're in regular contact with.

Your baby is growing fast! Muscles are growing stronger too, enabling them to stretch out a bit more with semi-controlled movements. Their face is now complete with eyelashes and eyebrows, and their eyes are making small movements left to right and can notice light through their still-sealed eyelids. What's more, your baby will be more sensitive to touch, so touching or poking your belly may cause them to react with a kick or poke back!

Everyone feels their baby's movements at different stages, but you may be starting to feel tiny flutters as your baby continues to flex their muscles. Don't worry if you haven't felt anything yet - at 10-11cm long, your baby is still small so it may be a while yet!

Nothing much will have changed for you this week. You may be seeing an increase in bump size, but other than that it is business as usual!

WEEK 17

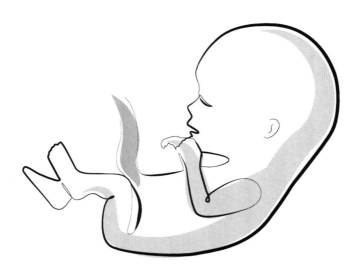

To support your baby as they develop strong bones, it is recommended that pregnant women take a 10mg supplement of vitamin D, as this helps the baby with their bone growing in the first few months after birth. You can also boost your vitamin D intake by eating foods such as mackerel, eggs, and salmon - all rich in vitamin D. Good levels of vitamin D reduce the development of a condition known as *'rickets'*.

Watch out baby, you may be continuing dancing around your roomy pad, but things are going to get a bit tighter! Now over 12cm in length and over 140grams in weight, you are growing at a rapid rate and planning permission will surely be declined for an extension - it's gonna get cramped in there! Baby is growing a layer of baby fat, even though its skin is still translucent, and its heart is finally being regulated by the brain, remaining around twice your own heart rate at 140-150 bpm.

All set for when your baby grows big enough to put their sticky fingers all over the place, their unique finger and toe prints are in the making this week!

For mum, weight gain can feel quite rapid at present, and you may be gaining as much as 1-2lb per week. Remember to take some bump pictures for the album so you can see your growth progress. You may also still be feeling fatigued, constipated, and a bit sluggish, but the nausea should be subsiding by now, fingers crossed!

This week is also a good time to have a think about which antenatal classes you may like to attend. Head over to *Let's Talk Birth and Baby* to sign up to a FREE antenatal class - they're the best around!

WEEK 18

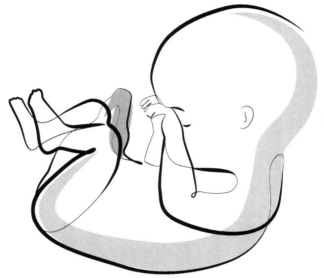

It can be easy to get yourself into a tizz if you haven't felt any movements yet, but don't worry, some people do feel them around this time, others don't start to feel anything for another few weeks - both are completely normal.

Your baby is continuing to put weight on and is now around 190g *(about the same as the amount of butter that goes into a cake - why not make one in celebration!)*

As your baby dances and kicks around, their muscles are gaining strength and cartilage is progressing into solid bone. You may feel your baby hiccup as it develops that skill, and its finger and toe prints now make your baby one of a kind.

Their nervous system is becoming more and more extensive with each passing day as all the message pathways and their protective *'myelin'* covering are put into place.

You may have started to notice that your hands and feet are a little puffy - especially towards the end of the day or in hot weather. This is quite normal but shouldn't be excessive. This is down to the excess fluid your body will be holding onto. If you are worried that you may be swelling up more than is considered normal, contact your midwife.

This week may be also around the time that you start to experience some discomfort in your pelvic area, while your muscles and ligaments start to relax due to a hormone called *'relaxin'*. In addition, as your bump grows, you may be altering your posture slightly and will be unable to comfortably lay on your back. Consider signing up to a prenatal Pilates or yoga class, which can really help strengthen your muscles and keep your joints functioning with ease.

If pain persists, it may be worth seeing a physiotherapist or osteopath to get some help with your skeletal alignment and muscle strain to ease your pain. You can also join *Let's Talk Birth and Baby's* Specialist Women's Physio, Nikki, on her *'Pelvic Girdle Pain Workshop'.* You can find her details in *'Our Experts'* on page 12.

WEEK 19

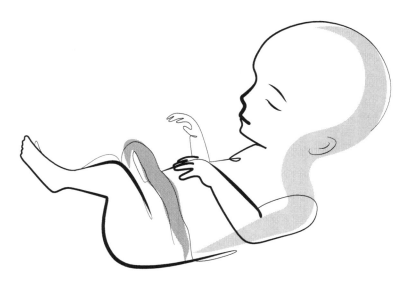

Now around 15cm in length and weighing over 240g, your little one continues to grow at a rapid rate and is now the size of a large mango. As your baby piles on the grams, their skin becomes less translucent and arms and legs much more in proportion.

All the senses are becoming increasingly sensitive, ready for the outside world when life will be one big sensory overload in the first few weeks. A layer of protective substance, called *'vernix caseosa'*, covers your baby this week. This greasy cheese-like layer, which stays until just before birth, prevents your baby's skin being all wrinkly from the amniotic fluid - a bit like how your fingers and toes get after a long bath. Although still too early to confirm, hair colour as pigment has not yet been determined, but your baby will be starting to grow tiny hairs on their scalp.

You may hopefully be feeling more definite kicks this week, which can be a really reassuring part of pregnancy, even if you don't enjoy the sensation, as they become more frequent. As the baby gets bigger and bigger, you may experience indigestion or heartburn, which can be uncomfortable. If you find that you are really struggling, you can speak to your midwife or GP. Sometimes a glass of cold milk may help.

Due to the increase of hormones and your growing baby, you may also feel a little breathless. Although this is normal, it can also be a sign of anaemia, so if you find you are really struggling, speak to your doctor.

If you haven't already needed to, you are probably finding that now is the time that you put your usual wardrobe to one side to make way for maternity clothes to fit your ever-growing bump. Time to shop!

WEEK 20

Put the baby on the scales this week and you will see a weight of around 300g and a measurement of 23cm - getting bigger by the day! You should have your anomaly scan booked for this week, which will take a good look at your baby's internal organs and growth, and you'll finally be able to find out *(if you want to)*, whether you're having a girl or a boy.

If it's a girl, her uterus and ovaries are now fully formed. If it's a boy, his testes will also be present. Otherwise, lots of activity going on inside that growing tummy of yours. If you lie down and relax, you may even be able to see as your baby swims around.

Your baby is swallowing and excreting every day, which helps with the development of the digestive system. *'Meconium'*, which is your baby's first poo, is forming in the digestive system too and is made up of dead skin cells, amniotic fluid, and digestive secretions. This will be passed in the first couple of days following your baby's arrival and will be black with a tar-like consistency - yum.

Now you're halfway, you may be starting to feel a little more breathless as your uterus pushes up towards your lungs and pushes your abdomen forward to make your bump more prominent.

Throughout pregnancy, your red blood volume increases significantly, and you are at risk of becoming anaemic, so ensure that your diet includes a good source of iron, as this is needed for haemoglobin, that carries the oxygen around your body. Lima beans, kidney beans, and green leafy vegetables are all high in iron.

Now is a great time to get booked onto your chosen antenatal course if you haven't done so already. We, of course recommend *Let's Talk Birth and Baby* classes with our Official Midwife Louise Broadbridge.

YOU'VE MADE IT HALFWAY.

WEEK 21

Only 4 months to go until you are holding your little one in your arms! Your baby is now roughly the size of a large banana, with ever decreasing room to spin, twist, and kick you out of at least a few hours of much-needed sleep!

For your little one, sleep is becoming a regular part of their routine with them now sleeping almost as much as a newborn. Their taste buds are now developing as all of those tasty meals you have been having in the outside world are now also tasted by your baby within their amniotic fluid. It's swallowed to help them practise swallowing and digesting food, key skills they will need for the outside world.

This amniotic fluid also provides nutrition and hydration for them in the womb. They'll get a taste for whatever you're eating, so it's time to start introducing them to a whole range of foods - veggies, fruits and tastes that can help them be less picky once they're at weaning age.

Their limbs are now finally in proportion to their body, and bones inside them are firming up, meaning their movements are now more controlled and less twitchy.

WEEK 22

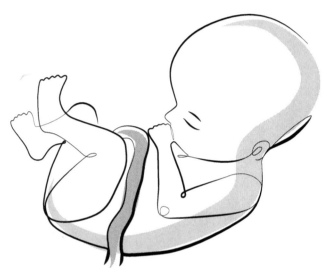

You may be starting to notice a pattern in relation to your baby's movements by now. We have moved away from asking mums to *count the kicks*, and now ask that you be aware of what is normal for your baby. Some babies move more during the night whilst you are at rest, some like to do their kick boxing during the day. If you have a placenta that is situated at the front *(anterior)*, movements may feel a little muffled. However, you should always get checked out if you are worried.

Hands and feet can start to become a little swollen from this point in, which there is usually nothing to worry about. Pop your feet up at the end of the day and make sure you wear comfortable shoes. If they get really swollen though you need to let your midwife know, as your blood pressure may be creeping up.

You will need to give your employer your MATB1 form soon. This can be requested from your midwife and is needed to process your maternity pay. You can start this at any point from 29-weeks and are entitled to a year off from work, irrelevant of your length of service. However, getting paid past 39-weeks will depend on your length of service and your employer's maternity leave policy. See 'Maternity Leave' on page 124 for more info on your rights, how to tell your employer, and answers to other common questions you may have.

As you have probably now realised, baby is all about growing from here on in. Now weighing in at around 430g, your growing baby is roughly 28cm in length. Preparing for the weaning stage in about 10 months' time, gums are developing, tooth buds and their first milk teeth will arrive just a few short months after arrival. Did you know that babies are born with both their milk teeth and their adult teeth above them already in their jaw?

Eyes are formed, but you will have to wait a little while to know the true eye colour, as for some babies, the colour at birth is not the result!

WEEK 23

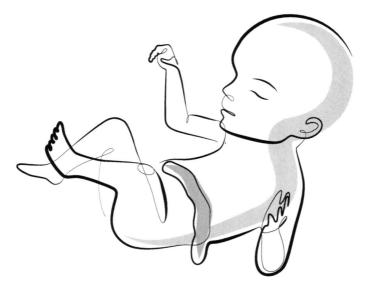

You should be well and truly feeling those kicks now! With slightly less room to kick around in, those feelings should be much more pronounced as their arms and legs get stronger and stronger.

Be careful what you say now though, as the baby is listening to every word! They will get used to daily sounds and will recognise your favourite music, as well as the sound of yours and your partner's voices.

As you head towards the end of the second trimester, and the end of month 5, you may start to experience some practise contractions also known as '*Braxton Hicks*'. These tightenings can be a little alarming at first, as your stomach can go rock hard. However, they shouldn't be too painful and should come and go at irregular intervals.

This week marks the point where a large amount of weight gain will likely begin for your baby. Their weight will likely double over the next four or so weeks. With this, will come some saggy skin due to skin developing faster than fat, however in their face, a pinky red hue will emerge thanks to the development of veins and arteries close beneath the skin's surface.

A new thing you may notice around this time is some skin discoloration occurring between your belly button and pubic area, this is, like with many pregnancy symptoms, because of various pregnancy hormones. This is called the *'linea negra'*. Do you know the old wives' tale about gender predictions from that line? Apparently, if it doesn't go beyond your belly button, you may be having a girl! Obviously, as with any old wives' tale, there is not much proof of this, but it's fun trying to guess if you don't know already!

WEEK 24

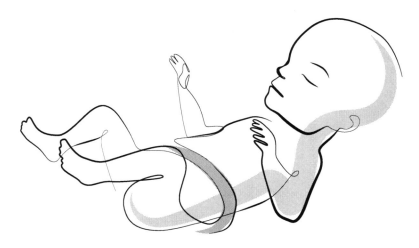

Pretty as a picture, your baby's face is just about fully formed, getting ready for all those photographs to give to grandma and grandpa!

Continuing to grow, your little one is gaining around 3-4 ounces a week and is around a foot long now. With each ounce, their body is filling out as they take in all those precious nutrients you are giving them through the umbilical cord and via their amniotic fluid. They are tasting more and more as their taste buds get even more sensitive. Their hair is also as white as snow as it is yet to have any pigment.

At 24-weeks' gestation, although your baby would be tiny, should they be born now, they have reached the point of viability and would be cared for in the neonatal unit. In preparation for the outside world, their lungs are getting stronger and stronger. As they mature, a substance called *'surfactant'* is appearing, which keeps the *'alveoli' (tiny air sacs)* open as they practise breathing in and out.

One thing you may be experiencing at this point in the pregnancy, is a level of numbness or tingling in your fingers and wrists. This sensation is called *'carpal tunnel syndrome'*. This occurs when the fluid causing swelling in your lower extremities is redistributed when you begin laying down. This redistribution puts pressure on your nerves going through your wrist and can also take the form of pain or a dull ache. Another annoying side-effect, but the light at the end of the tunnel, is that this will slowly disappear once you are no longer pregnant.

To add to the already growing list of side-effects during pregnancy, you may find that you start to experience itching, especially on your tummy, as your skin stretches to accommodate your growing baby. In most cases, pregnancy-related itching, whilst annoying, is usually nothing to worry about. However, if your itching becomes excessive and is especially noticeable on your hands and feet, with a worsening at night, it is important that you contact your maternity department as it may be a sign of a more serious condition known as *'obstetric cholestasis'*. More information on this condition can be found in our *'Pregnancy Complications'* section on page 74.

WEEK 25

Although you are still feeling reasonably energetic, your bump may be starting to make you feel a little more breathless. This is caused by your baby taking up more room now it's doubling in size but could also be down to anaemia. You will have a blood test at 28-weeks to check that your iron levels are okay, but if you find that you are really struggling, it may be worth speaking to your GP.

Haemorrhoids are a horrible side effect of pregnancy. Again, caused by the added pressure of your baby on your digestive system. Couple this with some constipation and you may find yourself suffering. Make sure you keep hydrated and have lots of fibre. This should hopefully keep your stools soft, so you won't need to strain.

It is difficult not to stress about weight gain especially in the second trimester when the baby is piling on the ounces but try to eat in moderation and partake in some regular, light exercise.

Baby is just over 33cm now, longer than a school ruler and will weigh around 650-700g, heavier than a basketball, but around the size of a head of cauliflower. One major milestone your baby will have made during this week, is that they will be able to begin practising breathing. This comes due to their nose being developed enough that it starts working. Breathing will be a key skill for them early on to keep their little organs working in the real world. Despite this, their lungs will still only be in the development stages, meaning they are not quite ready for the real thing just yet.

Throughout pregnancy, it is important that you are vigilant about your dental hygiene. The demands of pregnancy can take its toll on your teeth and gums, which can lead to long-term conditions such as *'gingivitis' (receding gums)* and *'inflammatory gum disease'.* As well as being entitled to free prescriptions, you are also entitled to free dental healthcare, on the NHS throughout pregnancy, so it may be time to take advantage.

WEEK 26

It is not known exactly why pregnant women are more prone to leg cramps, but you may find yourself suffering with this unpleasant muscle contraction - especially during the night. Try getting your partner to flex your foot back towards you to relax the muscles. Gentle leg and ankle rotations before bed may also help.

Baby has grown another inch and piled on over 200g in weight - it's growing fast now!

This week's big baby milestone is that their eyes will now be open! With the retina now being fully developed, your little one can now see the limited world around them in your uterus, but this will make the big wide world they are soon to enter more interesting for them.

One thing you may notice once your baby is born, is that their eye colour may change, this is perfectly normal, and any changes will normally have occurred by the six-month mark.

Unfortunately, at this stage of the pregnancy you may notice an increase in insomnia, which is the last thing you'll need! Some things you can try to tackle this include daytime exercise/fresh air, as well as limiting liquids before you go to sleep.

What may not help however, is that your baby is in the process of learning various movements they will need when they enter the world, for example pedaling *(which will eventually evolve into walking)* and stretching, which will make sleeping more difficult, sorry mumma!

WEEK 27

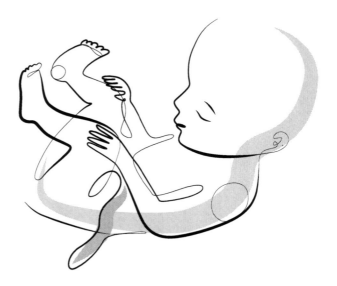

You've almost reached the end of the second trimester! Be thankful for any pregnancy glow you are experiencing *(sorry to all those mums out there that feel they are far from glowing!)*. Over the coming weeks, you may find some of those early symptoms return, as everything, including your stomach, starts to get just a little bit squished.

Sleep may be starting to be disturbed as you struggle to get comfortable. Women are now advised to avoid sleeping or laying on your back as this can increase the risk of stillbirth. The optimum position is to sleep on your left-hand side to increase the level of oxygen and nutrients that reach the baby. If you find that you can only sleep on your right-hand side, this is still considered safer than sleeping on your back.

TOP TIP: Try changing the side of the bed you sleep on as you may find it easier to sleep facing away from your partner or over the side of the bed!

Another centimetre in length from head to toe gained, a major milestone for your baby is reached during this time in the pregnancy - they can now begin to recognise individual voices. At this point, their ears and hearing have matured where they are able to identify some voices, or at least some slightly muffled equivalents of your voices that they hear through the various layers covering them at this stage.

Your baby now has more taste buds than they will at birth, making everything you eat a delight, or shock to their palette once ingested via their amniotic fluid. If they don't like what you've eaten, they'll swiftly let you know about it! Mums have reported they've felt a sharp kick or hiccup from their little one after eating spicy food for example. Here's your chance to start trying new food and seeing what the baby likes!

For your body, a somewhat more unwanted change may be underway, stretch marks! Unfortunately, it is estimated that at least half of all women[29] get them, however, these marks do not stay as vivid as they start out, but fade over time. It may be worth keeping your skin moisturised morning and night, drink lots of water and manage your eating habits to avoid rapid weight gain and reduce risk of stretch marks.

A slightly less happy symptom you may be beginning to experience at this stage, if you've not suffered from it so far, is some swelling around some of your extremities *(ankles, feet, and hands)* otherwise called an *'edema'*. These occur due to fluid buildup in tissue because of your increased blood flow and pressure from your uterus. Though it is normally nothing to worry about if the swelling is excessive talk to your doctor as it may be a sign of pre-eclampsia. You can get some relief from the swelling by trying some light exercise such as walking and avoiding sitting or standing for too long.

THIRD TRIMESTER

THE COUNTDOWN BEGINS!

You've entered the final 3 months of pregnancy before your little one enters the big wide world. Your baby has a LOT of growing to do in these last few months, gaining about 2kg and growing around 12cm in this time. You'll be grateful for a maternity belt *(if recommended by your midwife or physio)* and moisturiser to give you some extra support and stop the itchiness that stretch marks can cause as your bump grows by the day.

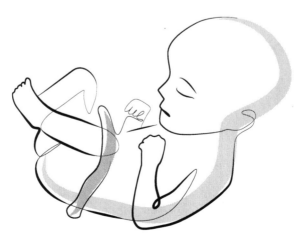

Unfortunately, pregnancy symptoms can rear their ugly head again this trimester with aches and pains being the most prevalent. Constipation, heartburn, swelling, and increased vaginal discharge being others you can expect. You'll want to get some maternity clothes for these last weeks as your bump certainly won't fit in those floaty dresses you've been getting away with wearing these past few months with a smaller bump.

Baby will hopefully start getting into its head-down position during these few months too, and as space gets tighter and tighter, they'll move further back into the pelvis, this time in preparation for their exit. You'll finally get your breath back now they're starting to move away from your lungs and give you a little more space to inhale.

You'll want to start thinking about baby names, your birth plan. It's time to get the nursery in order and pack your hospital bags as you prepare for baby's arrival very soon!

YOU'RE ALMOST THERE

UNDERSTANDING YOUR BABY'S GROWTH CHART

Every woman in the UK is provided with an individualised growth chart that will map and follow your baby's growth throughout the final trimester of your pregnancy. The charts are individualised to consider the height, weight, ethnicity, and parity *(how many babies mum has had before).*

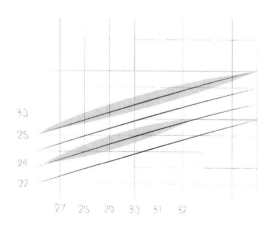

The charts produced after inputting all this information will have the 10th, 50th and 90th centile lines which will later show what your baby's current weight is after the fundal height measurement, and where it is expected to be by your next appointment, compared to other babies at the same gestation. These charts are used alongside fundal height measurements.

Your first measurement will be taken from your 20-week scan, and later, from 28-weeks, your midwife will measure your bump from the top down to your pubic bone. That measurement, taken in centimeters, is then plotted on the chart too.

From 26 to 28-weeks, your midwife will measure your bump at each appointment. Sometimes the measurements trigger a referral for a growth scan. This would happen if:

- The first measurement was below the 10th centile/ higher than the 90th centile.

- Later measurements showed a lack of growth (static growth).

Individualised growth charts are a really good way of keeping track of growth, however, measurements are subjective so there is a margin for error. If you see a different midwife, there may be a variance in the way you are measured.

COMMON TERMS YOU MAY COME ACROSS

AC - Abdominal circumference (around the abdomen).

BPD - Biparietal diameter (across the head).

CENTILE - Lines on growth chart to show expected growth (e.g., babies in 50th centile means 50% of babies at same gestation are same weight).

EFW - Estimated fetal weight.

FH - Fundal height.

FL - Femur length (length of thigh bone).

HC - Head circumference (around the head).

SGA/ LGA - Small/large for gestational age.

TCD - Transverse cerebellar diameter (across the cerebellum in the brain).

HYPNOBIRTHING

Hypnobirthing uses self-hypnosis, breathing and relaxation techniques throughout labour and birth to facilitate a calmer and more positive delivery. For anyone that has never done any kind of meditation or relaxation practise, the concept of hypnobirthing can feel a little bit like a walk on the wild side. However, there are some fantastic benefits to giving hypnobirthing a try.

Here are our Official Midwife's thoughts on hypnobirthing:

"AS AN EXPECTANT MUM, I DECIDED THAT HYPNOBIRTHING WAS NOT FOR ME AND WAS FAR TOO 'OUT THERE' FOR ME TO MASTER. I WAS FORTUNATE WITH MY LABOUR, AND I CAN NOW LOOK BACK ON MY EXPERIENCE POSITIVELY, DESPITE IT BEING A BIT OF A BUMPY RIDE! NOW THAT I AM A MIDWIFE, I WOULD LOVE TO KNOW WHETHER I WOULD HAVE HAD A DIFFERENT EXPERIENCE HAD I USED HYPNOBIRTHING TECHNIQUES.

I HAVE WATCHED SOME FANTASTIC BIRTHS WITH WOMEN WHO HAVE TAKEN TIME IN PREGNANCY TO PRACTISE THE DEEP BREATHING AND RELAXATION. SURPRISINGLY THOUGH, THE WOMEN THAT HAVE DONE JUST THAT, AND HAD EMERGENCY C-SECTIONS ARE OFTEN THE ONES THAT REPORT THAT HYPNOBIRTHING HELPED THEM NAVIGATE THE UNEXPECTED".

Our advice when considering hypnobirthing:

Find a class that encourages mum and partner to explore all different types of delivery. Learn what forceps, ventouse and c-section deliveries can be like and what you could expect.

Visualisation is compelling, but ensure you visualise all the different scenarios, not just a water birth *(obviously imagine a water birth too)* - that way you have prepared for every eventuality and every setting.

Breathing and relaxation practise is vital during pregnancy. Having the skill to recognise when tension enters your body quickly, will allow you to switch on your relaxation skills and keep unwanted body tension at bay.

Another tip - don't change the word *'contraction'* to *'surge'* as most hypnobirthing instructors suggest! Doing this is a little detrimental to you sometimes. Your midwife or doctor uses the word *'contraction'* 100s of times a week, and if they forget that you have asked them to use a different term, it can throw your concentration off and have the opposite effect to the goal of relaxation.

For a fantastic hypnobirthing workshops, visit *Let's Talk Birth and Baby,* where you can be guaranteed a midwife-led class that will give you all the amazing benefits of hypnobirthing, without some of the fluff!

CAESAREAN SECTIONS

There's not a lot you can control whilst in labour. The baby might not want to come out yet or may want to enter this world a little early or a little late. Some labours are quick and easy, some are long and complicated. It's worth remembering that no two labours are the same, even for the same woman. If the time comes and you either elect for a caesarean or have an emergency section, then one thing is for sure - you're not alone. 1 in 4 births occur this way[30] and are widely performed across the UK, so you're in safe hands.

Here's a list of things you should know ahead of your due date about caesarean sections:

YOU'RE CONSULTED AT EVERY TURN

The doctors and midwives will explain everything to you in detail - the risks, the eventualities, the options you have and make sure you fully understand everything before deciding. If you have a specific birthing plan you'd like them to follow, make sure this is communicated to them upon arrival and double-check they are aware of it as you get closer to birth.

YOU WON'T FEEL A THING

During most c-sections, you're given a regional anaesthetic, which numbs you from the breasts down. This allows you to remain awake during the procedure. It also means you can have your birthing partner in theatre with you for support, to cut the cord and hold the baby, as they would during a vaginal delivery, until you're able to sit up again. Whilst surgeons are accessing the baby through your lower abdomen and subsequently stitch you back up, you won't feel any pain, even if you're awake the whole time. Sometimes you're even able to watch the surgery on a monitor so you can watch your little one enter this world. Common choices for anaesthesia include a spinal block and an epidural block. In some emergency cases, however, general anaesthesia is needed, and your partner may not be allowed to be with you.

RECOVERY IS SLOW

A c-section is a major surgery. Your surgeon must cut through and sew up 7 layers made up of skin, fascia, and muscle, therefore it's normal to feel a little shaky and uncomfortable after the procedure. Most women are sent home within a few days, and once you're home, it can take your body months to completely heal. Even then, your muscles will be continuing to strengthen over the months to come.

The healing process can also be quite painful, especially when standing or sitting down, or lifting/holding a baby. You'll need to take care not to put pressure on your lower abdomen.

YOU'LL NEED LOTS OF REST

Rest when your baby rests - though unrealistic, it's great advice when it comes to caesarean recovery. Healing from this major surgery can take a while, so make sure you listen to your midwife about the dos and don'ts post-birth. Lifting heavy objects *(including the baby)* or pushing yourself too much can cause significant discomfort and slow down the healing process. Do your best to take some time out to heal. Another little tip is to hold onto your incision site when you cough or sneeze, but most of all, look after your body.

VAGINAL BIRTHS ARE STILL AN OPTION FOR YOUR NEXT PREGNANCY

VBACs - *(Vaginal births after caesarean)* are quite common in second and third pregnancies. Compared with undergoing a second caesarean, a VBAC would mean a faster recovery and a shorter hospital stay. VBAC might also appeal to you if you wanted a vaginal birth initially but were unable to for whatever reason.

If you opt for a VBAC, you will be advised to have your baby on the obstetric-led unit so that you and your baby can be monitored closely. Having a vaginal birth after a caesarean does however carry a slightly increased risk of uterine rupture *(>0.5%)*[31]. This is where the caesarean scar

on the uterus can break open and requires an emergency c-section to get the baby out safely. For the majority of mums-to-be however, a vaginal birth following a previous caesarean is completely safe and studies suggest it is safer that a repeat c-section - so definitely something to consider.

Overall, c-section recovery will be slower than a vaginal birth, however, the easier you take things in the earlier days, the quicker your recovery will be. Continue with gentle movement, but don't overdo it.

WRITING A BIRTH PLAN

Your birth plan is a record of your wishes and instructions for care before, during and after labour. You don't have to create one, but they are helpful to give you some peace of mind knowing you have a *'plan'* in place. Discussing your birth plan with your midwife, gives you the opportunity to ask any questions and find out what to expect during labour.

It's also an opportunity for your midwife to get to know you, help understand your feelings and your priorities during labour, and allows your birthing partner to know what you want too. Let's face it, you're going to be too occupied pushing a human out to ensure your labour is as close to your plan as it can be.

Your birth plan is also personal to you. Every birth is different, and every mum-to-be is different, so this will be a clear indication of your wishes. It will include details of your medical history, your current circumstances (i.e., consultant-led, whether you're a single parent-to-be) and have noted down what is available at your maternity service that you'd like to utilise.

It's worth noting, these plans aren't set in stone, you are able to change your mind at any time. You will need to stay relatively flexible however, if complications arise with you or your baby, or if certain facilities aren't available to you at the time of birth. Writing a birth plan gives you the opportunity to consider all the difference scenarios your labour and birth may cover and in doing so, gives you confidence to make the right decision for your circumstances

WHAT TO INCLUDE:

- Where and how you want to give birth.

- Desired pain relief options.

- Use of forceps or ventouse (intervention or instrumental delivery).

- Your choice for/against a caesarean section.

- Your baby after the birth (skin to skin, delayed cord clamping, cord blood banking, placental use).

You can also use this opportunity to think about what your birth partner can do to support you throughout labour, whether that's coaching you through hypnobirthing, keeping you cool, or DJ'ing your labour playlist.

Your midwife might give you a form to fill in, or you can provide your own. It's a good idea to always keep a copy of your birth plan with you and have additional copies for your birth partner handy too. We've put together a plan for you in the next few pages for you to print out and fill in to take with you.

MY BIRTH PLAN

Name: _____ Due date: _____

Where I
want to
give birth: ☐ Hospital ☐ Birthing unit ☐ At Home ☐ Undecided

Name or address of birth location: _____

BIRTHING PARTNER

☐ I want someone with me ☐ I want more than one person with me ☐ I'm not sure

Name of birthing partner(s): _____

Relationship to you: _____

FORCEPS/VENTOUSE DELIVERIES

☐ I've had the procedure explained to me and understand it may be necessary during my labour

☐ I'd like this procedure explained to me in more depth

☐ I'd like my partner or companion with me

CAESAREAN DELIVERY

☐ I've had the procedure explained to me and understand it may be necessary during my labour

☐ I'd like an elective c-section

☐ I'd like my partner or companion with me

ACTIVITY DURING LABOUR

☐ I would like to move around ☐ I wouldn't like to move around ☐ I don't mind ☐ I'm not sure yet.

POSITIONS *(tick all that apply)*

☐ In bed with pillows ☐ Standing ☐ Sitting ☐ Kneeling

☐ On all fours ☐ Laying on one side ☐ Not sure yet

☐ Other *(please specify)* _____

MONITORING

☐ I have discussed with my midwife how I would like my baby's heart to be monitored

Chosen method: _____

MIDWIVES/NURSES/DOCTORS IN TRAINING

☐ I don't want a trainee present ☐ I don't mind

PAIN RELIEF OPTIONS

☐ Breathing & relaxation ☐ Hypnobirthing ☐ Gas & air *(entonox)* ☐ Massage

☐ Acupuncture ☐ TENS machine ☐ Pethidine ☐ Epidural ☐ None

☐ Other *(please specify)* _____

EPISIOTOMY

☐ I understand it may be necessary ☐ I'd rather not have one

BIRTHING EQUIPMENT

☐ Beanbag ☐ Birthing ball ☐ Mats ☐ Stool ☐ TENS machine ☐ Pool

☐ None of the above ☐ I'm not sure if I want to use these yet

☐ I will bring my own ☐ To be provided if available

SPECIAL FACILITIES

☐ LDRP room *(labour, delivery, recovery, postnatal rooms)* ☐ Birthing pool *(if available)*

☐ I'm not sure yet

☐ Other *(Please specify)* _____

SKIN-TO-SKIN CONTACT

☐ I'd like my baby placed straight on me ☐ I'd like my partner to hold them first

☐ I'd like my baby cleaned before given to me ☐ I don't mind

☐ I haven't decided yet

Any specific requests: _____

OTHER CONSIDERATIONS

☐ Myself or my partner would like to cut the cord ☐ I'd like the clamping of the cord delayed

☐ I'd like a lotus delivery ☐ I don't mind

PLACENTAL DELIVERY

☐ I would like an assisted delivery ☐ Let it deliver naturally ☐ I don't mind

☐ I would like to keep the placenta   ☐ Please dispose of it   ☐ I'd like to donate it

If you'd like to keep the placenta, have you arranged for collection?

☐ Yes   ☐ No

FEEDING MY BABY

☐ Breastfeeding   ☐ Bottle feeding   ☐ Mixture   ☐ I'm not sure

VITAMIN K

☐ I consent to Vitamin K being given to my baby   ☐ I do not consent

SPECIAL REQUIREMENTS

☐ I will need an interpreter as English is not my primary language
☐ I will need a sign language interpreter
☐ I have special dietary requirements
☐ I and/or my partner have special needs
☐ I would like certain religious/cultural customs observed *(give details below)*

ADDITIONAL COMMENTS

NEWBORN ESSENTIALS

Not long to go now until your little one is finally here, so it's time to start kitting out the nursery with everything your baby may need in the first year of its life. We've put together a checklist for you of everything you could possibly need or want, to help you shop, add to your baby shower registry, or ask relatives for their pre-loved pieces so you've got everything prepared for their arrival.

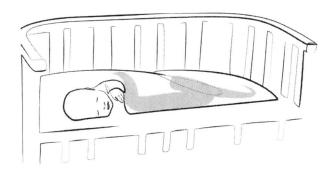

Nesting is likely to start in a few weeks so having all this ready and waiting will give you something to organise and beautify once your nesting instincts kick in.

NOT ALL THE BELOW WILL BE APPLICABLE TO YOU, AND SOME, YOU MIGHT NOT NEED AT ALL. JUST CROSS OUT WHAT YOU WON'T NEED, TICK OFF WHAT YOU BUY AS YOU GO AND HAPPY SHOPPING!

FURNITURE

☐ Cot & mattress, mattress cover, fitted sheets

☐ Changing pad/mat

☐ Moses basket/bassinet/side sleeper/crib

☐ Nursing chair

☐ Wardrobe/chest of drawers

CHANGING & BATH TIME

☐ Flannels

☐ Bath insert

☐ Cotton wool pads

☐ Creams & lotions

☐ Soap & shampoo

☐ Nail trimming kit

☐ Hairbrush

☐ Baby wipes

☐ Nappies or reusable nappies & liners

☐ Nappy cream

☐ Bath thermometer

☐ Nappy bin/bags

☐ Soft towels

ELECTRONICS

☐ Baby monitor

☐ Room thermometer

☐ Night light/lullaby/white noise machine

☐ Baby body temperature thermometer

☐ Nasal aspirator

TRAVEL

☐ Car seat & base

☐ Sun blinds

☐ Pram/buggy/travel system

☐ Rain cover/sunshade

☐ Changing bag with changing mat

☐ Snowsuit

☐ Hat/mittens/booties

☐ Travel cot

☐ Baby carrier/sling

CLOTHES

☐ Sleepsuits/long sleeve onesies

☐ Short-sleeve suits/vests

☐ T-shirts/dresses

☐ Leggings/trousers

☐ Cardigans/jackets

☐ Socks

☐ Sleep bag

FEEDING

☐ Dribble bibs

☐ Breast pump, nipple covers & creams

☐ Milk storage bags

☐ Muslins

☐ Bottles, teats & bottle brush

☐ Steriliser

☐ Bottle warmer

☐ Nursing pillow

☐ Nursing bra

☐ Breast pads

Just remember, babies go through quite a few outfit changes from spit-up, poonamis and dribble, so make sure you stock up and in lots of different sizes, making note of what season it will be when your baby will fit into each size. This will save on your washing loads and means you don't have to feel guilty buying a whole host of different outfits and cute clothes.

If you're looking for a helping hand during pregnancy, to get some of these newborn essentials for free, or for less, head to *YourBabyClub. co.uk* and take advantage of our freebies, discounts, competitions and more.

PACKING YOUR HOSPITAL BAG

Preparing for your stay in hospital when you're about to give birth to your perfect little baby, is an exciting time, much like packing for a holiday *(except holidays do not involve squeezing a human head through your pelvis, okay poor analogy - sorry!)*, Packing for the big day can be exciting though, after all, you're on the home stretch. As you enter your third trimester, it would be a good idea to start thinking about what you're going to need, want, and all the *'just in case'* items to pack, ready for the moment your baby arrives in this world.

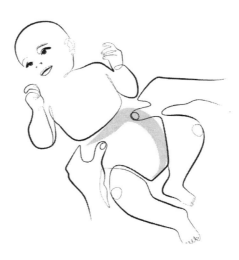

You can start packing your hospital bag whenever you want to, but it's a good idea to have your bag ready from 34-weeks onwards.

If you're feeling totally clueless about what you need to pack, try not to worry. Here's what you should think about adding to your bag:

FOR MUM – LABOUR AND DELIVERY

☐ Maternity notes

☐ Lightweight dressing gown

☐ Socks

☐ Slippers & flip-flops/ sandals

☐ Lip balm

☐ Massage oil/body lotion

☐ Water spray & sponge or fan

☐ Own pillow(s)

☐ Books/magazines/movies on tablet

☐ Eye mask & earplugs

☐ Spare clothes & underwear Enough for about 2 days

FOR MUM – AFTER DELIVERY

☐ Nightdress or oversized T-shirt and comfy shorts

☐ Maternity pads/pants

☐ Nursing bras & breast pads

☐ Toiletries including toothbrush and toothpaste

☐ Glasses/contact lenses

☐ Phone & charger

☐ Snacks & drinks

☐ Comfy clothes to wear home & shoes

FOR BIRTHING PARTNER

☐ Snacks & water

☐ Phone/camera/video camera (plus chargers and batteries)

☐ Spare clothes and underwear

☐ Toiletries including toothbrush

☐ Small pillow

☐ Entertainment

☐ Cash (for vending machines/ on-site cafe)

FOR BABY

☐ Babygrows

☐ Muslin cloths & bibs

☐ Socks, scratch mittens & booties

☐ Blanket/ swaddle

☐ Nappies & nappy bags

☐ Wet bag for dirty clothes

☐ Wipes

☐ Vests, shorts/leggings, jumpers, dresses

☐ Going home outfit

☐ Hats

☐ Ready-made formula bottles if bottle feeding

☐ Any colostrum you may have harvested (in a cool bag with ice packs)

☐ Car Seat/carrier

Once you've got these essentials together, make sure to choose a bag that is not too bulky, but allows easy access without having to rummage around trying to find a pot of nappy cream or a clean pair of knickers you'd rolled up in the bottom.

A great tip would be to group things in little zip seal bags, or luggage organisers, keeping all your toiletries in a separate toiletry bag to things for baby, your clothes separate from baby's, as well as a spare bag for any dirties ready for the wash when you get home.

Remember to label each bag too, so your partner or midwife can help you with getting things.

You could also pack an extra bag of another days' worth of clothes for you, your partner and your baby and leave it in the car just in case you need to stay a little longer than expected. This will save your partner needing to drive home and back again, particularly if you don't live that close to where you are giving birth.

COUNTING KICKS

For many expectant mums, feeling those first baby movements can feel a little bit like the Motherland! The prize for surviving all those pesky pregnancy symptoms and looking a little peaky whilst the world is oblivious to the tiny human growing inside. Those kicks, once they start, can be a regular reassurance that you have a growing baby inside and once they really get strong, an opportunity for your partner to feel connected. That said, not all women like the sensation of feeling their baby move, so don't stress if it is not a part of pregnancy that you relish - it's not uncommon.

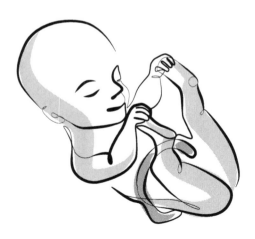

Aside from being a reminder that you have a baby growing inside you, your baby's movements are also a good indicator of their overall wellbeing. An active baby is generally a happy baby. Just like when we are unwell, we slow down. Your baby is no different. Therefore, keeping an eye on your baby's movement is so important. As is getting checked anytime you have any worries.

WHEN SHOULD I START FEELING KICKS?

Baby should start to make themselves known between 16 and 24 weeks of pregnancy, with some first-time mums not feeling anything until after 20 weeks. It is a myth that baby's movements slow down in the later stages of pregnancy, so if you haven't felt your baby move by 24-weeks, or notice a reduction in movements, contact your midwife so that you and baby can be checked over.

WHAT DO THEY FEEL LIKE?

In the early days, feeling your baby's movements may just feel like little flutters in your tummy before your little kickboxer starts landing some serious kicks and punches and you are then left in little doubt that your baby is live and literally, kicking!

A common occurrence is baby experiencing hiccups! It is perfectly normal for babies to have hiccups as they get used to swallowing. What is important, is that baby's movements are otherwise the same. So, hiccups with normal movements - worry not. Hiccups with a change in movements - get checked.

Once your baby starts to move, you will start to get a feel for what is normal. They will have periods of rest and activity, and by being conscious of their activity, any time you feel their normal activity changes and you are worried, please call your midwife.

A reason why getting checked out is so important, is that a reduction in movement could indicate that all is *not* well. If that is the case, it is far better to learn this sooner rather than later, so that you and baby can get any treatment needed. Remember, doing this could save your baby's life.

PERINEAL MASSAGE

The perineum is the area of muscle between your vagina and back passage and forms part of the support given to the pelvic floor, which aids control over your lower internal organs. Most first-time mums will suffer some degree of tearing during childbirth. However, research has shown that massaging the perineum can help to stretch more easily during the birthing of your baby.

Massage increases the elasticity of the muscle which, in turn helps with stretching and can reduce the need for episiotomy *(a small cut made to facilitate the delivery of your baby)*. It is particularly useful if you have previous scar tissue or a rigid perineum from long term activities such as horse riding or dancing.

SUGGESTED POSITIONS

- Prop yourself up using pillows on a bed or a sofa.

- Lay back in the bath with one leg over the side.

- Stand with your leg up on a stool in the shower *(be very careful though as your balance may not be as it should be)*.

- Sit on a clean, open toilet seat with legs wide apart.

These will make the massage a bit more comfortable as your hips and back need support and bump can get in the way quite a bit at this stage too.

Massaging your perineum from 34-weeks can reduce the risk of trauma in this area anD increases blood flow which will later aid recovery.

HOW TO MASSAGE

Starting from 34 weeks either you or your partner can perform the massage.

Using an oil is essential, however, expensive oils are not necessary. For many years, midwives have recommended using almond oil, which is a natural and odourless oil and does the job perfectly.

- Use a small amount of oil.

- Ensure you are in a comfortable position.

- Place one or both thumbs within the back wall of the lower vagina.

- Gently press down towards the back passage.

- Then move from side to side for 3-4 minutes at a time.

This should result in a slight burning and stretching feeling; however, it shouldn't be painful. It's an idea to practise your hypnobirthing or slow breathing techniques while you massage to stay nice and relaxed.

Getting into a routine of doing these 3 to 4 times per week will hopefully reduce the significance of any tearing.

COLOSTRUM HARVESTING

Throughout pregnancy, your breasts are also changing in preparation for feeding your baby. In the latter weeks, they will even start to produce a liquid known as *'colostrum'*. This highly concentrated milk is packed with goodness and has everything from protein to nutrients, to those all-important antibodies that help to protect your baby by building up a healthy immune system.

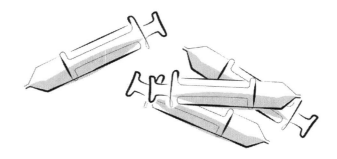

Colostrum is packed with white blood cells, which help to guard against and fight infection. These clever cells work hard to produce antibodies which in turn, neutralise any nasty bacteria or viruses your baby may encounter. This amazing milk really is the gift that keeps on giving, with all its vitamins and minerals that help keep skin, vision, and immune system in tip top working order.

We could write pages and pages about the benefits of colostrum, but all you really need to know is that it is, basically, super milk for your baby.

WHAT IS COLOSTRUM HARVESTING?

When women have their first pregnancy scan at around 12-weeks when an official estimated date of delivery (EDD) will be given. We all know however, that very few babies arrive on that date and so, rather than our bodies producing vast quantities of milk in anticipation, we produce colostrum. As we have said, this contains everything your baby needs for a healthy start but does lack that volume that your mature milk will provide when it arrives around 3 or 4 days after baby is born.

In recent times, women have been advised to harvest their colostrum, if possible, from 37-weeks onwards and store in a clean container in the freezer. Why? Well, those first few days whilst you are getting breastfeeding established, can be an anxious time for new parents as they get to grips with getting the baby's latch right and even getting them to open their mouth.

Up until recently, worried parents have often turned to formula to bridge the gap between those first few days when the milk production system is getting going and when milk finally arrives. However, we do know that giving baby formula instead can impact the supply and demand process as baby will be much more satisfied and less inclined to spend time at the breast. This is not ideal when we need baby to get that milk production system up and running.

HOW TO HARVEST YOUR COLOSTRUM

Having a few 1- or 2-ml syringes *(the non-needle kind)* safely stored *(there is no limit to how many, just keep going)* can feel like a real lifeline and give you confidence that your baby is getting some milk whilst you navigate this new and wonderful journey. It is worth noting that if you try colostrum harvesting and you don't manage to get a single drop, that this is not an indicator of your future milk supply. If you can get some - fantastic - if not, don't worry, your baby will be able to get all the milk they need by just going to the breast.

1. First, you need to be relaxed and have a clean, sterile, 1 or 2 ml syringe *(you can order these online quite cheaply).*

2. Imagine your breast is a clock and make a 'C' shape around the breast with your thumb at 12 o'clock and your other fingers at 6, outside of the areola.

3. Gently squeeze and release, avoiding any dragging down towards the nipple. Keep doing this until liquid is released from the nipple, which you collect into the syringe. It may only be two or three drops; this is totally fine.

4. Once the flow slows, move your hand around so that you are squeezing all the ducts inside the breast - so thumb at 3 o'clock and other fingers on the opposite side at 9.

You may not get much on the first attempt, but keep trying, it should come eventually, even if it's a tiny amount.

If you're really struggling, you could take your syringes to one of your midwife appointments and ask her to help you get started.

WEEK 28

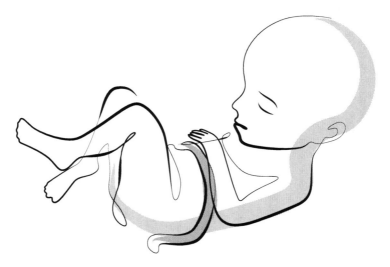

At 28-weeks, you should have a midwife appointment to check how things are progressing. Your midwife will want to take a blood test to check that your iron levels are as they should be. As you are probably aware, women do lose blood during labour and birth. Should your iron levels come back as 'low', you will be prescribed iron tablets - your midwife will let you know if you need them. Being low in iron can also make you feel extra tired and quite breathless, so if you do find you are suffering with these symptoms, let your midwife or your GP know.

Have you been told off by your partner for snoring? Another common occurrence as your nasal passages and mucous membranes in the nose become a little swollen thanks to something called 'pregnancy rhinitis', which is extremely common. All will be resolved once the baby arrives though - then they really won't get any sleep!

At this point in your pregnancy, your baby is beginning its work to be in the proper position for birth. This will mean very soon that their head will be facing downwards, ready to enter the world. Now weighing in at over 1 kilo *(around 1.1kg)* and measuring about 38cm in length, your baby is just less than half the weight they will be at birth. The average baby in the UK weighs between 3.2kg and 3.4kg at birth and measures 51cm head to toe. Check with your midwife to see what your baby's projected birth weight will be - you could be in for a big one!

Throughout your pregnancy, your baby will have been learning a variety of things from the real-world skills book and the latest thing on their list, is blinking. Some of the skills they will have already been working on also include breathing, coughing, and sucking. All of which will be key when they enter the world - another great sign that they are nearly ready!

You may begin to experience sciatica towards the latter stages of the pregnancy, which in simpler terms is shooting pains that start around your buttocks and then down the back of one or both legs. This can also occur through a feeling of numbness or tingling instead of shooting pains. Have a read of *'Pelvic Girdle Pain'* on page 148 if you haven't already, for more information on how to manage this.

WEEK 29

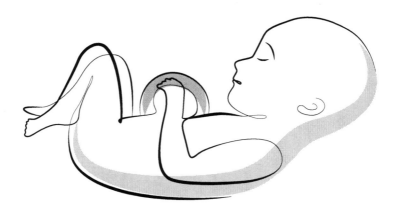

If you'll remember, since around week 20, a white cheese-like substance known as *'vernix'* has started to cover your baby's skin. This protective layer is thought to protect the skin from prolonged immersion in fluid. In addition, it is suggested that the substance has antimicrobial properties that protect the baby against infection. As the next few weeks come and go, the amount of vernix on the baby will decrease but unless your baby is very late in arriving, there will still be some visible after birth. Don't rush to wipe it off though as it is thought to be very beneficial to the baby and great for their skin. That said, if your baby has had a poo whilst still inside, this vernix may have a yellowy-green appearance - in this case you will probably want to wipe it off!

Baby is now 40cm long and weighs around 1.3kg - about the weight of a large water bottle. As the space around them has shrunk, you may not be able to feel proper kicks anymore as their legs cannot extend much. You're more likely to feel elbow jabs and knee pokes at this point. Be mindful of your baby's routine of movements going forward and get checked if you notice a difference.

One thing you may notice around this time *(or maybe not notice as much, due to your growing bump)* is the emergence of varicose veins. These are nothing to worry about. During pregnancy, your blood volume increases, and pregnancy hormones cause your veins to relax. Varicose veins can be painful for some pregnant women; however, many feel no discomfort at all from them.

To help minimize or even prevent them, try to keep your circulation going. This can be done by avoiding sitting or standing for long periods, this can be done by regularly adding some exercise to your routine. By adding this to your routine early, you may find it brings further benefits later in the pregnancy.

WEEK 30

You're probably feeling a little sleep deprived and ready to lump anyone that recommends you *"get some sleep now before the baby arrives"*. What can be just as frustrating, are the vivid dreams that may have made an unwelcome return. Don't worry, dreaming you give birth to a rabbit in the middle of the supermarket is not a prediction of future events!

You may start to notice that you are itching quite a bit, especially on your tummy. This is due to the skin stretching as your baby grows. Keep it moisturised and stay hydrated to prevent stretch marks. Itching can also be a sign of something more serious - obstetric cholestasis, so if you find that the itching is unbearable, especially on your hands and feet at night, you must let your midwife know.

The big bit of growth currently going on inside you, is to do with your baby's brain. It will no longer be smooth, instead it's beginning to take the more distinctive form with grooves and curves to allow for more brain tissue to form.

This lovely new brain your little one is forming will at this point, also be taking control of the temperature regulation they will be thankful for in the outside world. This means they will also be losing the hair which previously did this, known as 'lanugo'. You may find some remainders of this hair on your baby's back and shoulders when they are born.

Around this stage of the pregnancy, you may also notice some of the less appreciated early symptoms of pregnancy re-emerging, with one of the most notable culprits being heartburn. Be sure to keep some pregnancy-safe heartburn remedies handy in case the day comes where this returns for you. When it does, find ways of cutting down on foods that are likely to cause it, for example fried or fatty foods, as well as fizzy drinks. If it gets bad, it's time to pay your GP a visit.

YOU'RE NOW THREE-QUARTERS OF THE WAY THERE.

WEEK 31

With around another kilo or two to gain in weight, your baby has just 8 weeks to double or triple in size! Be sure to keep up your moisturising routine, as a lot of women begin developing stretch marks at a much faster rate in the last weeks of pregnancy.

Your need to frequently urinate is likely at its peak this week, mainly down to the fact you have a baby's head bouncing on your bladder! To add insult to injury, you may find you need to wee even more at night too. This is due to the fluid that causes your hands and feet to swell during the day finding its way to the bladder to exit your body. One silver lining - you can start the day with your usual slender ankles!

Leaky boobs may also be a factor when choosing what to wear at this point in your pregnancy. Your body's getting ready for breastfeeding and is starting to produce colostrum to meet your baby's needs in the first few days following delivery. Make sure you read *'Colostrum Harvesting'* on page 209!

Now able to use and understand all five of its senses, the baby is developing mentally, as well as physically. One slightly different thing you may notice, is that your baby's periods of being awake are much more noticeable. This is since they have begun sleeping for longer periods of time. As your baby is getting bigger, you'll notice an increase in back aches and pains. This is because your back is curving to accommodate the growth occurring on the other side of your body. To try and tackle this, why not try to incorporate some prenatal yoga or Pilates into your routine? By doing this, you will not only be able to relieve some of these new-found pains, but it also gives you a great way to relax and focus before the big day.

Another thing to be wary of at this stage, is the wonderful thing of 'pregnancy brain'! Yes, unfortunately as you get further into your pregnancy, your brain cell volume reduces meaning you can become prone to forgetfulness and being generally less 'with it' than you might usually have been. To tackle this, why not try noting things down more, either on a device or on paper and try and delegate as much as you can to reduce the number of things your brain is trying to remember.

WEEK 32

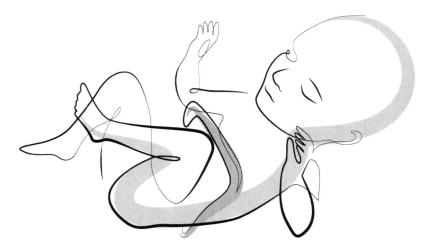

Hopefully your baby is planning on entering the world head first and will be starting to turn to face head-down into the pelvis if they aren't already. This is known as a *'cephalic presentation'*.

Don't worry if your baby is still pointing towards the stars - there is plenty of room for changing position yet, despite the ever-shrinking amount of space left in your uterus thanks to how much your little one is growing.

At around the 43cm mark and weighing 1.8kg, your baby is growing at a rapid rate - ready for all those cute baby clothes you have bought! Its previously saggy skin is filling out as they start growing more fat tissue and their skin is now finally opaque!

One thing you may begin to notice at this point is the stronger emergence of *'Braxton Hicks'* contractions, these are nothing to worry about and are merely *'practise contractions'* as your body gets ready for your big day. These contractions will increase in frequency the nearer you get to your due date. To stop feeling these contractions, simply move, or change position. If you are sitting, stand, if you're lying down, sit up, and so on. This is also a great way of identifying the difference between these contractions and contractions you feel during labour - real ones won't go away.

If you find that larger meals make you feel uncomfortable, something you may want to try is eating a little less, more frequently. As your uterus takes up more space, many find their appetite to be very reduced, however by eating little and often, you can help keep yourself energised as well as reducing the risk of feeling dizzy or faint between meals.

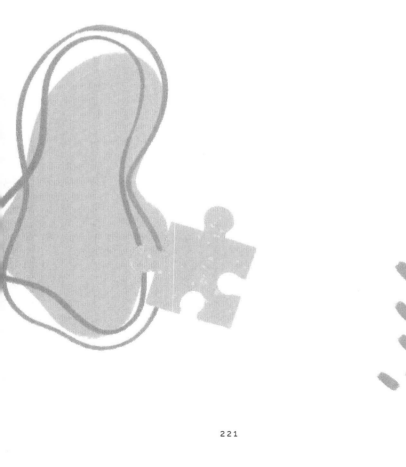

WEEK 33

Tired? We'll bet! You are likely still at work but do try to rest when you can - especially if you are struggling to sleep at night. Are you able to alter your working hours a little to go in later? A lay-in may make all the difference!

As your tummy gets bigger and bigger, you may be noticing increased back ache. This is a normal complaint in the late stages of pregnancy, even throughout the whole 9 months. However, you may want to consider pregnancy Pilates or aqua-natal classes, as both activities can ease your discomfort. Get your GP to refer to you a physiotherapist if you are really suffering.

Now that the uterine wall is thinning, your little one is getting a greater idea of what day and night is and is beginning to close their eyes to sleep and open their eyes when they're awake. As much as it might not seem it when they're with you in the world, your little one does now understand sleep!

Have you started to worry about how this growing baby is able to come through such a small exit? Luckily, your baby's head is nice and squishy to allow it to navigate its way into the world. Because a baby's skull is not yet formed solid, it has 4 separate plates which can move and overlap to make it possible for their heads to squeeze through the birth canal. Some babies are born with a cone-shaped head where it elongates towards the back of the head, but don't worry, it won't stay like that. The bones will soon relax back into a normal skull-shaped curve within a week or so and takes 9-19 months for their skull to fully form - so watch out for that 'soft spot' at the top until then.

Another great thing about your baby at this point, is that they now have their very own immune system. This will of course, be an extremely important and beneficial development for your baby once they enter the real world.

WEEK 34

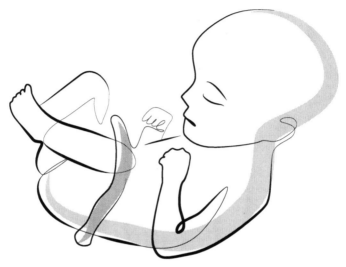

Starting to get ready for take-off, if you have an organised baby, they may be starting to get into the correct position and be moving lower down into the pelvis. This is called *'engagement'* and results in you having more space in your abdomen and your lungs being less squished - you can finally breathe! You may even be able to put the heartburn tablets away as your heartburn settles a little.

Don't go getting all excited just yet. This act of gravity may well result in you needing to go to the toilet even more than before if that is at all possible!

Have you and your partner had a date night recently? If this is your first baby, these next few weeks will be the last of you being a family of two, make the most of it now.

Some of the growth your little one will have experienced this week, will be things such as having nearly complete fingernails and if it's a boy, his scrotum will now be fully formed, and his testicles are slowly making their way down to their final destination. Baby is now around 45cm long and nearly 2.2kg.

For your body, a somewhat more unwanted change may be underway, stretch marks! Unfortunately, it is estimated that at least 1 in 2 women get them[29], however, these marks do not stay as vivid as they start out, but fade over time. It may be worth keeping your skin moisturised morning and night, drink lots of water, and manage your eating habits to avoid rapid weight gain.

One thing you could consider starting at this stage in the pregnancy would be perineal massage. These massages gently stretch your perineum, covered in 'Perineal Massage' on page 207. By doing these massages, you can help in reducing the chances of significant tearing during labour.

Another thing you may be experiencing at this stage is some changes to your vision and should be reported immediately to your midwife. This is because of those annoying pregnancy hormones, and it can cause a variety of different changes to your sight. Some of these changes could include blurry vision, more near/farsighted than usual and less ability to tear up/cry.

These changes are only temporary; however, it may be more comfortable to wear glasses rather than contact lenses during this time. One thing to keep in mind, is that some more serious vision changes can be a sign of pre-eclampsia, so be sure to mention any changes to your doctor or midwife to make sure you are properly checked and okay.

WEEK 35

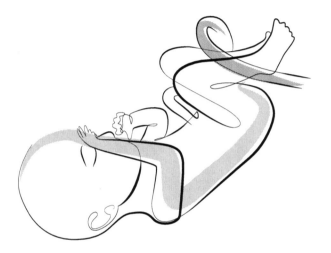

Space really is at a premium - your baby continues to pack on just over 200g per week and is just a couple of centimetres off its final birth length. That said, it is a myth that babies don't move as much because of the lack of space.

You may notice a change in the sensation of the movement, however, as the baby isn't able to practise those roundhouse kicks anymore. But you should still feel the baby wriggling around in there. If you are ever worried about baby's movements, get checked out.

Baby is growing even more brain cells this week and is settling further into their new head down position in your pelvis.

Despite coming towards the end of your pregnancy - hopefully just 5 weeks left - you are likely to find yourself once again needing to dash to the loo every 5 minutes. This time however, unlike in the first trimester where it was pregnancy hormones causing this unfortunate side effect, since your baby is in head down position it is pressing on your bladder, as well as giving you an increased likelihood of peeing after sneezing, coughing, or even laughing... Sorry!

One thing to ensure is that despite this, you do not cut down on fluids. Instead, always try and empty your bladder completely. One way which can help to do this, is to lean forward while peeing and also try some kegel exercises as a way of reducing potential incontinence.

GET THOSE KEGELS IN!

WEEK 36

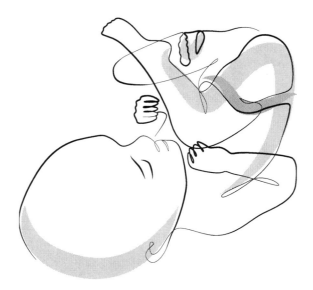

You are likely to have a midwife appointment this week. Your appointments should become more frequent now as it is important that your blood pressure and urine are checked on a regular basis to ensure you are not developing pre-eclampsia.

You may be asked if you have started to consider your birth plan. This is an opportunity to write down things that are important to you during labour such as your preferred pain relief options and your plans for how you are going to feed your baby. Tips on what to include, as well as a template to fill in can be found in *'Writing a Birth Plan'* on page 193.

Assuming everything is fine at this appointment, you are likely to be given another date to see the midwife again in a couple of weeks' time. You are so nearly there!

Your baby will now be weighing around 2.7kg and its digestive system is ready to take in their first milk, marking the start of their continued growth in the outside world.

One thing you may be experiencing at this point, is an increase in pelvic pain. To tackle this, try relaxing with your hips elevated, pelvic exercises, warm baths and prenatal massages can all help too. If you are really struggling with pelvic girdle pain, head to *Let's Talk Birth and Baby* for their physiotherapist-led workshop.

One benefit of this stage of the pregnancy is that since your baby is dropping slowly into your pelvic cavity, the pressure being put onto your diaphragm is relieved. This means you can take bigger, deeper breaths than you would have been able to throughout recent weeks.

Remember, during the later stages of the pregnancy, make sure you are continuing to note any changes surrounding the movement of your baby. If you are worried, do not hesitate to contact your midwife if there is an irregular change in movement frequency or an unusual change in the patterns of your baby's movements.

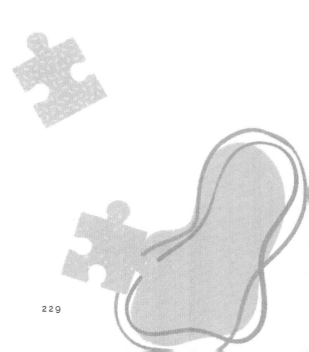

WEEK 37

Although your due date is not for another 3 weeks, you are now actually classed as being at *'term'* - baby is done cooking! It can be expected that your baby will arrive anytime between now and 42-weeks of pregnancy, but let's hope you don't have to wait another 5 weeks.

If you are planning on breastfeeding, you can now start your colostrum harvesting this week, which will be the gift that keeps on giving in the early weeks. If you have been to antenatal classes *(hopefully Let's Talk Birth and Baby ones)* you will be aware of the signs of labour and what to do when the time comes, if not, head to *'Am I in Labour?'* on page 238.

Despite this being quite a way along in your pregnancy, your little one is still gaining weight and function. At this point, your baby is growing by around 200g a week in the form of super cute and squidgy fat and is getting ready for the big wide world waiting for them, by practising things such as breathing, sucking their thumb, and moving.

Something to consider at this stage in the pregnancy - "*is everything ready?*" Very few babies arrive on their due date, meaning you won't be guaranteed that extra week of shopping or that day to test the baby gadgets, so try and make sure everything you need is in place ready for your big day.

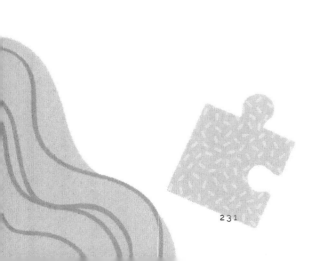

WEEK 38

Only a couple more weeks to go, or maybe less! Your baby now has fully matured lungs which are continuing to produce a substance called *'surfactant'*. This substance prevents the lung walls sticking together once breathing starts. The vocal cords are ready for their debut - that first cry will be one of the most wonderful sounds you've ever heard.

Hopefully your baby is head down. If not, you will have had an appointment with the consultant to discuss your options for delivery and any plans to try and turn the baby.

Your baby is also experiencing numerous smaller changes throughout this time, all of which will be equally as important in the long run. They are adding fat, improving their nervous system, and improving certain brain functions, all in readiness for when they enter the world. Their *'vernix' (that greasy substance protecting their skin from going wrinkly)* is starting to shed, as well as their *'lanugo' (fine hair covering their body)*.

For your body, the main thing that will be happening at this point, is that your baby will begin dropping into your pelvis further, which in turn brings benefits such as easier breathing, but also brings with it increased pelvic pressure.

You may also find that you begin experiencing some of the things you would usually expect to have during the early stages of motherhood. Most notably, leaky breasts! Time to crack out the breast pads and start colostrum harvesting if you haven't already.

You may be experiencing some additional vaginal discharge and could lose your mucous plug at any time. This gooey glob of mucous has been plugging the cervix for the past 9 months, keeping everything inside. Don't be alarmed, it can have traces of blood in it and is gross, but it's all part and parcel. If you have any suspicions that your waters have broken, you must give the hospital a call. Has your baby's eviction notice been served, we wonder?

YOU'RE ALMOST THERE!

WEEK 39

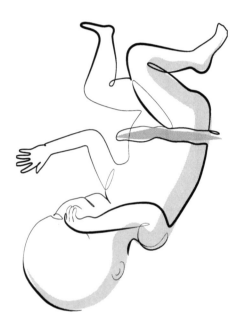

Time to nest. The urge to get your house in order may leave you tempted to climb ladders and fix the leaky roof. Trust us, you are far from invincible at this point and your sense of balance is a little off-kilter - save the high-up jobs for your other half! Feel free to dabble in some light chores if you must, or search for some local cleaning companies online and get someone to do it all for you so you can put your feet up - you're almost there!

With all this activity, you may be starting to feel some mild contractions as things start to happen. Best advice: unless your waters break, carry on as much as you can. Early labour, especially when it is your first baby, can stop and start. Getting psyched up too soon can leave you exhausted before the curtain even goes up.

Make sure you learn the difference between real contractions and Braxton Hicks as they can feel very similar. A lot of pregnancies are wrapped up between week 39 and 40, so make sure your hospital bags are packed and ready to head out the door, when you feel the time is right.

Your baby will be at their full weight by this point, with just their brain growing by the day, ready to soak in the world and new experiences, sights, and sounds.

These last few days will drag, especially if your baby decides to stay in a little longer. You may also be struggling to sleep, with your mind active and body uncomfortable. Sorry to tell you this, but you're just going to get more and more uncomfortable until the baby is born, as it wriggles and moves into their final head down birthing position deep in your pelvis. Hopefully, you are on maternity leave now and can have a nap in the afternoon and get your feet up to give your back and pelvis a rest.

SIT BACK, RELAX, LET YOUR BODY HAVE A BIT OF R&R BEFORE IT'S TIME TO PUSH.

WEEK 40

By week 40, your baby may have arrived already or be due any day this week. For 1 in 10 mums-to-be, their baby decides they don't want to be evicted quite yet and hang on past 42 weeks[33].

Everyone deals with reaching this milestone differently. For some, reaching their due date doesn't change anything, for others it can feel like a bit of an anticlimax. Don't worry if you are feeling a little emotional too, you are about to become a mum - it's an emotional time.

Your baby will be at full birth weight by week 40 and can be anything from 6 to 12lbs. If you have a larger baby, it may be suggested that you are induced. The pros and cons will be discussed with you.

For smaller babies, your body is still providing all the nutrients your baby needs, as well as antibodies needed to fight infection following birth, so sit back and wait until your baby is ready. This could only be for a further week if your midwife thinks it's safe to wait.

You can use this time to perfect the little one's nursery, think about finalising names if you've not yet decided and get all your hospital bag contents packed and ready to go.

So when will you start feeling those all-important contractions? Some women, even when overdue, start experiencing Braxton Hicks contractions. If they don't increase in frequency and severity or go away after some light activity - they are just *'practise'* ones. Once you've had Braxton Hicks, you'll know it when the real ones come, trust us!

One event however, that's not always guaranteed, are your waters breaking. Less than 8-10% of women experience a true rupture of the amniotic membrane[34], and if it does, it won't be that bucket-dump you see in movies. It's more like a trickle or small gush, like the little accidental wees you may have done as your pelvic floor has been weakening - except your waters will be clear and odourless!

When you're ready, your contractions are regular, and dilation has started. It's time to head to the hospital or birthing unit ready to meet your baby! The next few pages should help you know what to expect and give you some guidance on birthing positions, but just remember - you can do this!

AM I IN LABOUR?

By the time labour starts, most women are well and truly ready for baby to arrive. However, it can be a little nerve wracking. Try not to worry! No two women or labours are the same. Some can have fast deliveries and others have slow ones.

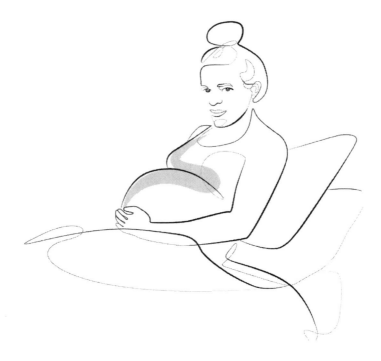

EARLY LABOUR SYMPTOMS MAY INCLUDE:

- Your mucus plug that has been covering your cervix may be expelled
- Waters breaking
- Contractions
- Cramping *(like period pains)*
- Feeling constipated, bloated, or pain in your stomach
- Diarrhoea or sickness

It's essential to call your midwife if your waters break and they will let you know when you should go into hospital.

AT THE START OF LABOUR:

- Keep walking or moving if you can.
- Drink fluids and have regular snacks.
- Try relaxation and breathing exercises we covered in *'Hypnobirthing'* on page 188.
- Have your birth partner rub your back – this can be a great pain reliever.
- Take paracetamol.
- Have a warm bath.
- Use your TENS machine.

HOW DO I BRING ON LABOUR NATURALLY?

There are tonnes of old wives' tales surrounding bringing on labour, including things like having sex, eating spicy foods, exercise, nipple stimulation, raspberry leaf tea, acupuncture, eating dates and ingesting castor oil. Though most are complete hogwash, women have reported some success with a few of them, so can't hurt if you want to give them a go. However, eating spicy foods can cause an upset stomach - not something you likely want when you're pushing a baby out! Midwives also advise against the use of castor oil, as it can cause irregular and painful contractions.

Our Official Midwife's best advice is to try nipple stimulation. But mainly, remain relaxed and calm and it will happen on its own.

9 times out of 10, if your baby hasn't come yet, it's because you or baby isn't quite ready. Midwives will arrange a date for induction once you are 41 weeks with the view to baby being born before 42.

WHEN TO CALL THE HOSPITAL

Everyone's labour is different and women will come into labour at different points in their pregnancy. Some babies are born prematurely, others are born at *'term' (37-weeks onwards)*. Some are delivered late. Once they are ready to enter the world, it can be both exciting and a bit unnerving when your waters break, and you're left wondering *"what do I do now?"* It's easy to assume you should head to the hospital at the first sign of contractions, but that may end up in you being sent home to wait until contractions are closer together.

If you're expecting your first baby, it's sometimes difficult to tell whether you're in early labour or not, as for some, it could last for a few hours or even a few days. The irregular contractions or tightenings you may feel, can signify that your cervix is softening, the baby is getting into position and your pelvis is getting ready. These pains will feel a lot like period cramps.

WHEN SHOULD I RING THE HOSPITAL?

- If your waters break.

- If you have vaginal bleeding.

- If you have been having regular contractions lasting at least 60 seconds *(every 2 to 3 minutes)* and are likely having these for quite a few hours.

- If you need pain management.

- If you have concerns regarding your baby's movement.

Having confirmation from a midwife that it is finally time to have the baby, or to just wait a little longer and watch some TV, can also be reassuring. When they tell you to come in, head straight there.

WHAT IF I THINK SOMETHING IS WRONG?

Call your midwife or hospital straight away if:

- You're having proper contractions and have not yet reached full term.

- You feel there have been changes to your baby's regular movements.

- Your contractions are too severe for you to cope with.

WHEN DO I HEAD TO THE HOSPITAL?

Being in your home surroundings is often a great comfort and can help labour run smoother, with higher levels of oxytocin keeping you calm. But once you're ready, you've spoken to the hospital and your contractions are coming thick and fast, it may be time to make a move. Once a midwife has confirmed you're in established labour upon your arrival, fingers crossed, it shouldn't be too long now.

If you have been given any information specifically related to your individual circumstances, please follow those instructions.

BIRTHING POSITIONS

Labour doesn't always look like what it does on the TV. Laying on a hospital bed with your legs up in stirrups and knees by your ears isn't the most comfortable or most effective position for all women whilst helping your baby into this world. Birthing can look quite different to different people too, introducing birthing balls, bean bags, a stool, or a birthing pool into the mix can give you many more options for a less strenuous birth.

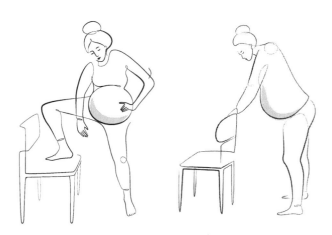

These days, you can move around and change position as much or as little as you'd like during labour. You can walk around, change positions from laying on your back, to on all fours, move from the birthing pool to the bed and back to a position you find most comfortable - do what feels right for you.

Generally, women are much more relaxed if they can move about, even whilst in active labour, so it's important to remember that unless physically or medically impossible, try lots of different positions until you find one that works for you. Studies have suggested that laying on your left-hand side with your right leg elevated, can reduce the risk of significant tearing - one to bear in mind. Your midwife will be able to support you in whichever position you prefer to be in so, don't worry and get yourself as comfortable as possible.

Below and on the previous page are some of the most common alternative positions to laying on your back that women get into during labour.

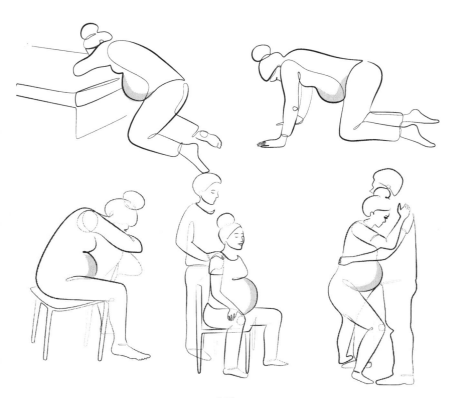

10 THINGS PEOPLE DON'T TELL YOU ABOUT LABOUR

Despite us not even realising it, we all have a picture in our minds of what labour and birth look like. We have all heard our friends' stories of how their little one made it into the world, but what *didn't* they tell you?

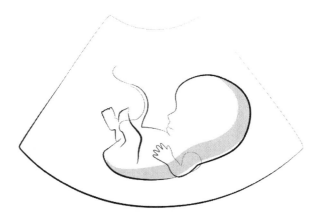

Here is our Official Midwife's breakdown of 10 things no one tells you about labour and birth.

1. It rarely happens like it does on the TV. Sometimes you may not even know if your waters have broken. You may just get a trickle rather than a soap opera style gush!

2. Your mucus plug! - It's not pretty and can look a bit like Shrek has got a cold and sneezed into a hanky. It sometimes comes out in one big blob *(about the volume of a raw egg)*, or it may come out bit by bit over the space of a few days.

3. Eating spicy foods is not a good way to evict your baby! All this does is aggravate your tummy and may tip you into labour BUT who wants to be in labour with an upset tummy, especially with all that pushing! Just wait and let nature take its course.

4. Giving birth by caesarean is still giving birth - don't ever let anyone make you feel bad for having one - even if it was an emergency decision. You're still a mum and a warrior that will look after her baby, even after having major surgery!

5. Bleeding in labour is not normal. If you experience any bleeding, you should call the midwife or nurse to get things checked out.

6. Once you get to the pushing stage, it is rarely over in 10 minutes with your first baby. The pushing stage can take up to 2 hours - sorry.

7. When women say they don't know how to push, their midwife will probably tell them to imagine they are trying to have a big poo! The muscles we engage to birth our babies are the same as the ones engaged to open our bowels! - Who knew!

8. As well as pushing your baby into the world, you may well open your bowels too. Don't be embarrassed though, it means you're pushing right, and midwives are good at clearing things away before you even know it's happened.

9. Labouring and pushing your baby into the world are just the first and second stages of labour. There is a third stage when you must deliver your placenta. This can take up to an hour if you decide to have a physiological *(drug free)* third stage. If

you opt for an assisted 3rd stage *(injection to help things along)*, this is usually done and dusted within 20 minutes.

10. No matter how much you say that all you want is to go to sleep whilst you are in labour, you will never feel more awake or more in love than when your baby is put in your arms. Making points 1-9 more worthwhile, plus the tea and toast you'll get on the ward will be the best you've ever tasted!

BONUS INSIGHT:

Epidurals are not like they were in days of old when your legs were like cement. You will still be able to change position and may also be able to use a birthing ball whilst leaning on the bed - if your partner is there to make sure you don't topple off!

WHAT HAPPENS AFTER BIRTH?

You've done it mumma! Your baby is finally here. What a relief! Your placenta has been delivered too and you're now enjoying your rest, cuddled up with your new baby, excited to share the news with the whole family. But what happens before you take them home?

If you've seen newborn babies on TV or in films, you'd be forgiven for thinking that they are born all nice and clean. In real life, your newborn is likely to be a bit wrinkled, more purple and covered in a whole manner of fluids and gunk. They might still have a waxy white substance called 'vernix' on their body and fluid, mucus, and blood from the actual birth. They may also be quite hairy! This hair is called 'lanugo' and helps to protect your baby in the womb. It should disappear quite quickly though.

You'll be encouraged to enjoy skin-to-skin contact with your baby as soon as possible after birth and you can do this even if you have had a caesarean section. It may be the case that your partner is offered the chance to hold the baby against their skin too, as that helps with their bonding.

THE FIRST FEED

If it is your wish to do so, you will be supported to initiate breastfeeding during skin-to-skin time. Your midwife can help you with positioning and attachment to minimise the risk of suffering with sore nipples.

If you are formula feeding, you will need to bring pre-made formula with you in your hospital bag. These are sold pre-mixed, so you won't need to mix powder and water on the day. Your midwife and the other staff at the hospital will help you with whatever you need, so don't be afraid to ask. Your baby will want to feed roughly 8 times in 24 hours, but this may not be evenly spread and varies from baby to baby.

FINAL CHECKS

There are a few tests carried out on your baby after their birth, but none of them are painful and your baby won't remember them! The first is the 'Apgar' test, which is done at one minute and again at five minutes after the birth and again after ten minutes. Your baby will be given a score of 0-10 for breathing, response, heartbeat, colour and muscle tone. Most babies will score between 7 and 10.

The midwife will also measure their weight, length *(if you want them to)*, head circumference, and temperature after delivery. Before you are discharged, a full examination of your baby also takes place, checking their vitals, anus, hips, eyes, and genitals.

There may be additional tests required, such as if your baby was breech at birth, or if the doctor suspects your baby has jaundice. They should also check for tongue tie *(particularly if the first feed didn't go well)* and keep checking in with you as to whether they've pooed and peed yet. Again, this is routine and nothing to be concerned about, they just want to make sure the baby is perfectly happy and healthy before they send you home!

If at any point you feel overwhelmed or aren't sure what to do, how to do it, or just need some rest following the birth and your partner has nipped home, the midwives are on-call to help ensure baby is happy and give you a little rest too. They can answer any questions you have.

Once all the checks have been completed on you and your baby, you will be given

information on safe sleep guidelines and advised of when your midwife will be popping by to see you at home.

TIME TO TAKE BABY HOME AND START YOUR LIFE AS A BIGGER FAMILY!

TAKING YOUR BABY HOME

You've read all the books *(you're almost done with this one too!)*, you've done all the classes, your baby is finally here, but theory is somewhat different from practise and now it's time to put your knowledge to the test. You're taking your baby home! Taking your baby home can be both exciting and daunting without the help of midwives talking you through everything as it happens, but you'll feel much more relaxed when you're back in your own surroundings.

CAR SEATS

Whether you're taking the baby home in the car, catching a taxi, or getting a lift from family, you'll need a car seat suitable for newborns (Group 0+) to safely transport them. Choosing the right car seat includes comparing their compatibility with your car, which you can search on the car seat's website. You'll also want to check whether they have an ISOFIX base which makes fitting them as easy as clicking them into place. Ensure your car seat complies with current i-Size (ECE R129) regulations which makes it mandatory for babies to remain rear facing until they are at least 15-months old and car seats are to be bought by your child's height, not their weight[35].

The weight of the seat is also important if you'll be removing the seat from the car often, particularly if you're recovering from a c-section. You'll want something lightweight so as not to strain your wound. Just remember, it's both dangerous and illegal to put a baby rear-facing in a front passenger seat with an active airbag turned on. Always turn the airbag off if strapping your baby in here. It is also not advisable to put your baby in a forward-facing seat anywhere in the car at this age, as this is not safe. Having them in the back of the car, in a rear-facing seat protects their neck, spine and internal organs[36] if you were to have an accident. Many car seats these days can stay rear-facing until around 4 years old.

It's also worth noting, babies shouldn't be kept in a car seat for more than 2 hours[37].

HOME

Once you're home, your nursery is all set up, you've got a side sleeper or cot next to your bed for the first 6 months and you're just happy to be home with a cup of tea in hand.

Baby is settling into its new environment, taking in all the sights, sounds and smells - sensory overload! If your partner has been home in between the birth and you being discharged, they can set everything up for you ready, making sure the food shop is done or dinners are pre-prepared and you're fully stocked with nappies, wipes, breast pads and most importantly, chocolate.

THE FIRST NIGHT

It's okay to be a little overwhelmed the first night once you're home and you've no longer got a bustle of midwives around you to help with everything. It's common for new mothers to not get any sleep the first night either, because hey, there's a new human in the house and they're completely reliant on you and your partner for every little thing. You may also experience night sweats as your hormones are settling down post-baby, so getting some sleep, even when your baby is fast asleep, is near impossible. Once your head does finally hit the pillow, it'll likely be time for another feed!

Breastfeeding can hurt at first, as your baby learns to suckle, and you learn to get into the flow of it. Getting the latch right may take a few days. The discomfort is even worse at night, but just try to stay calm as your body adapts to its new function as a feeding vessel for your baby. If you feel more pain than you think normal, or are really struggling to get it right, do call your midwife so they can get some support to you ASAP.

YOUR FIRST POST-PREGNANCY POO

Something you've probably been dreading, particularly if you tore during labour. After labour, before being sent home, your midwife will run through some poo positions

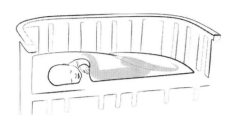

with you to ensure you don't strain. Ask your midwife or doctor if they would recommend a laxative to help soften things up, so you're able to go 'number 2' without pain or strain. Raising your feet (on a stool or hefty book) and leaning forward may help too and don't forget to breathe! It may take a few days to go successfully, but make sure you keep your midwife up to date when you see her, on concerns around your first bowel movement - they're used to it, don't worry!

SUPPORT ONCE YOU'RE HOME

Once you are settled, the midwife should come and visit you on the first day after you've been discharged from the hospital to check on you and your baby. There's no set number of visits you will have from your midwife, they'll visit you for as long as you need their support. This is usually 2-3 visits, just to get you settled and happy with everything and ensure you are recovering, and the baby is feeding well.

Your health visitor will also visit usually around 10 days after you've been discharged from hospital. They are trained midwives/nurses and will help you and baby stay happy and healthy. They usually either visit you, or you can see them at your local children's centre or GP surgery.

Don't be afraid to ask any questions that pop to your mind, even if you think they're silly questions. They're there to help you and make sure you're comfortable and confident in your baby's needs, feeding schedule, and how to identify anything they may need.

FEEDING, CHANGING, BATHING AND SLEEP

Your full milk will come in after about three days and your baby should be having at least 8-12 feeds in a daily routine. Every baby is different however, and some will need feeding more or less than others. Being born is exhausting, so the few days after birth, your baby may want to sleep lots.

Feeds can take anywhere from 10 minutes to an hour, so have the remote, tablet, or a book handy! It's quite intense to begin with, you'll feel like you don't even have time to pee or shower, as baby wants feeding every 5 minutes, but it will settle into a regular feeding pattern. They will also sleep for around 18 hours every 24 hours, but this could be coupled with plenty of wakeups. They won't fully know the difference between night and day yet, so expect some broken sleep at night-time.

When washing your baby, and they have their umbilical cord stump still clamped, try to keep the area around it as clean as possible. Cotton wool pads and water is the best option for this. Do not try and remove the clamp or cord as it will naturally fall off when it has completely dried. However, do have a look daily for any signs of soreness or infection. Your midwife and health visitor will check this as well. Until it has fallen off, you can still give your baby a bath, just ensure it is fully dry afterwards. As an alternative, you could give them a 'top and tail wash' each day, especially between their little toes and between skin creases.

To ensure your baby sleeps safely in their cot, Moses basket or side sleeper, it's important to keep your room between 16-20°C, with a well-fitting, lightweight sleep bag or swaddle. No toys, blankets, or pillows around them, and they should sleep on their backs. It's safest for babies to remain in your room for the first 6 months, so you're able to monitor them and make night feeds much easier.

It's likely you'll already have experienced baby's first poo *('meconium', which is black and tar-like)*, whilst at the hospital. Yep, black poo is totally normal. If your baby is breastfed, their poos will be softer and more frequent compared to their formula-fed counterparts which will have firmer, less frequent, more pungent poos. After the first couple of poos, your baby's digestive system kick-starts, meaning their poo will become more browny green after a few days.

They will usually wee 2-3 times per day too until day 3, when wees will become more frequent until they're a week old, when they'll be urinating 6+ times a day alongside their now yellow poo.

Get those nappies ready! You'll likely need a whole 22-pack for the first week alone.

If you're new to reusable nappies, it is usually recommended waiting until they're at least 6-weeks old to start and gradually introduce them into your nappy cycle until you get into a routine of using and washing them. There are some great biodegradable eco-friendly disposable nappies on the market to use in the meantime too.

INTRODUCING YOUR BABY TO SIBLINGS

Your new bundle of joy is finally here and your other child has been asking for months when their new sibling will be ready to play with them. Some children are excited that they will be a big brother or sister, but for others, it can be daunting that they're no longer the only child, or the youngest. Of course, having a new arrival is a massive change for the whole family, but it may take a few months in the lead up to birth to prepare them emotionally and mentally that there's a new family member on the way.

Here are a few ways you can prepare your child for their new sibling:

BUMP BONDING

First thing's first, talk about the baby openly, get your child to speak to your bump, feel the kicks, listen to the heartbeat, and look at the scan pictures, so they know that a new baby is coming. If you have any friends with newborns, or see a baby on the street, you can draw your child's attention to it, showing them that there's one in mummy's tummy. This is so they can better associate *'baby'* with an actual baby. Talk with them about all the fun things they'll be able to do when they're older and show pictures of you and your siblings when you were little, to help with the association.

INVOLVING THEM IN DECISIONS

Let them help you prepare for the baby. Get your child to pick out clothes, bedding, toys, and nursery decor to make them feel more involved. Get them to pick a special cuddly toy or blanket that the baby can have when it's born that is a present from your older child. They will feel happy when you come home, and the baby has this with them. Ask them their opinion on baby names and even ask for ideas.

Make them your chief toy tester, a super important role to make sure the baby will like it too - this can also introduce the concept of sharing if your child knows that the toy will be played with by the baby too. You can even sort through their old toys, asking if the baby can play with each one.

PREPARE THEM FOR YOUR HOSPITAL STAY

It's also essential to prepare your child for the time you will be in the hospital. Make it seem like they're getting a special treat and spending time with nanny and granddad or with friends, away from mummy and daddy and that you are going to come back with a fantastic present - a sibling! If they are old enough, you can explain the situation more maturely. Again, you can make sure they know you are taking their extra special gift for the baby with you and will show it to the baby once it's here. You could also get them to physically give their gift to the baby once they can visit the hospital, or when you arrive home.

It can also be a good idea to get a present from the baby to give to your child, so they feel extra special to meet them.

ONCE YOU'RE HOME

When the new baby arrives home, try to do something special for your older child. In a small child's eyes, there's a big difference between meeting the baby in the hospital and the baby coming home to live with you, in their space. It's essential to make them feel they are getting just as much attention as before.

Be sure to maintain your bedtime story routine, have some 1-2-1 time with them whilst the baby is sleeping with both parents together and individually, as well as time with the grandparents too - who better to spoil them! Also, make sure they get some calm playtime with the baby, even if it's just lying on the activity mat together, or watching TV with the baby next to them on your lap. This bonding is essential and can make for some strong sibling bonds later.

If you are still breastfeeding your older child under 2, make sure you give both adequate bonding time with you; expressing so your partner can feed your baby whilst you're with the eldest, or feed your eldest whilst your partner feeds your newborn.

Finally, you can take them on special outings or do things they love, but space these things out, so they don't start expecting treats every day, forever!

How ever you prepare your child for a sibling, introducing them to your child in the home environment can be a slow process. It can take a few weeks for your child to accept the significant change, or it can take a matter of hours. Just listen to your child's cues and go at their pace. Don't force it and they'll be inseparable in no time!

INTRODUCING YOUR BABY TO YOUR DOG

FIONA BIRD

BABY & CANINE RELATIONSHIP SPECIALIST

Up until this point, your faithful friend(s) have been the centre of your universe, so it may take a little time for them to accept the new addition to the family. Having a baby is a wonderful time in your life, however, it can give us many things to think about too. The relationship between your favourite canine and your new baby is often a topic that is not considered yet is so important. You will want these

two important beings in your life to love each other as much as you love them.

TOP TIPS

- Start preparing your dog early for the changes which will inevitably happen before the baby comes home.

- We can do many things, such as changing our dogs' routines, so they don't feel put out when their usual 7am walk doesn't happen, or their dinner is a bit later than usual.

- Get them used to the *new normal'*, by introducing new sights, sounds and smells.

- Make new house rules to make life easier for yourself - no one wants a stressed dog barking behind the newly erected stair gate once baby is home.

- Reduce the amount of time your loving hound lays on the settee next to you and encourage them into their own, very comfy bed, so that your baby can be laid safely down next to you.

- Stop unwanted attention from your dog wanting to *'help'* with nappy changes. This is done with an effective *'leave'* command.

- Over excited greeters jumping all over you and your visitors can be quite frightening when it comes to bringing babies in the house, so you can look at how to reduce this and other unwanted behaviours.

- To stop you worrying that the dog will enjoy playing a game of chase around the dining room table with baby toys or clothes, you can redirect their energy into controlled play. Handing them one of their own toys or a treat-filled rubber chew to keep them occupied will do the trick.

- Teach your dog to walk nicely on the lead will also be a great help to stop you and your pram being taken off at speed in the direction of their favourite park when out for a walk.

For more information, tips, and classes on this topic, Fiona Bird runs a regular *'Barkers and Babies'* class through *Let's Talk Birth and Baby*. Her contact details for 1-2-1 sessions can be found in *'Our Experts'* on page 12.

HOW WILL YOU FEED YOUR BABY?

As we quickly figure out, when it comes to babies, everyone starts to share their own opinions on what you're doing, whether you want them to or not. *'Breastfeeding vs bottle feeding'* a baby is an age-old, controversial topic and is an important decision to make for parents. So, let's help give you as much information on both so you're able to make an informed decision that's right for you and your baby.

IS BREAST BEST?

'Breast is best' as a message can spark many disagreements and many of you will have heard repeatedly. Plainly speaking, breastfeeding is something health professionals and respected professional health and medical bodies like WHO and Unicef encourage. Breast milk is biologically designed to be your baby's only source of nutrition. It's the safest, cleanest, and richest source of nutrition and contains countless antibodies that will protect them against many childhood illnesses.

Breast milk can provide all the nutrients and energy that your baby needs throughout the first months of their life, and it is recommended this is done exclusively for at least the first 6 months of life *(and up to 2 years old for optimum nutrition)*[38]. Once they reach 6-months, solid food should be introduced, and breast milk used to supplement a varied and colourful weaning diet of proteins, vegetables, fats, and carbohydrates.

PROS OF BREASTFEEDING

Practically speaking, breastfeeding is convenient and can be a much cheaper option. It is always fresh and at the perfect temperature, whether you're at home or out and about. You can feed your baby directly, pump, or do a mixture of both for convenience. Once established and *(hopefully)* pain-free, breastfeeding can be a beautiful time for mum and baby, as all other tasks and activities are put on hold.

From a physical perspective, breastfeeding really is incredible. It cuts baby's risk of many things:

- Infection
- Vomiting
- Diarrhoea
- Sudden infant death syndrome
- Leukaemia
- Cardiovascular disease later in life

It also lowers mum's risk of:

- Breast and ovarian cancer
- Osteoporosis *(weak bones)*
- Obesity
- Cardiovascular disease

Breastfeeding burns lots of calories, so it's important to have some healthy snacks and water nearby and maintain a rich diet whilst breastfeeding.

There is evidence to support that breastfeeding lowers your risk of developing postnatal depression, due to the release of *'oxytocin' (our happy hormone)*. However, it is important to remember that not everyone has an easy time with breastfeeding and getting the latch right is the key to getting your fix of happy hormones.

It's also worth noting, that breastfed babies' poo is non-odorous and is more frequent, softer, and paler in colour until solids are introduced at 6-months.

CONS OF BREASTFEEDING

Unfortunately, as mentioned, getting the latch right can be a big hurdle. Whilst you're getting the latch right and getting the hang of breastfeeding for the first time, women often experience sore or cracked nipples, which can be difficult to navigate. However, once you have had good support, you should find that breastfeeding is comfortable.

Mastitis and other infections, as well as engorgement, can also cause difficulties breastfeeding, which may be severe enough to make you want to stop breastfeeding altogether and switch to formula. But again, these can

often be avoided by getting the latch correct.

BOTTLE FEEDING

Bottle feeding doesn't always mean formula feeding. You can still give all the same nutrients mentioned above by using expressed breast milk. But typically, when people refer to *'bottle feeding'*, they're talking about formula feeding, so let's look at what the differences are as well as the pros and cons.

All formulas are manufactured to a very high standard, to include all the ingredients recommended and to meet the criteria set by the World Health Organisation *(WHO)*, which ensure that formulas provide your baby with all the right nutrients that they require to thrive. They also regulate how they're marketed.

PROS OF BOTTLE FEEDING

Formula feeding can be a more convenient option, as it gives mums some more freedom and allows others to get involved too. Although breastfeeding women are protected by law, many mums do still feel uncomfortable breastfeeding in public and therefore this is not a consideration when formula feeding. Unlike breastfeeding, which really does all come down to mum, formula feeding gives partners an opportunity to spend time feeding baby whilst mum gets some well-earned rest.

CONS OF BOTTLE FEEDING

Formula can take longer for your baby's stomach to break down, thus giving fuel to the idea that it keeps babies fuller for longer, but this slow digestion may also mean the baby is more prone to constipation, wind, bloating and pain - this is one of the main downsides.

Unlike breastfeeding, where you only really need boobs (and a pump and bottles if you want to express too), bottle feeding does require a bit of kit. You'll need bottles, a range of teat sizes, as well as some sterilising equipment. You may also want to invest in a bottle warmer to help safely warm baby's bottle. There are lots of different types out there too, that include anti-colic and anti-reflux bottles and ones shaped like real boobs to simulate breastfeeding.

Another difference between breast milk and formula can be found in the baby's nappy. Formula-fed babies tend to have more solid poos, and poo less often, as well as being super stinky. They'll also be darker in colour.

Whichever feeding method you choose, just know you are doing great. If you have trouble breastfeeding, be sure to speak to your midwife or health visitor once you're home to get some guidance on getting the latch right. If you're ever worried about your baby's weight, regardless of feeding method, consult your healthcare provider to check everything's okay. If you need any help or advice about formulas, which is best, if your baby suffers from allergies (CMPA in particular), and you need some dairy-free formula, speak to your midwife or GP who can recommend some or prescribe you what your baby needs.

IT'S NOT ALL OR NOTHING

With the right support, most mums can breastfeed successfully. Just remember, breast vs formula feeding isn't an *'all or nothing'* choice. You can enjoy a combination of the two if that is your preferred method. However, it is important to understand how this may impact your milk supply and must be done in a way that minimises the risk of infections such as mastitis.

The physiology of breast milk production is a complex topic and understanding how the process works can give you a major head start with your breastfeeding journey. For an in-depth class, covering both breast and formula feeding, check out *Let's Talk Birth and Baby's 'Infant Feeding'* class.

YOUR BREASTFEEDING JOURNEY

Breastfeeding is a skill that you and your baby learn together and it can take a little time for you to be fluent in this wonderful new language. As we have discussed on page 209, colostrum harvesting is a great way to get ready for the next phase of growing your baby; only from birth onwards, you literally are growing them on the outside too!

It is helpful to understand how the breastmilk production system works, so that you can understand how and why things can seemingly change - just when you thought you had breastfeeding sussed!

As your body gets ready for the arrival of your baby it starts to make colostrum, which will give your baby lots of goodness during the first few days. Colostrum is protein-rich and full of nutrients, and gentle on baby's developing digestive system so is easy for them to digest.

SUPPLY AND DEMAND

The first few days of milk production are hormone-led, with a dig drop in those pregnancy hormones from the point your baby is born, making way for the milk production hormones to get to work.

After this initial *'kick-start'* to the provision of milk, all later supply is triggered by milk removal. As your baby removes the milk by suckling at the breast, the body recognises the need to replace what has been removed and more milk is produced. Basically, supply and demand.

INCREASED DEMAND

Those first few weeks whilst you and baby are getting into the swing of things, can be the most demanding and it may feel like you get very little break between feeds.

If you find that baby is feeding more frequently than usual, it is likely because they are going through a growth spurt and are needing a little more attention. In addition, they are asking your body to switch things up a little to provide them with all the additional nutrients they need now they are that little bit bigger.

GETTING THE LATCH RIGHT

One of the main reasons women struggle with getting breastfeeding going, is associated with the latch.

To get started, make sure you are comfortable, get your baby's head and body aligned and bring them close to you, facing your breast.

It is important you bring your baby to your breast, rather than bring your boob to your baby, as the latter can result in poor attachment, as well as back and shoulder pain for mum.

Remember, just like us, your baby has a hard and a soft palate. To minimise the risk of trauma to your nipple, you want your baby to draw as much breast into their mouth, so that your nipple is just pressing on the squishy soft palate right at the back of their mouth as possible. This will also help your baby get good feeds.

BREASTFEEDING SUPPORT

Breastfeeding is a wonderful way to feed and spend time with your baby. If you want some additional support, talk to your health visitor in the first few weeks after birth and remember, you can always sign up for *Let's Talk Birth and Baby's* FREE weekly *'Bumps & Babies'* group or their *'Infant Feeding'* antenatal class if you want to know a bit more ahead of baby's arrival.

EXPRESSING & STORING BREAST MILK

When breastfeeding, sometimes it becomes preference to express *(pump)* your milk in order to supplement feeding, or to allow your partner to take some of those never-ending night shifts with baby. Expressing can either be done by hand or by using a manual or electric breast pump. How often, how much and for how long you express, will depend on you.

REASONS TO EXPRESS

- Social freedom - if you need to leave baby for a short time or if you are returning to work.

- Engorged breasts - you feel your breasts are uncomfortably full.

- Poor latch.

- Sharing feeds - your partner may want to help with feeding.

- Boost milk supply.

It may take a few days or even weeks for your milk to come in or flow steadily. Feeding baby as often as possible can help with this. Choose a time when you are calm and relaxed and have a bit of time on your hands to start. Sometimes, expressing in the morning can be easier when your breasts are fuller. If you're wanting to express regularly, try to do so consistently.

HAND EXPRESSING

Expressing your milk by hand in the early days before your milk fully comes in, means you don't need to buy or borrow a pump straight away. It allows you to target a particular part of the breast which can be handy if one of your milk ducts is blocked. You can catch the milk with a sterilised bottle or container as it flows. However, it may be quite a task to hand express if you're wanting to do this long-term, by which point, you can move onto a pump - manual or electric.

STEP BY STEP

1. Wash your hands with soap and warm water.

2. Gently massage your breasts to help your milk flow

3. Hold your breast with one hand and form a 'C' shape with the thumb and forefinger on the outside of your areola with your opposite hand, to target the milk ducts.

4. Begin squeezing forward gently. Avoid squeezing your nipple directly. This shouldn't hurt.

5. Release and repeat, moving your hand around your breast to target all your milk ducts.

Your milk should start to flow slowly like a dribble at first, then like a weak tap. If no droplets appear, adjust your finger positioning. When the flow slows from one breast, it's time to start on the other. Alternate breasts until no more milk is coming out.

EXPRESSING WITH A PUMP

There are manual *(hand-operated)* and electric breast pumps available, as well as single and double pumps. Which one you buy is totally personal preference. Some are louder than others and some require more equipment, so shop around and find the best one that suits your needs. If you do not want to buy one, you can also hire them.

With some electric pumps, the suction strength can be altered, so take it slowly working your way up through these settings. It's not advisable to whack the strength up high straight away, as it can damage your nipple and ducts. You'll also need to find the right size funnel to fit your nipples. As we all know, nipples come in all shapes and sizes! A pump should never cause you bruising and should always be sterilised before use.

STORING BREAST MILK

Storing breast milk allows you to feed your baby from a bottle and allows your partner or another caregiver to do the same. You can store breast milk in special breast milk storage bags or sterilised containers which take up little space and are cheap to buy.

SHELF LIFE

- Fridges - 5 days at 4°C or lower.

- Ice compartments - 2 weeks.

- Freezers - 6 months.

- Coolers with ice packs - 24 hours after being cooled in the fridge.

Storing small quantities will help to avoid waste. Remember to label and date your milk if you're freezing it, so you know how long you have left to use it. Once served, it should be consumed within an hour and any remaining in the bottle should be thrown away. Do not refridgerate milk that has already been drunk from.

DEFROSTING FROZEN BREAST MILK

Frozen breast milk is still good for your baby and is easily defrosted in the fridge. You can also defrost it quickly by placing the container in warm water or holding it under a running tap. Once defrosted, use immediately and do not re-freeze.

HEATING BREAST MILK

Some babies prefer warm milk, as it would come out of your breast, so you can warm the milk by placing it in warm water, the same way you'd defrost a frozen bag.

Never microwave breast milk as it can cause hot spots which can burn your baby.

DONATING SURPLUS MILK

If your milk supply produces more milk than your baby can drink, it can be a lovely idea to donate your surplus milk to neonatal units and premature babies across the country where their mothers' milk hasn't come in yet or are unable to breastfeed.

The nutrients in breast milk are perfect for NICU babies to help them grow strong.

Charities such as *UKAMB* have been set up to provide milk banks where new mothers can take their bagged milk and help save a life. Check out their website to find out where your nearest milk bank is and how to store your milk ready for donation.

HAVING DIFFICULTY EXPRESSING?

Like with breastfeeding, expressing can take some time to get the hang of. However, if you are finding breastfeeding difficult, or it's unusually uncomfortable to express, talk to your health visitor as they will be able to help.

THE BREAST MILK RAINBOW

Yep, just like baby poo, your breastmilk can come in a wide variety of colours. It can vary as your milk comes in following childbirth and cycle through all sorts of colours as you eat different foods. Changes in breast milk colour is not usually a cause for alarm. What you eat and how your body works are a big part of those fluctuations.

GOLDEN YELLOW

In the first few days after birth and even for a few weeks beforehand if you're harvesting, your milk will be a golden yellowy colour. This is called *'colostrum'*. This is thick, nutrient-rich milk, filled with proteins and high in fat that tides your baby over until your mature milk comes in. Its major role is to contribute to a healthy immune system and sustains baby - by giving them important antibodies and prepares the digestive system for bigger feeds.

BLUISH WHITE

From around day 5-10, you produce what is called *'foremilk'*. This is milk is packed with lactose and is low in fat and calories. Its consistency is thin and watery and is white with a blueish hue.

CREAMY WHITE

Your milk has arrived! Around day 11-14, you produce what is called *'hindmilk'*. This is high in fat, high in calories and much thicker, richer, and creamier than foremilk. This is the milk that easily satisfies your baby's hunger and gets them all sleepy. It also helps them feel fuller for longer.

ORANGE OR YELLOW

Sometimes your colostrum can be a little orange or yellow, however this is totally normal. Frozen breast milk can also turn this colour can also be caused by food dyes, or if you've eaten a lot of orange foods such as carrots and sweet potatoes.

GREEN

Like with your urine, green foods such as kale, asparagus, spinach and seaweed, or supplements can alter the colour of your breastmilk and give it a green Hulk-like hue.

BLACK

Some women are given the antibiotic *'minocycline' (or minocin)* and this can turn breast milk black. If you're on these antibiotics, you may be advised to pump this milk to keep up your supply, but not feed it to your little one.

PINK, RED OR BROWN

Not always normal, these colours can be caused by several things. The more normal explanations include beetroot and food dyes that have entered your system.

The not so normal reasons your milk turns this colour, could be because of a cracked or damaged nipple, which is causing blood to enter the milk supply. *'Rusty pipe syndrome' (when old blood is left inside of the milk ducts from vascular breast engorgement)* and increased blood supply to the breasts could also be the culprit.

Pink or brown could also be an indication of an infection called *'mastitis'.* If this colour milk persists, do head to your GP to get checked out.

WHEN TO TALK TO MEDICAL PROFESSIONALS

As you can see, breast milk that changes colour from what you'd consider as *'normal'* isn't usually a cause for concern. However, if you notice your milk *(when pumping, by your baby's spit-up, or from leakage on your breast pads),* is an odd colour or has changed from one colour to another with no apparent cause, contact your health practitioner who can either put your mind at ease, or run some tests to ensure all is okay.

DISPOSABLE VS. REUSABLE NAPPIES

Nappies are a staple for any baby whether they're newborn or leading up to potty training at about 2.5 years old. During this time, they will go through around 4000 nappies. Whilst we've come a long way since the terry-towels and safety pins of our childhoods, disposable nappies are in fact losing popularity and the cute covers, environmentally friendly reusable alternatives are becoming more widely used. They're now even being stocked in supermarkets.

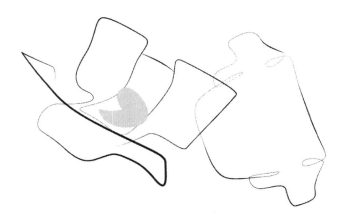

With a growing focus on environmental concerns such as landfill and the production of single-use plastics, many parents are switching to reusable nappies, or at least looking at more eco-friendly options. Did you know it takes over 500 years for nappies to decompose[39]? That's a lot of rotting poo polluting our air since they were first invented 70 years ago. Every nappy ever worn is still here and will be for another 400+ years - gross!

REUSABLE NAPPIES

A reusable nappy can be washed, either in the washing machine, boiled, or washed by hand. They can be bulkier than disposables, especially if you are using a high absorbency insert or liner, but a single, adjustable nappy can be used and reused right through to potty training and even passed on to relatives or friends who are expecting or saved for your next child. They wash up new and retain their monetary value so you can even list them for sale online.

When using disposable nappies, you'll likely go through more than 30 nappies in the first week alone, with each one being wrapped in a nappy bag with wet wipes and sent off to the landfill where it will stay for the next

500 years[39]. Can you imagine just how many you would go through in the first year?

COST COMPARISON

The cost of reusable nappies can vary greatly. A single reusable can be anywhere between £5 and £40, which can be compared to buying single-use nappies at around £4-7 for 12 or more in a pack. In the first year alone, disposables can cost between £750 and £970 (depending on whether you go for own-brand or branded nappies). In contrast, reusable cloth nappies, inclusive of the cost of washing, can cost as little as £132 per year[40].

Until they're potty trained, here's what they'd cost:

DISPOSABLES = £1.8K-2.4K

REUSABLES = £340

That's huge savings, possibly even enough for the baby's first holiday!

You are also able to borrow reusables from local *'Nappy Libraries'* for a small fee and return once your baby is potty trained - a great initiative to keep local landfill pollution down.

ECO-FRIENDLY DISPOSABLES

But of course, like with anything baby-related, everything is a personal choice, and many parents enjoy the convenience of disposable nappies, particularly if they don't have easy access to a washing machine. There are therefore lots of options available, different sizes, different fits and absorbencies, styles, brands, and levels of decomposition. Brands are emerging more often that claim their nappies, *(yes, including what your child leaves in them)* are completely biodegradable and compostable, meaning you can still have the convenience of a disposable, with the bonus of reducing your carbon footprint.

Though none on the market are truly 100% compostable *(usually only between 60-80%[41])*. To ensure they actually decompose, you can't send them off to landfill in your black bin or put them in a nappy bag. You'd have to take them to an industrial composting facility, or compost them in your own garden, as your usual brown compost bin will not accept nappies - even the biodegradable kind. Hopefully, a service to properly compost these nappies will emerge in coming years. Until then, we can only buy them knowing they are using less single-use plastics, and thus better for the environment than non-eco-friendly brands.

MAKING THE SWITCH

If you do want to make the switch to reusables, it's worth noting that for the first 6 weeks, it's probably easier to get some eco-friendly disposables due to the sheer amount you'll go through in the first few weeks, without putting a strain on your time to wash and dry enough for each nappy change multiple times a day.

The two most common types of reusable nappies are shaped/pocket nappies and all-in-ones. Shaped/pocket nappies have an outer waterproof cover *(or 'wrap')* with an insert/liner to absorb the wees and poos. The liners can either be washed or are made of biodegradable materials that can be disposed of. The outer cover comes in a huge variety of colours, designs and styles. Once you have one, you'll want loads more, simply because the designs are so cute. The advantage of these being, that they have lots of poppers on the outside that make it possible to use on babies from newborn until they're potty trained. The all-in-one is what it says on the tin - the cover and the insert are combined, which can make for a slimmer nappy and a quick nappy change. They will need separating however, before they're washed.

CLEANING & DISPOSAL

Once these nappies have been soiled, you have a couple of options for dealing with the pooey ones. If it's solid enough and you can get it off the nappy, scoop it off with a tissue and flush the poo down the toilet. Or if just a wee or light soiling, you can chuck it straight into the washing machine. It's worth noting that breastfed babies' poo is water-soluble *(at least that is, until they're weaning)*, therefore will not need to be rinsed before they're washed. Simply dry pail them until you've collected enough for a wash.

Once they are on to solid foods, you might also want to use a pre-wash cycle to loosen anything that's really dried in or scrape off any lumps beforehand. If you buy around 10-15 reusable nappies and liners, you can wait for a load of nappies to be ready to wash, rather than washing one at a time to save on energy costs.

If you do have separate liners, either dispose of them, or wash the liner. The outer cover won't need washing unless it was a super explosive poo! It's best to separate the liner from the cover before washing, and you can pre-soak if necessary.

It is recommended that you wash your nappies at 60-degrees but check the manufacturer's guidelines carefully. You can dry your nappies outside or on an airer. Some can even be tumble dried.

Washing your reusable nappies make them more absorbent, so aim to wash them at least three times before you start using them. Don't use fabric softener in the washing machine as this can affect the absorbency and can also irritate your baby's skin.

WHICH WILL YOU CHOOSE?

Once your baby goes into childcare, or is looked after by family/friends, check they are set up for or familiar with reusable nappies. You may need to provide them with enough nappies to last a full day, plus some spares if they only offer disposables.

Reusable nappies are a cheaper long-term option than disposable nappies but do require an additional amount of commitment in terms of washing and drying.

Whilst they do reduce the amount of waste going to landfill, you do need to balance this off against the potential increase in energy used for washing *(and possibly drying)*, but there'll still be a tremendous saving to be had.

Before you commit, make sure you do your research and find a solution that suits your needs. You are of course, also able to chop and change as and when convenient.

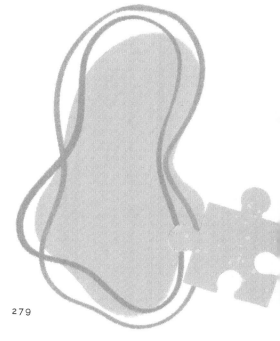

BABY POO COLOURS & WHEN TO BE CONCERNED

Something every parent has to deal with and probably what you were least looking forward to confronting... your baby's poo. But did you know it can be a whole spectrum of colours and consistencies? Runny, firm, dark, light, green, black, brown, and yellow. Whilst some are normal, here's a little guide on what to look out for and what the different colours mean.

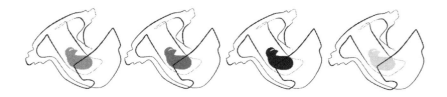

WHAT DOES A HEALTHY POO LOOK LIKE?

The first few poos your baby does will be called *'meconium'*, a gooey, black, treacle-like poo made up of cells, amniotic fluid,and waste that built up whilst they were in utero. Whether you're breast or bottle feeding, their first few poos will be this way.

Once this is cleared from their system, their normal poo will depend on how they're fed. It usually goes from black to green, to yellow.

When breastfeeding, their poos will be runny and more yellow in colour, with no smell and a bit grainy - a bit like mustard.

If formula-fed, their poos will be more browny in colour, be quite smelly and have a firmer consistency.

Once your baby reaches the weaning stage at around 6-months, their poos will be firmer, darker, and smellier as their food filters through into their poo.

POO COLOURS

Here's a few examples of different colour poo when it's normal and when it's not:

GREEN POO *(normal)*

This can be quite a shock when you first see it, but normally isn't a cause for concern. Poo is often green like pesto during the transition period following birth. If your baby is otherwise happy and isn't showing signs of distress or discomfort, all is fine and normal.

YELLOW POO *(normal)*

Whether it's bright, mustard, or neon yellow, these are all completely normal and not a cause for concern. In breastfed babies, this is how poo looks. However, if it is bright yellow and runnier than usual, this could be a sign of diarrhoea, which you may want to speak to your GP or paediatrician about to ensure your baby isn't losing too many nutrients/fluids.

BLACK POO

After the first few poos, where black poo will be their meconium and totally normal, after weaning, a black stool could mean there is blood coming from your baby's digestive system. However, it could also mean they have eaten something dark in colour, for example, blueberries. You will need to get your GP to confirm this.

RED POO

If you see traces of red, it can indicate that there's blood in your baby's poo. Talk to your GP or paediatrician for their advice on what might be causing it.

Bear in mind that there can be many harmless reasons for red poo, for example, babies can swallow blood during labour, or if your little one is already eating solids, red foods like beetroot can tint your baby's poo.

WHITE OR GREY POO

If you open your baby's nappy to find a whitish or grey coloured poo it is advisable to contact your doctor as soon as possible. Stools this colour could indicate a digestive or liver problem that should be investigated.

ORANGE POO

This is often seen in breastfed babies and is totally normal. It occurs when colouring is picked up from their digestive tract.

ANY OTHER COLOURS TO LOOK OUT FOR?

If any poo colour causes you concern or it doesn't quite fit into the colour descriptions seen here, do get in contact with your midwife, health visitor, or GP, who can help put your mind at rest or offer advice on what could be causing it. Always better safe than sorry.

DEVELOPMENTAL BABY MASSAGE

AMY TRIBE

DEVELOPMENTAL BABY MASSAGE PRACTITIONER

Touch is a newborn baby's first language. Your touch provides their introduction to the world and gives an immediate and effective way for you to bond with your baby. Developmental massage can be practised at any stage in these first 1001 days and beyond.

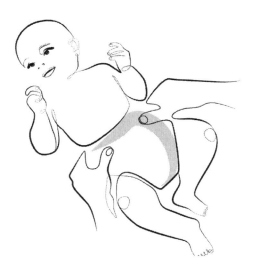

The use of baby massage to provide relief for commonly seen ailments in babies is well-recognised and is used from day 1 to release birth trauma and help baby relax into the world.

The areas we focus on in the very early days, are most commonly the tummy and the *'phrenic nerve'*. The tummy is the home of the *'enteric nervous system'* - often called the *'baby brain'*. Developmental baby massage practitioners always say, *"if you can relax the belly, you will relax the baby".* The phrenic nerve sits right at the top of baby's spine and is vital to their physical and emotional well-being. It feeds directly into the diaphragm, therefore controlling baby's ability to take deep abdominal breaths, feeds the immune system, releases the tummy, and opens the chest.

Tummy massage also provides effective relief for colic, trapped wind and other gastro issues. It also helps them enjoy tummy time and sets them up to hit their motor-milestones safely and healthily.

As you massage your baby, they also release *'oxytocin',* the love hormone, which will deepen the connection and encourage secure bonding and attachment for both you and baby.

TOP TIPS FOR BABY MASSAGE:

- Always use warm, open palms to massage.

- When massaging the tummy – never push in, never squeeze, and always work clockwise!

- Avoid hip massage for the first 6 weeks of baby's life as they aren't properly developed yet.

- Put your phone away & keep the eye contact – this is their time with you!

- Work from the feet upwards as this is less intrusive to start with.

- Start them early to prevent colic, trapped wind and encourage tummy time.

Amy runs The *'Baby Buddha'* classes with *Let's Talk Birth and Baby*, which provides you with everything you need to know to give your bundle of joy the very best start in life and guide them through their first 1001 days. For contact details to book onto a class, you can find Amy in *'Our Experts'* on page 12.

SAFE SLEEP GUIDE

Unfortunately, the reasons why some babies die suddenly from something known as *'sudden infant death syndrome' (SIDS)* are usually unknown. It is known however, that placing your baby on their back to sleep reduces their risk of SIDS. Exposing a baby to cigarette smoke, co-sleeping, or letting your baby overheat, increases the risk of SIDS. If you have any concerns, head to the NHS website for more detailed information about what you can and can't do to ensure your baby sleeps safe.

HOW TO KEEP BABY SAFE

Although SIDS is rare, there are things you can do according to the NHS[42], that significantly reduces the risk:

- Don't expose your baby to cigarette smoke during pregnancy or after birth.

- It's not considered safe for babies to sleep on their side or stomach when newborn. Once your baby starts to roll over however, there is no need to worry if they roll off their back while sleeping.

- Keep your baby in your room, in their cot or Moses basket, for the first six months.

- You should keep the room where your baby sleeps between 16 and 20°C.

- Don't let your baby overheat because of too much bedding or clothing. Use room thermometers to gauge the tog sleepsuit they should be wearing, if any.

- Keep toys, pillows, blankets, bumpers, and mobiles away and out of reach from baby's sleep environment to prevent suffocation.

- Breastfeeding for at least the first two months, halves the risk of SIDS.

- Some research suggests using a dummy may reduce the risk of SIDS[43].

- Use a good, firm, completely flat, waterproof mattress with no raised or cushioned sides.

- Do not fall asleep next to your baby, or with them on your lap on a chair or sofa.

- Do not co-sleep if you smoke, drink, take drugs, or are extremely tired, as there is an increased risk you can roll over whilst asleep and suffocate your baby. The risks of co-sleeping increase if your baby was premature or had a low birth weight.

- Never cover the baby's face or head while they are sleeping. To stop your baby wriggling under the covers, place them in the 'feet to foot' position at the base of their cot[44].

- If using a cushioned sleeping nest or pod, do not allow your baby to fall asleep. The raised cushions can be a suffocation hazard.

HELP, MY BABY WON'T SLEEP

CARLA BERLIN

PAEDIATRIC SLEEP CONSULTANT

If there was a single secret to getting your baby sleeping all night, every parent would be getting 8 hours of uninterrupted sleep each night! There are so many factors that affect how well your child sleeps, we want to share with you some top tips that should really help improve your little one's naps and nighttime rest.

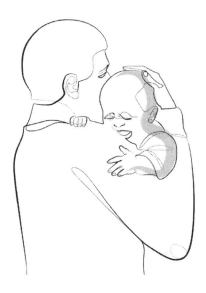

TEACH YOUR CHILD TO FALL ASLEEP INDEPENDENTLY

Every parent has the end goal to teach their child to fall asleep unassisted, so that when they wake in the night, they peacefully put themselves back to sleep.

Though many parents see this as impossible, there is a way to teach this. This most definitely does not mean leave your baby to cry until they fall asleep due to exhaustion, *(that does not teach them anything)* and can lead to separation anxiety and child psychological trauma. You can instead, support them through the whole journey towards this lifelong skill.

SLEEP REGRESSION

We often talk about the dreaded *'4-month regression'* too. Although it may not feel like it when they are waking up constantly throughout the night, this is in fact progression. As well as your child developing physically, their sleep cycles have matured, so this is a great time to start teaching your child to self-settle. At the newborn stage (0-3 months), you can practise putting your baby down a little more awake each night but be aware that they may need a little bit extra support. You may therefore need to use a more of a hands-on approach. Don't be afraid to sometimes use the likes of a sling or pram to get them that little extra sleep!

YOUR CHILD'S ROOM SHOULD BE VERY DARK

Have you heard of *'melatonin'*? It is the sleepy hormone which signals to your brain that it is time to rest. This is increased in darkness. A slight bit of light has been shown to reduce those melatonin levels in our bodies.

Let us give our baby's the best chance of sleeping well, by ensuring their room is pitch black for naps and nighttime sleep. So dark, that if you put your hand out in front of your face, you would not see it.

The same applies to morning, if the light starts coming through the curtains, melatonin levels will drop and can contribute to those early wake ups. If you don't have blackout blinds or they still let some light in around the edges, you can always do a DIY job yourself, or there are some great velcro blackouts available.

TOYS AND MOBILES SHOULD BE KEPT FOR PLAYTIME

They may look cute, but toys and mobiles in cots often over-stimulate a baby and will keep them awake longer. As well as sometimes being unsafe, toys are often associated with playtime, which is exactly what you don't want when you're putting your baby to bed.

Again, mobiles over the bed have music and lights which don't always encourage sleep.

LIMIT TOTAL DAY SLEEP

When a baby has a bad night's sleep, parents often let them catch up the next day and let them sleep more than what's age appropriate. All that happens in this instance, is the following night they sleep badly again, and they have entered into a vicious cycle with more night wakings. Always try to give them the right amount of sleep in the day, so that at night, they go down to bed easily and are not over or under tired.

HOW MUCH DAY SLEEP SHOULD THEY GET?

Here is a guide as to how much sleep they should have during daylight hours. *(Be aware that some babies have higher or lower sleep needs so these are just averages).*

0 TO 12-WEEKS - total day sleep should be between 4-6 hours *(this gets less each month)*.

3 TO 5-MONTHS - total day sleep should be between 3.5-4 hours.

6 TO 11-MONTHS - total day sleep should be between 2.5-3.5 hours.

12 TO 18-MONTHS ON 2 NAPS A DAY - total day sleep should be 2 hours at most.

AFTER 1 NAP TRANSITION - total day sleep should be 3 hours at most.

WAKE TIMES

When you catch your baby at the right time when they are not over or under tired, getting them to sleep and staying asleep will run a whole lot more smoothly! This applies for both naps and bedtime, and it really is about finding that sweet spot.

Below is a guide for wake times but adjust accordingly

for your own child's sleep needs:

0 TO 12-WEEKS: 1-1.5 hours

3 TO 5-MONTHS: 1.5-2 hours

6 TO 8-MONTHS: 2.5-3 hours

9 TO 11-MONTHS: 3-4.5 hours

12 TO 18-MONTHS: 4-5 hours

18-MONTHS PLUS: (usually until about 3 years): 5-6 hours

NO SINGLE NAP SHOULD EXCEED 2 HOURS

If a nap is longer than 2 hours, it often steals some of the night's sleep. This can result in a struggle to get them to bed at night, as well as more night wake ups and early morning rises. The only exception to this, is when your child is on a 1 nap schedule.

Some children will sleep for 3 hours and go to bed at night no problem!

BEDTIME SHOULD BE BETWEEN 6PM AND 8PM

We often hear parents say, *"I put my baby down late, at about 9-10pm hoping they then wake up later in the morning".* This rarely works!

You will instead have a super overtired child, which will lead to more wake ups and they will probably still be arise at 5-6am.

Somewhere between 6-8pm is an ideal bedtime, because the sleepy hormone melatonin naturally surges during this time in a baby. So, you should take advantage of the hormone being high before it starts dropping again.

TRY TO NOT MAKE FEEDING THE LAST STAGE IN THE BEDTIME ROUTINE

Often the last stage of a baby's bedtime routine is a bottle of milk or a breastfeed. When this is the case, they can go drowsy and without knowing it, you are assisting them into the first stage of sleep. This means they never really learn properly to fall asleep on their own and instead rely on the bottle or boob to feel sleepy.

Then when they wake in the night, they need the milk to send them back to sleep. Sound familiar? The best thing you can do, is bring the feed to the beginning of the bedtime routine, out of their nursery, so they disassociate feeding with sleep and then teach them to settle themselves. Either before or after the bath is ideal.

When your baby wakes and makes a noise, try to wait a short while and see what they do.

The slightest whimper and parents often rush to their baby. It's parents' instinct - we get it! But just by waiting a short while, you are giving them the opportunity to try and put themselves back to sleep on their own.

Did you know that it takes a baby 3-5 minutes to fully wake? So do try and wait this long. By going in before this, you may wake them up when they were just making noise as they transition between sleep cycles *(they are noisy little sleepers!).*

CONSISTENCY IS KEY

Routine and predictability - baby's love this and they thrive knowing what's coming next. Their little internal clock, called their *'circadian rhythm'*, starts expecting sleep at certain times of the day if you begin offering it at the same time each day. If you can give your baby as many naps in their cot, all at similar times, this really helps to improve their sleep.

For more information or help with your baby or toddler's sleep, you can contact our Sleep Expert, Carla, directly. Her contact details can be found in *'Our Experts'* on page 12. She also runs newborn and 4-18 months sleep workshops with *Let's Talk Birth and Baby,*

that provide you with the knowledge and techniques to start improving your baby's sleep. You can check out the available dates to book on the website.

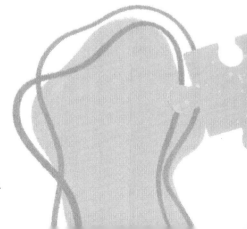

WHAT IS COLIC?

It is not unheard of for parents to feel like they have the whole parenting of a newborn thing sussed, then BAM, along comes colic. Despite it affecting up to 1 in 5 babies[45], it can still come as quite a surprise and can feel quite isolating. Having a baby that is crying for hours at a time can be frustrating and just a little overwhelming.

If your baby cries excessively and ticks the perfect storm of 3: cries for 3 hours a day, at least 3 days a week, and has done so for 3 weeks, following a trip to the doctor, and being given a clean bill of health, it's likely they are suffering from colic. A newborn will usually cry for an average of 2 and a half hours per day total, and this peaks at around 8-weeks of age.

DOES MY BABY HAVE COLIC?

Do they:

- Cry to the point they are red in the face?
- Arch their back?
- Pull their knees up to their chest?
- Clench their little fists?
- Cry for really long periods of time?

If so, it's likely they have colic. But don't worry, it's quite common and is treatable.

WHAT CAUSES IT?

TRAPPED GAS

Generally, the first question to ask. - *"Are they being winded?"* And *"are they taking in lots of air during their feeds?"* If so, this could be getting trapped in their tummies causing discomfort and bloating. When they are born, babies have an immature digestive system, which is fine as this develops over time, but in the early weeks this can mean that the milk takes quite some time to digest. By 3 or 4-months of age, this should start to improve, but it does take time.

THE FOURTH TRIMESTER

Pregnancy is broken down into 3 trimesters whilst your little one is getting ready for the outside world. However, even when they are earth-side, they are still very much dependant on their mother to continue this development. Known as the *'4th trimester'*, the 3 months following birth can be a little overwhelming as they experience the wonders of the world.

Everything has changed for your baby. They have spent the past 9 months in a dark and cosy womb and are now facing the bright sunshine and clear sounds of earth. Babies often experience a sensory overload, resulting in them being a little fussy and reluctant to settle outside of the arms of their mother.

OVER-STIMULATION

Ever heard of the *'witching hour?'* A seemingly happy baby suddenly turns up the volume and goes from nought to screaming in 5 seconds flat and then stays there for the next few hours. This can feel like everything you are trying to do is rejected and you start to doubt your abilities. Don't do that! You are doing great.

One of the key things here, is to look out for your baby's cues and try to make sure that they are getting enough sleep time during the day. Dumb down stimulation in the run up to the usual time of baby being unsettled - one sign is baby not making eye contact and looking away.

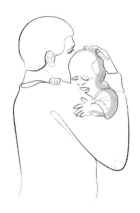

COW'S MILK PROTEIN ALLERGY

Otherwise known as CMPA, a cow's milk protein allergy is your baby's gut reacting to the milk proteins, whey, or casein, in their milk. Babies can be miserable and the days for parents can be long and anxious, as your baby may cry for most of the day.

Symptoms of a cow's milk protein allergy can include:

- Eczema
- Mucus in poo
- Constipation
- Wheezing when breathing
- Vomiting
- Blood in poo

The only way to take away baby's discomfort, is to take away the dairy element of their feed. If you are breastfeeding, try eliminating dairy from your diet and if you are formula feeding, you can get a prescription for hydrolysed formula milk from your GP.

DELAYED SENSITIVITY TO COW'S MILK

In some cases, your baby can get along well with their milk in the beginning but still seems to suffer with bloating and trapped wind. This is often coupled with being a little constipated or fussy when feeding. This is not necessarily an allergy but can be because of your baby having an immature digestive system and therefore is not able to digest the milk efficiently.

Cutting dairy out of your diet *(if breastfeeding)* may reduce these symptoms in your baby or, if formula feeding you could try a comfort milk.

However, keep in mind that you do sometimes swap colic symptoms for constipation as the milk is a little heavier to reduce reflux. The proteins in comfort milks are smaller and therefore place less pressure on baby's digestive system.

REFLUX

Having a baby that is sick after every feed can be quite stressful. Babies are born with an immature digestive system which results in the oesophageal sphincter not closing as firmly as it should. In some instances, this allows all a baby's feed to come back up and can cause discomfort for baby. Baby will often arch their back and cry excessively. One thing that can help is holding baby upright for longer after feeds to allow the milk to digest. As baby gets older and they can sit upright for longer periods, the signs and symptoms of reflux often diminish.

TONGUE TIE

Another thing to consider is whether your baby has a tongue tie *(also known as 'ankyloglossia')*. A tongue tie is a small strip of skin that connects baby's tongue to the bottom part of the mouth, known as the *'lingual frenulum'*. In many cases, this therefore doesn't cause a problem, but it can hinder baby's ability to move their tongue properly and therefore cause issue when feeding. Babies with a tongue tie often struggle to latch on to the breast well and tend to take in more air. Mums often suffer more with sore nipples too.

Your baby will often take in much more air than if there wasn't a tongue tie. This can result in more trapped wind and colicky behaviours. In some cases, it is recommended that the tie is snipped to divide the skin and allow freer movement of the tongue and improve feeding. Tongue-tie can however (though very rarely) grow back, so it's worth checking regularly if you're having issues with their latch or feeding.

COLIC REMEDIES

Have a baby with colic? Then you'll probably have been desperately trying to find a solution. Luckily, there are lots of different remedies out there, some new, some as old as the hills. The right remedy will depend on the cause of the colic, and it is important to remember that there may not be a total solution, but there are things that you can try.

Infacol, gripe water, and colief are traditional products that can help. However, it is worth noting that many products do contain chemicals and as such there has been a recent move towards more homeopathic remedies.

Chamomilla granules, nat phos, and infant probiotics are often used instead. When making your choice, it is so important that you ensure products are well researched and tested and pass as suitable for infants.

Breastfeeding mothers could also enjoy a nice cup of chamomile tea which can help to calm baby via your milk. Adding fennel or peppermint to the mix could also help to settle sensitive little tummies.

BABY MASSAGE

As covered in 'Developmental Baby Massage' on page 283, touch is so important for babies as they are still developing the ability to communicate through other methods. Making gentle stokes, massages and cuddles are babies' first language. As well as being a comfort to babies, it can also really help with any digestive problems and encourage the tummy to relax and release any trapped wind.

Stroking baby's tummy in a clockwise direction, directly targets the digestive system and encourages movement within to ease discomfort. In addition, the love hormone, 'oxytocin' is released alongside the body's natural pain killing hormone, 'endorphins'. Massage really is a win-win.

BACK INSIDE

Your baby never felt more secure than when they were in the womb, so recreating some of those sensations may help to calm baby. Wearing baby in a sling, gentle rocking and swaying, the playing of white noise, or the sound of heartbeats and swaddling may also be a source of comfort for your baby.

BABY WEARING

Babies like to be cuddled! So, using a carrier or sling can

be an ideal way to comfort your baby whilst moving around. The closeness gives your baby the sound of your rhythmic breathing and your heartbeat at the same time - just as they had in the womb. This calm and comforting position can trigger your baby's *parasympathetic nervous system* to kick in and trigger the *'rest and digest'* instinct in your little one. This slows down baby's heart and encourages the digestion of food. In addition, the nature of the carrier encourages baby to be in an upright position and therefore doubly aids digestion. All that gravity keeps milk where it should be and can reduce those reflux symptoms too.

COLIC HOLDS

We have all held a baby and bounced and rocked them in a bid to settle their cries. These movements mimic the womb and are often really comforting to baby as they are transported back to the rhythmical movements of the womb.

'Tiger in the tree' hold can be great for babies as it can help to provide pain relief to any tummy discomfort.

With your baby on their tummy across your arm, their head should be supported by your inner elbow. Rub your

baby's tummy and gently rock to give a calming effect by reducing stimulation.

If you need any help with diagnosing or treating colic, talk to your GP or health visitor who may be able to advice on your options.

WHAT IS BABY REFLUX?

Reflux is a term you may hear quite frequently from mums and dads in the first years of parenthood. It describes healthy babies who are very unsettled, and in some cases, bring up a lot of their milk. Reflux itself means regurgitation, which is the movement of food from the stomach into the oesophagus *(food pipe)*.

In some cases, babies can be diagnosed with reflux when what they have could be digestive discomfort, ongoing disturbed sleep and colic that they didn't grow out of. Babies are prone to vomiting very easily. Their stomach exit isn't a proper valve and therefore up to 73% of normal babies do vomit/regurgitate their food in the first month of life[46]. There are also loads of babies formally diagnosed with reflux, who have never spit-up anything. Paediatricians only tend to show concern if a baby isn't putting on weight and seems excessively upset by crying more than usual. Of course, bringing up milk is messy, but not always a worry or immediate sign of reflux.

SILENT REFLUX

This is a slightly different style of reflux which you may also experience. This is where the regurgitation only comes into the oesophagus or mouth and is rarely seen as vomit. This is the only difference between reflux and silent reflux, so the term 'reflux' can be either type.

Reflux is frequently used as a catch all term, so there are many reflux myths that you may have been told, which we want to dispel for you here.

THERE'S A DIFFERENCE BETWEEN REFLUX AND REFLUX DISEASE

There are two medical terms you may come across when it comes to reflux, gastro oesophageal reflux *(GOR)* and gastro oesophageal reflux disease *(GORD)*. Despite these different terms, the only difference from a medical point of view, is that the disease version causes *'marked distress'.*

Reflux, however, is not a *'disease',* there's no underlying pathology or symptoms that you can pin 100% on reflux itself. In fact, it is more accurate to call reflux a symptom.

For a baby who has either GOR or GORD, there should be no difference in how they are supported and treated.

As a symptom, reflux has multiple causes, and the causes of reflux can be understood by simply looking at the patterns in symptoms and behaviours that your baby is showing. Some common causes of reflux in babies can be found on the next page:

SYMPTOMS OF REFLUX

- Having a predominantly liquid diet.

- Spending long periods lying flat.

- Premature birth resulting in reduced muscle development.

By looking at reflux in this way, the underlying causes of your baby's reflux can be resolved, and some parents can sometimes even see improvements in their baby within days, which all comes through simply having a better understanding of it.

REFLUX IS NOT 'NORMAL'

Even for babies who are happy, reflux is anything but normal.

It's true that our body's ability to regurgitate air and stomach contents is normal, however it isn't *'normal'* to be in constant, or frequent, recurring discomfort or pain from simply eating or drinking.

A method you can use to help assess the symptoms of your baby, is to put yourself into the scenario of if you were to visit your doctor and describe your baby's symptoms as your own, would you be happy being told *"it's normal"* and *"you'll eventually grow out of it"?* Or would you want to know why it's happening?

So, if you have been told your baby's discomfort is normal and you personally feel that it isn't, trust those parental gut instincts of yours and act on it, as you know your baby better than anyone else.

DON'T WAIT FOR YOUR BABY TO GROW OUT OF IT

Another thing to remember is that you don't need to wait for your baby to grow out of it. For a rather high number of children, they never grow out of it. So why gamble with your child's *(and your own)*, comfort, sleep, happiness, and sanity, when you could be free of reflux within weeks when you look at it as a symptom and take specific action to support them?

SO, WHAT CAN YOU DO?

Reflux itself is a symptom, so there are a range of factors that can cause or contribute to reflux occurring. This means that there is no one-size-fits-all answer.

The best way to start tackling your baby's reflux can be as simple as asking yourself *"what is causing my baby's discomfort?"* Once you've asked yourself this, note down anything you think of, as this may come in handy in any future appointments surrounding the reflux or even for finding your own remedies. Some ideas to get you started for minimising reflux in your little one could be:

- Feeding your baby in an upright position.

- Burping your baby more frequently before and after feeding to reduce air buildup.

- Feed your baby smaller amounts but more frequently.

Your baby is always telling you exactly how they are feeling, even if they may not have words yet. Instead, they are using crying, movement and even their behaviour to communicate. As a parent, it's your job to play detective to uncover what they are saying

to help guide you to the best way you can support your baby. You can often tell a baby is refluxy, as a common sign is baby wriggling their head around to try and get comfortable.

If you are concerned at all with your baby's digestion, discomfort, or excessive crying, it's always best to see your GP or paediatrician with these worries. They may be able to prescribe things like a proton pump inhibitor such as omeprazole or suggest some dietary alterations if an allergy is suspected.

BASIC BABY FIRST AID

Seeing your baby injured or unresponsive can be extremely scary, particularly as they're so small, so you may feel anxious about performing any first aid on them. Even something as simple as a slap on the back can save their life. In the event of an emergency, call 999 immediately and keep them on the phone while you perform some of the basic first aid recommended for under 12-months-olds. They can help guide you through it and give you updates on the ambulance's location.

WHEN THEY'RE UNRESPONSIVE

If your baby is unresponsive, tap them on the foot and call out their name. Never shake a baby. Call 999 or 112 immediately. If still unresponsive, you need to check they are breathing. To do this, put two fingers on their forehead and one below their chin and gently tilt their head back. This opens their airway and allows you to bring your ear to their mouth to listen for breathing. Wait 10 seconds.

If they are still not breathing, begin CPR resuscitation until the ambulance crew arrive. If they are breathing, but not responsive, put them in the recovery position and wait for the ambulance.

RECOVERY POSITION

If they're unconscious, but breathing, put them in the recovery position.

For a baby, this involves cradling them in your arms with their head tilted downwards, towards your elbow and their body facing towards you. Keep checking their breathing and pulse until the ambulance arrives.

RESUSCITATION

As with checking their airway, tilt your baby's head back and take a small breath. Place your lips wide over their mouth and nose to form a seal. Blow very softly for one second until you to see their chest rise. Allow it to fall again and repeat 5 times.

This should be quickly followed by 30 chest pumps. For an infant, you should place two fingers in the center of their chest over the breastbone. Press down one third of the baby's chest depth and release, allowing the chest to rise. Repeat 30 pumps quite quickly - about two per second *(Sing Bee Gees' Stayin' Alive if you need a rhythm to stick to)*. Keep your other hand on the baby's tilted head to keep their airway open.

Give 2 more rescue breaths and repeat 30 pumps, followed by 2 breaths, until an ambulance arrives, or your baby becomes responsive.

CHOKING

A choking baby can send a mad wave of panic through you, but it's important to act quickly. You can usually tell when a baby is choking as they will be unable to cry, cough, or breathe, or they'll have a puffy, red face. If you can see the obstruction, and you are able to pincer it out with two fingers, do so. If not, do not attempt to remove it. Instead, slap it out.

Lay your baby face-down over your thigh, supporting their head with your hand with their bottom higher than their head. Give them five blows firmly on their back using the heel of one hand between their shoulder blades[47]. If back blows do not clear the blockage, turn them over and give up to five chest thrusts with two fingers, whilst supporting their head. Check their mouth each time. If it still does not dislodge the blockage, call 999 and repeat the cycles on their back and chest until it dislodges, they become unresponsive, or until paramedics arrive. If baby becomes unresponsive, start CPR.

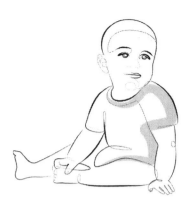

BURNS

If your baby gets burned or scalded, put the burn under cool running water for a minimum of 20 minutes. Once the 20 minutes are up, take off any tight clothes to prevent fabric sticking to the burn and cover it loosely with cling film to prevent infection. Do not wrap the area as it needs room to swell. A piece of cling film over the area will be fine. If the burn is on a foot or hand, a clean plastic bag will suffice. Do not use any creams, ice, oils or gels on the burn or break any blisters the burn may have caused. Take your baby straight to A&E. If your baby has burned through clothing, try not to take this off them as peeling off the fabric could peel off skin. Cool under water for 20 minutes and take them to hospital where the medical staff can decide what course of action to take.

FEVERS

A fever in babies is when their temperature exceeds 38°C. Fevers are the body's instinct to fight off infection, however a very high temperature can lead to seizures, so you need to act quickly to bring it down.

The first point of call is a cool sponge to bring their body temperature down. Try giving them a sip of cold water and the correct dose of baby ibuprofen or paracetamol should also help. Try putting them in front of a fan and removing some layers of clothing, as this too can help bring down their temperature rapidly. If it is still not settling, call the doctor or take them to A&E.

MENINGITIS

Under 5s are most at risk and can deteriorate very quickly with meningitis, so it's important to know what to look for and call 999 or take them to the hospital urgently if you think they may have it.

Symptoms to look out for:

- A high temperature
- Flu-like symptoms and feeling unwell
- Pale, blotchy skin
- Cold hands and feet
- Pain in their limbs and joints

Not every child will experience every symptom and if the illness has progressed, they may also be suffering from:

- Severe headaches and neck stiffness.
- Vomiting and drowsiness.
- Light sensitivity.
- Floppiness and bulging soft spot (the 'fontanelle').

The last to show up, is a rash consisting of red or purple spots that won't fade or disappear when you roll a glass over them. Until help arrives, keep your child as cool as possible and treat their temperature with either paracetamol or ibuprofen.

Whilst these are just a few of the emergency situations your child may face, there are many other hazards in the home and just as many ways to treat them. You can buy baby first aid kits online and take a basic first aid course as part of your antenatal classes or separately too.

Our Official Midwife from *Let's Talk Birth and Baby* offers a *'Baby First Aid'* course that covers burns, fractures, choking, poisoning, injuries, and convulsions as well as the basic CPR.

POSTNATAL RECOVERY

NIKKI KELHAM

SPECIALIST WOMEN'S PHYSIOTHERAPIST

Congratulations! You grew and gave birth to another human being. You are literally incredible! Your body has undergone one of the biggest challenges it will ever go through and needs time to recover and heal well. Whether you've had a vaginal birth or a c-section, your body has undergone a lot of trauma and needs to be rehabilitated back safely and effectively, back to full function.

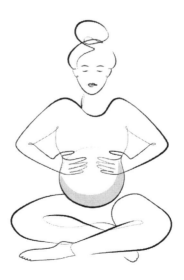

The first few weeks are all about getting nutrient dense foods and plenty of liquids to assist in your healing. Gentle movement *(in the form of short walks, when you feel ready)* and stretches, will keep you from becoming chair shaped. There is no shame in taking painkillers when you need them as tears, episiotomies, c-sections cause genuine pain.

You can begin breath work *(that we covered in 'Pelvic Girdle Pain' on page 148)* as soon as you can feel your pelvic floor *(this may take several days, depending on the trauma of your labour and birth)*. This is a great way to focus on tummy breathing and relaxing your pelvic floor, as well as starting to get them to contract too.

After 6 weeks, *(this may be longer and that is totally fine)* you may feel like you want to start doing some exercise. Postnatal Pilates, yoga or other postnatal-specific classes can be a good place to start. If you have it in your budget *(and highly recommended)*, a 'Mummy MOT' would be a great place to begin. This is a specific postnatal assessment where a specialist physiotherapist will look at your posture, your function and test for any tummy gap *(diastasis recti)*.

They will screen you for any bladder/bowel/prolapse/sexual dysfunction and give you a tailored plan of how to start your rehab.

Strengthening from the inside out is the best advice that we can give you. Exercise should not be rushed into as you can cause yourself injury and postnatal complications. The pelvic floor muscles are still healing 3-6 months *(sometimes longer)* after giving birth and if you have had a c-section, you have undergone major abdominal surgery.

WHEN TO SEEK HELP

It is common to have some leaking *(urinal/fecal)* for a couple of months after giving birth, however if this is something that is not improving, it is best to seek help.

If you are experiencing symptoms of heaviness, dragging, or bulging in the vagina, these could be symptoms of a prolapse. These are common, though again, it is best to get yourself checked out.

For ongoing pain in your pelvis, tailbone, groin, during sex, certain movements, or around your c-section scar, there is always something that can be done. Please do not suffer in silence!

For a great session on postnatal recovery, you can join Nikki over at *Let's Talk Birth and Baby* in her *'Postnatal Recovery Workshop'.* Details can be found in *'Our Experts'* on page 12.

POSTNATAL HEALTH & WELLBEING

The first weeks at home can be a daunting, but exciting time for many parents as you get used to your new life with a newborn. Once you've left the hospital or midwifery unit, it's understandable that you may feel apprehensive about being on your own, but your confidence will increase each time you hold your baby. Midwives, GPs, and health visitors will see you whenever you need following birth, to check in on you and baby, ensuring everything is okay both physically and mentally.

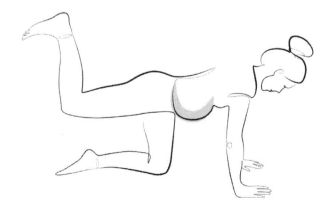

TAKE CARE OF YOURSELF

Though it may feel like every minute of your day and night is spent running around and tending to your baby's every need, it's important that you take time to look after you too - this goes for both parents.

You both must make sure you are taking time for yourselves where possible, supporting each other and staying active and healthy, so you can better care for your little one. The first few months are exhausting and challenging, so it's also important to give yourself *(and each other)* time to rest. It may be tempting to use the time baby sleeps to catch up on chores but try to use that time to sleep and ask for help if you need it - perhaps someone to help you do some of the housework or watch the baby so you can rest in the first couple of months.

STAY HEALTHY

Exercise is a great way to not only stay in shape, but it's also a good way to de-stress and get some fresh air. Take the baby out on a stroll or go running with the buggy, do short 20-minute home workouts, or go for a light swim - anything to release those endorphins, strengthen your body and clear your mind.

Alongside this, make sure you maintain a healthy diet, particularly if you're breastfeeding to not only keep you healthy, but ensure the baby is getting all the nutrients and vitamins possible through your milk.

SEEK SUPPORT

Relationships with friends, family and even with your other half, can change after you have a baby. Many women turn to their own mum or sisters who've had babies for help and support, but it's always a fine line between helping and interfering, so it can put a strain on relationships. Just try to let them know what help and support you want from them, so they know not to over-step.

Your relationship with your partner will also change somewhat. In those exhausting early weeks, you may both be tired, stressed, and irritable, so you both need to have some time alone, with each other and without the baby, to remind yourselves of how you were before your baby, and how you got to that point - love!

They can help you where and when you need them, just let them know what you need. Even if it's looking after the baby for an hour while you shower or taking a night shift and using expressed/bottled milk, remain supportive of each other and you'll be great parents.

Your feelings towards your baby may not all be positive either, especially when you're sleep-deprived. Don't ever feel guilty if you sometimes feel resentful towards your demanding mini-human or be alarmed at any emotion you may be feeling. Make sure you talk to your midwife or health visitor, or if you are anxious, worried, upset, angry, depressed - they are there to help.

TAKE CARE OF YOUR MENTAL HEALTH

'Baby blues' is common amongst women in the first week after childbirth. Women can feel irrational and emotional and burst into tears for no apparent reason be irritable or experience anxiety and/or depression.

Your body has just been through 9 months of extreme changes, hormones are all over the place and now your world has been turned on its head with a tiny being to look after. It's no surprise you may feel this way. What's more, it's totally normal and should only last a few days.

In situations where these blues don't go away, this can be a sign of postnatal depression (PND). As mentioned, if you've had a traumatic birth, and these blues haven't gone away, it can be an indication of PTSD (post-traumatic stress disorder), either alongside, or instead of PND, which may have been linked to you feeling out of control or anxious and afraid during the birth. 1 in 10 women get PND[48], so just know that you're not alone.

WHAT HELP IS AVAILABLE?

Help is available through your GP either by way of therapy, self-help practices, or medication. Many celebrities have spoken out about their experiences with postnatal mental health and raising more awareness about how the way you may be feeling is quite common. It can be reassuring to know that there is help there and that others are going through the same thing to make you feel less isolated and alone.

Loneliness can be another factor that can affect a new mother's mental health, particularly if it's their first baby. Cut off from friends who perhaps don't have children or finding it hard to find mummy buddies, even if you have friends and a great support network, it can be difficult to make time to see them and be 'you' again.

Many women struggle with their self-identity post-birth and feel like they've lost who they are. Therefore, it's so important to make time for yourself, use your family and partner to take care of the baby to give you some alone time, or time with friends.

You can also join postnatal groups near you, or if you took group antenatal classes, see if you can reach out to some other mums on there, mother and baby groups in your community, carer/parent, and toddler groups, and even playgroups will have lots of parents you can talk to and make friends with. There are even apps available to meet other mums in your area. The likelihood is, you'll find a mum who feels the same way and just wants someone to talk to who knows what they're going through.

If you are finding things particularly difficult, with any aspect mentioned above, do contact your GP or health visitor who can help you. You can also post anonymously on our *Your Baby Club UK Facebook page* for our *'Ask the Fans'* segment by dropping us a message. Parents and parents-to-be share their advice, leaving the ball in your court as to whether you want to reach out to them directly, or just take the advice they give. Although it isn't monitored by health professionals, you may get some valuable peer support. However, please contact your GP in the first instance.

PARTNERS GET PND TOO

MARK WILLIAMS

MENTAL HEALTH CAMPAIGNER

As an expectant mother, you are given a midwife, you'll attend classes from hypnobirthing to antenatal, pregnancy yoga to bumps and babies, get support before, during and after, particularly through any spells of anxiety or PND. But what about dads? What is out there for them during this huge change in their life?

Going into labour, there's midwives, nurses, doctors, consultants and more for mum. They focus entirely on your care and wellbeing during those hours of labour. Whether it's vaginal or caesarean, the focus is on mum and baby, and rightly so. But what is it like to be a new dad or partner of someone giving birth? Having asked a few partners about this topic, many of them said the same thing...

"I FELT UTTERLY USELESS!"

"NEWBORNS ARE SO SMALL AND FRAGILE".

"MY WIFE IS ALWAYS CRYING AND SHOUTING AT ME, AND I DON'T KNOW WHAT TO DO".

"THERE'S LOVE BUT SO MUCH FEAR AT THE SAME TIME".

"OUR LIVES HAVE CHANGED SO MUCH, AND MY MOOD HAS TOTALLY CHANGED SINCE BABY'S ARRIVAL, BUT I DON'T KNOW HOW TO ASK FOR SUPPORT".

Almost all dads and partners were glad when the newborn stage was over. They felt overwhelmed and didn't have a baby group to chat to others about how they felt. A few of the dads who were stay-at-home-dads or part-timers really focused on the loneliness of those days, much like mums do.

If your partner goes quiet, or when they disappear in front of your eyes, or start working late, please start that conversation. Because partners can get a form of PND too[49].

Partners can often also feel overwhelmed and unprepared but have little to no support network as everything is typically about the mum and baby. As much as dad wants to be involved, he can lose his role a little and, if we are all quite honest, us new mums can be shouty, teary, tired, and hormonal after birth and partners can't always cope with everything all at once.

Get them to talk to their doctor or health visitor, whether it be days later or even months later, as PND can manifest itself at any point in that first year and beyond. It can sideswipe them from nowhere or it can be a slow creeping thing. Don't be embarrassed to seek help or encourage him to do so. The gamut of emotions is real and both particular to him and yet shared by many too.

Many other partners struggle during the perinatal period with their mental health and early prevention is key for yourself, your partner, your family and the development of your child.

CHANGES IN BEHAVIOUR TO LOOK FOR:

- Substance abuse
- Anger
- Avoiding situations
- Physical health problems
- Personality changes
- Seemingly distant

RISK FACTORS:

- Fathers witnessing a traumatic birth.
- Fathers with undiagnosed disorders or existing mental health issues.
- Lack of sleep.
- Adverse childhood experiences.
- Partner with postnatal depression.
- Financial worries & isolation.

TOP FIVE TIPS FOR MANAGING MENTAL HEALTH

1. Speak with someone or a professional. It will not impact on their employment - it's a problem if it's affecting your whole family. Early prevention means a quicker recovery.

2. Exercise and healthy eating are important.

3. Sleep is vital for good mental health - there are consultants in this field that can help as well as lots of information online.

4. Baby massage, skin to skin and being in tune with your baby will be of benefit to you too.

5. Communication with your partner and joint hobbies which will stop feelings of isolation during the transition of parenthood.

Join Mark and Louise on their *'Wellbeing Workshop'* through *Let's Talk Birth and Baby* to get you and your partner fully ready for the amazing road ahead. You can find their contact information in *'Our Experts'* on page 12.

YOUR BABY 0-6 MONTHS

DR CARLY FERTLEMAN, MD, FRCPCH, MSC, MB BCHIR, BA (HONS) CANTAB, SFHEA, FACADMED

NHS CONSULTANT PAEDIATRICIAN

So your bundle of joy has arrived, you've gotten through the first few days and now the real hard work starts! Having a baby, whether it's your first child or third, can be challenging, and while it's important to remember that all babies are different and can develop at slightly different rates, here's a rough guide of what to expect and when.

1-WEEK OLD

Your baby is already developing quickly at one week old. They'll be able to hold on to your finger and start showing strong sucking reflexes. These are automatic responses that mostly disappear until later, as baby won't be able to consciously grasp and let go of objects until around 4 months.

You'll notice that they start rooting around on your chest for milk or open their mouth if you stroke their cheek as their feeding reflex kicks in. If you can, try to understand what your baby's hungry cues are, these movements help show you that they're hungry.

Your midwife will pay you a visit in the first few days to check your baby over and take certain measurements. It is very common for newborns to lose weight in the first few days or develop jaundice, so make sure they are feeding often and getting access to sunlight.

Don't be alarmed if your baby does lose weight - it's normal. Your baby will have a heel prick test too which tests for sickle cell disease, thyroid deficiencies, cystic fibrosis, and other medical conditions that may show up after birth.

2-WEEKS

Once your baby begins putting on weight, they will gain on average 25g per day.

They will be able to recognise yours and your partners' voices, smells around them and can see roughly 25 cm in front of their face. They might try to copy your facial expressions, such as sticking your tongue out and smiling.

Their hair and nails will be growing at a rapid rate, so you may want to give their nails a little trim whilst they're asleep.

3-WEEKS

By now, your baby will be looking more stretched out and their skin will be plumper and less wrinkled. Their skull should have settled back into a rounder shape by now too. They might be sleeping a bit less than the first few days, so you can start introducing the distinction between night and day - don't try and force it by keeping your baby awake for long stretches though. You are likely to still be doing at least one- or two-night feeds.

You will notice that the amount *(and level)* of crying increases and the cause may not always be obvious. Try to work through one thing at a time; check their nappy. Are they tired? Are they hungry? Are they bored?

If your baby seems uncomfortable after feeding, they may be suffering from colic or reflux, or have an intolerance to their milk. Check with your health visitor for advice on how to help your baby with this. For many babies, these are issues which only last a few weeks.

4-WEEKS

This is an exciting time, as your baby will find their own hands and feet, normally by accident! They'll be able to grab their feet and explore their hands with their mouths. Their grip is also getting stronger too.

Your baby's hearing will have developed further, and you may see them jumping or turning their heads towards a loud sound. Your baby may start trying to follow an object with its eyes as it moves closer to them too.

Now is a good time to start some 'tummy time' to encourage your baby to lift their head and build on their arm muscles. At 4-weeks, your baby may try to turn their head from side to side but you will still need to provide plenty of support.

1-MONTH

Your baby's development will pick up once they reach one month old. You will probably hear them making noises like gurgles and grunts and they will be even more receptive to sounds. From day 0, you should have been talking to your baby. Even if you're just describing what you're doing, it all helps with their development. Some parents go with the 'baby-talk' simplified English, but many studies have shown speaking to them normally as adults, better encourages their development and ability to understand you. At 6 weeks old, you should see baby's first smile by now.

2-MONTHS

Your baby will be able to see items that are further away from them. They will still respond better to bright and bold patterns and colours and you can encourage this with sensory boards, toys, or fabric touchy-feely books.

Your baby may be able to recognise familiar voices, especially those of close family members. Look for their response to songs or noises they may have heard in the womb too!

The arm and leg kicking that your baby loves to do, will become slightly smoother in its action and they might start waving their hands and feet around. They may start showing signs of wanting to roll, so take care if you have them up high for nappy changes.

If you have long hair or wear glasses, you may find that your baby reaches for them and doesn't let go. This is because their grasping reflex is not fully developed yet and can struggle to release their grip.

Although you are a few months away from teething, you may see your baby start to drool as they begin to produce more saliva. Make sure your baby has a bib or cloth around to mop it up, as it can cause soreness on their skin.

They should be sleeping in longer blocks by now, hopefully at night, but this is not the case for everyone!

You will be asked to book in for a six-week check-up at your GP surgery and this is a check-up for both you and the baby. Your GP will take measurements of your baby and check certain things such as reflexes and feeding. They may talk to you about contraception and any mental health issues you may be experiencing. Be completely honest and don't be afraid to ask for help if you need it.

At around 8-weeks, you will be offered the first set of vaccinations for your baby. Get in touch with your health visitor or GP surgery if you haven't been contacted. The first jabs immunise against the following:

- Rotavirus – *a nasty virus that is very contagious and can cause gastroenteritis.*

- DTaP/IPV/Hib – *this one vaccinates against diphtheria, tetanus, hepatitis, whooping cough, polio, and haemophilus influenza.*

- Meningitis B – *this protects against only the meningitis B strain.*

- Pneumococcal conjugate vaccine *(PCV) – this is for pneumococcal infections such as pneumonia and bronchitis.*

3-MONTHS

Now that your baby has more control of their hands and feet, they will start reaching for and responding to different textures and materials. They may be able to accurately hit an object in front of them, such as a toy dangling on a bouncer or mobile. Their arm and leg movements will be gaining in coordination and their joints will be strengthening.

You will see your baby smile a lot more and they will be fascinated by other people, especially other children, and their own reflection.

At 12-weeks, it's time for the next round of vaccinations, which will include the second doses of the rotavirus and DtaP/IPV/Hib jabs.

4-MONTHS

Your baby's senses will be developing rapidly, and you will notice that they will test out new things by putting them in their mouth. This will include anything that they can get their hands on, including you and your clothes! Ensure that there are no small or dangerous items within reach and think about your own

jewellery and clothing. Also make sure things are sanitised regularly.

Your baby will begin to see the differences between colours now, so you can introduce them to paler colours and more complex patterns. If you have any concerns about your child's sight, even at such a young age, talk to your health visitor and they can advise on getting it checked.

You may hear the start of some letter sounds coming from your baby and they will make different sounds for different emotions. They may start to imitate noises that you make too.

Some babies can roll over at four months, either fully or partially and may start to make a *'skydive'* type pose when they're on their tummy. This is a great sign that their muscles are developing. You should still provide adequate support for their head at this age, as they may not be able to hold it independently for long periods of time.

Teething starts between 3 and 12-months old, although you might not see the first tooth pop through for another few weeks. Some common signs of teething are excess dribbling, red gums and chewing on their fist or fingers.

You may find that the number of feeds that your baby wants decreases by month four. This is nothing to worry about, as your baby will be taking on more milk at each feed. If you are worried, keep a diary of the amounts and times of each feed and talk to your health visitor.

At 16-weeks you will need to attend your last set of immunisations until your baby is one. This round includes second doses of meningitis B and pneumococcal, and the third dose of DTaP/IPV/Hib.

5-MONTHS

Your first hug from your baby comes at around 5-months and they will also be holding their arms up, wanting to be picked up. Their focus will be more developed, and they will be able to follow a slowly moving object more easily. They may cry when you move something or if they can't see it anymore. This is because they don't understand the concept of object permanence yet. They think if they can't see an object, it no longer exists, and this can be very distressing for them - this goes for when you leave the room - no games of peek-a-boo yet we're afraid.

Your baby will be rolling more and may also be able to sit up for a time if they are supported with cushions or in a baby chair. You'll find that they do fall sideways easily though.

You may hear their first laugh and the range of sounds that they have will increase, especially in response to funny faces or smiles.

When it comes to sleeping, some babies will be sleeping for a five or six-hour stretch a night at 5-months old, but there is nothing wrong with your baby if they are not doing this. They may also have reduced their daytime naps. Check your baby's sleeping across a whole 24-hour period, if they are sleeping too much or too little in the daytime, it could be impacting on their nighttime sleep. Check out our pages on sleep earlier in this book or contact our Sleep Expert, who's details can be found in *'Our Experts'* on page 12.

6-MONTHS

You can start weaning your baby from 6-months if you want to, which is the minimum guideline age from the World Health Organisation, but you still can carry on breastfeeding until 24-months alongside. Before this point, breast milk or formula is enough nutrition for them and should still form a part of their diet until at least 12-months.

You can also expand the types of sensory play and other activities you do with your baby. At this age, they will be able to focus on smaller details now, such as an intricate pattern. Your baby will be moving around more and may start crawling from 6-months, although many babies crawl from 8 or 9-months. You will see your baby try to make the movements they need to be able to crawl, so try to leave them to figure it out for themselves. Tummy time is still great for building muscle strength in their arms and legs.

You may notice that your baby is expressing preference towards certain people at this age and becoming upset

when being held by others, possibly even by you or your partner. This is very normal and may continue for a few months. Try not to play up to these preferences and demonstrate to your baby that they are safe with others and that you are never far away.

DEVELOPMENT ANXIETY

As a parent and especially for first-time parents, you may be concerned that your baby is not keeping up with the expected development for their age. This is not helped by friends or family members offering *'helpful'* advice.

Keep in mind that all babies develop at their own speed and differing abilities. There is no correlation between the age that your baby started to crawl and their achievements in adult life. Try not to make comparisons to other babies and you won't win any favours by bragging about your baby either!

Even siblings will develop at different times, so don't assume that your next baby will follow the same timeline, or your baby doesn't develop at the same rate as your first.

If you do have any concerns, talk to your health visitor, midwife, GP, or paediatrician. Dr Carly Fertleman's book *'Your Baby Week-by-Week'* has an in-depth look at what you can expect each week following baby's birth, as well as how to care for them. Details can be found in *'Our Experts'* on page 12.

TEETHING

From around 10-11 weeks in utero, your baby's tooth buds start to appear, but don't actually break through the gums until they're around 6-months old after birth. The lower teeth erupt first, with the final top teeth coming through around 20 months later. When exactly your baby will start to teethe is difficult to predict, as all babies develop at different rates. However, there are a number of *'symptoms'* or signs that suggest it may be happening soon.

TEETHING SYMPTOMS

- Dribbling
- Chin or face rash
- Coughing
- Biting
- Pain or irritability
- Fussiness when feeding
- Diarrhoea
- Elevated temperature
- Difficulty sleeping
- Rubbing their cheeks/ pulling on their ears

Some babies breeze through their teething stage with not much bother, others have a hard time with it and it can be quite distressing seeing your baby in such discomfort.

WHEN WILL MY BABY'S TEETH COME THROUGH?

Your baby's teeth will come through at different times, typically the bottom front teeth arrive first, followed by the top front teeth, giving them that adorable buck-toothed smile, but the rest will fill their grin soon enough.

Here's the general, approximate order and time frame you should expect to see their teeth grow:

6 TO 10-MONTHS - central incisor *(bottom front)*

8 TO 12-MONTHS - central incisor *(top front)*

9 TO 13-MONTHS - lateral incisor *(top font)*

10 TO 16-MONTHS - lateral incisor *(bottom front)*

13 TO 19-MONTHS - first molar *(top)*

14 TO 18-MONTHS - first molar *(bottom)*

16 TO 22-MONTHS - canine *(top)*

17 TO 23-MONTHS - canine *(bottom)*

23 TO 31-MONTHS - second molar *(top)*

25 TO 33-MONTHS - second molar *(bottom)*

HOW TO SOOTHE A TEETHING BABY

When our babies cry, we just want to take their pain away and hold them close. Teething is one of those long, drawn-out stages every child goes through, and it can be a distressing time for both you and baby, but there are some ways to alleviate some of that discomfort for baby and give your ears a little break between cries.

- Give them something to chew on. Teethers that have been put in the fridge or freezer until cold *(but not solid)* are great for babies to chew on/gum. The coldness helps soothe the gums and can help stimulate growth as they chew.

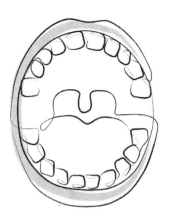

- Give them your hand. They'll be chewing on their hand most of the time during this stage, but sometimes a bigger hand and fingers can be a lot more soothing. Wash your hand thoroughly *(and trim your nails)* and use it to firmly massage your baby's gums. They'll likely bite down, but it really does help them.

- Give them some paracetamol. In some instances, teethers and hands just won't cut it and you need to crack out the painkillers. Once your baby is over 3-months old, you can give them baby paracetamol or baby ibuprofen to relieve their pain. Any teething gels are best left until you've consulted your GP due to their ingredients, however, there are also some more natural home remedies that can help.

- Chamomile is a natural anti-inflammatory, so you can dip a clean flannel in some chamomile tea and

pop it in the freezer *(not until its solid)* for your baby to suck on, or even keep it warm to room temperature for a more warm, soothing soak.

- Chilling a teething toy can also provide additional relief, but again, don't freeze it solid, as that will make it too hard for your baby's teeth and gums. If the item was in the freezer, be sure to let it thaw partially before giving it to your baby.

EDUCATIONAL TOYS

FOR YOUR BABY'S DEVELOPMENT

Whether they're aiming to be the next Einstein, or they just want a nice bit of colourful fun, your baby is going to encounter new things and learn new skills with the use of different toys and games as they grow up.

One thing many parents don't necessarily consider, is the numerous benefits that can come from getting your baby to engage with learning materials such as toys at as young an age as possible[50].

If you are looking to get your baby learning through play, the main thing you will be looking for, is toys or games that will trigger a variety of your baby's senses *(predominantly sight, touch, and hearing)*. Things that require them to move objects using their hands and arms will also help them develop a greater understanding of numerous basic skills they will need in day-to-day life.

As a result of this, the kinds of toys you are going to want to look for could include:

- Rattles
- Touchy-feely books
- A baby gym
- Learning cubes
- Shape sorting puzzles
- Toy musical instruments
- Stacking cubes or rings
- Play mats
- Bead mazes
- Mobiles
- Linkable rings
- Zip-seal bags filled with water and beads/sequins

WHEN TO INTRODUCE TOYS

You can start introducing toys such as play mats and colourful plush toys as early as 0 to 2-months. Holding a toy out in front of their face can encourage smiling, lifting, or turning their head, gurgling and other sounds, as well as making eye contact with moving objects. Tummy time can also help with this development.

From 2 to 4-months, they will be able to hold an object, such as a rattle, which encourages them to reach for items, improves their grip and release control, and their hand-eye and hand-mouth coordination as they start to explore bringing items towards their face.

Teaching object permanence with games of peek-a-boo with their toys can be introduced from around 4 to 6-months.

Most of all, spend some quality time with baby, speak to them and introduce them to as much as possible.

BABY SIGN LANGUAGE

AMY TRIBE

DEVELOPMENTAL BABY MASSAGE PRACTITIONER

Baby signing is one of the most popular activities you can do with your little one and it's easy to see why. The benefits for both parents and children are plenty - the most obvious being that it gives your baby the ability to communicate with you much earlier than they would ordinarily.

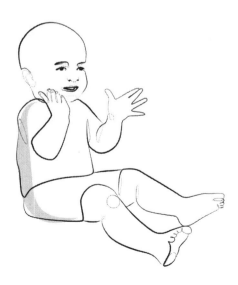

Being able to express their thoughts, feelings, when they are hungry or tired, or simply just when they need a hug, boosts self-esteem and confidence not only for them, but for you too. The ability to 'chat' with your little one encourages secure bonding and attachment to form, for both of you and this is vital to raising emotionally healthy infants.

Parents who sign with their babies will be given an insight into just how intelligent babies really are - their level of understanding from just a few months of age can be astonishing and watching their ability to communicate with you grow over time is incredibly rewarding.

There is now about two decades worth of studies supporting the use of baby signing. One of the most important studies conducted, showed 24-month-old babies to have more than a 3-month speech advantage over their peers. A year down the line, the trend continues - 36-month-old toddlers who signed as babies were talking like 47-month-olds - almost a year ahead of the average non-signing toddler[51].

WHEN TO START

Getting started with baby signing can feel daunting, but it doesn't need to be. Anyone can start signing with their baby at home. There is always a period of 'teaching' when you begin, though most parents start their journey when their little one is around 6 to 8-months old.

The advantage of starting then, is that you are likely to see engagement with signing relatively quickly, yet baby is still young enough to ensure you'll be using the sign for a while yet until they talk.

INDICATIONS THAT YOUR BABY IS READY TO START SIGNING INCLUDE:

- Pointing to things.
- Watching an object in your hands.
- An interest in picture books.
- Shaking/ nodding their head to mean yes or no.

STARTING POINTS FOR SIGNING

- Start with signs you know you'll use a lot e.g., 'eat', 'drink', 'tired' and 'mummy'.
- Try and incorporate a couple of safety signs e.g., 'hot' and 'hurt'.

- Choose signs for words your baby can't say yet e.g., *'toothbrush'* and *'cat'*.

- Pick some signs to avoid frustration e.g., *'more'*, *'all done'* and *'please'*.

- Involve everyone in the house who cares for/ interacts with baby for consistency.

Communicating with your baby as they start to figure out the world around them brings immense pleasure to both you and them - and the fun element of signing is undoubtedly why so many parents across the world are choosing to explore their baby's in-built desire to communicate.

You can sign up to one of Amy's *'Sing, Sign & Play'* classes through *Let's Talk Birth and Baby*. Contact details can be found in *'Our Experts'* on page 12. Head to our website to find out how to sign the above list and more.

YOUR BABY
6–18 MONTHS

DR CARLY FERTLEMAN, MD, FRCPCH, MSC, MB BCHIR, BA (HONS) CANTAB, SFHEA, FACADMED

NHS CONSULTANT PAEDIATRICIAN

When your baby reaches 6-months old, it's a milestone for both you and them. They'll have taken their first tastes of solid food and be moving around a lot more, perhaps even crawling by this point! It'll feel like the end of the *'newborn'* stage and the start of them being a little boy or girl.

6-MONTHS

There's a lot going on at six months and it can be overwhelming! You're likely having lots of conversations with your friends and family about weaning and you may have already started trying out some foods with your baby. There's no pressure on when you start, how you do it, or how long it takes for your baby to be eating a range of foods.

In terms of their physical development, you'll find that your baby is fascinated by the world around them. Their focus has improved so they can notice small details now and start reaching out for an experimental feel. They will love feeling different textures, like water, paper, and the grass outside. Helping your baby to experience lots of different items to touch is great for improving their attention span and curiosity, as well as practising for weaning.

Your baby's speech will be developing too, although they will only make short sounds by this stage. They will listen to everything you say and the sounds around them and will try to repeat things back. Even though you may feel a bit uncomfortable doing so, try to talk to your baby all day, such as describing what you are putting in the supermarket trolley, or what you can see on a walk. Using proper words, rather than 'baby-talk' can help develop their understanding and language skills faster.

7-MONTHS

Some babies start crawling from 6-months, with others not starting until around 9-months old. Some skip the crawling stage all-together and go straight to walking. There are lots of ways you can help your baby to start crawling, but you'll need a lot of patience. Your baby may be able to sit unsupported at this age and be able to move into a sitting position from laying down. There is likely to be a lot of rolling, so keep the floor clear.

Your baby will also be using their hands more and will be able to clap and hold an item in both hands soon. You may notice that your baby can support their weight on their legs if they are holding onto you or a piece of furniture. It's unlikely that they will be able to stand for a long time though, so make sure you are there to support them sitting down or from toppling over. Do not however, place them in a seated position on the floor unless they are easily able to get out of it by themselves, as well as being able to stay seated upright without support.

You can help strengthen your baby's legs by helping them to bounce, either in a baby jumper or with you holding their waist.

If it hasn't already started, your baby may start teething now. Look for signs such as excessive dribble, sore gums and your baby chewing furiously on objects and their fists. Teething starts with the bottom teeth and then the top ones follow soon after. You may be able to see a white patch in their gums as the tooth pushes its way through.

8-MONTHS

Your baby may be well on their way to crawling now or may have already begun, so you'll probably see lots of the 'skydive' pose. If you can, allow your baby to figure it out for themselves and develop their own crawling style. It could be a commando crawl, bum shuffle or even on their knees. Try to challenge them by placing a toy or drink slightly out of reach so that they need to move to get it.

You'll also find that your baby tries to pull themselves up, using furniture or your legs. This is part of their progression to walking. Make sure that

your baby has a soft landing if they fall and cannot reach anything inappropriate if they start to cruise along. If you have long curtains, it may be a good idea to hook them over the curtain rod or fence the area off, so your baby doesn't pull on them.

Your baby will be more expressive at this age and be able to clap at something they like. They are also able to use their fingers to pick up smaller objects, especially food that they want to eat.

Separation anxiety can kick in at this stage too, especially if you are heading back to work - again with object permanence, they don't realise you still exist if they can't see you. It's nothing to worry about and it really is just a phase. Whilst it can be very upsetting for you, stay strong and stick to your guns. You'd be surprised at how easily your baby can be distracted by something else and forget all about missing you. You can help your baby transition into childcare by sending them with items they are familiar with, or that remind them of home or you.

9-MONTHS

If your baby has started crawling, you'll notice that their speed and range of movements increases month on month. They may even be walking along with the help of a walker or holding your hands. They might try out a step or two by themselves but don't be disappointed if they don't start walking until much later. They are likely to sit down with a bump. You don't need to buy any 'proper' shoes for your baby until they are walking unaided, but it doesn't hurt for them to have some soft-sole shoes for cruising or playing outside. Make sure the footwear has plenty of room and non-slip soles. Look for slipper sock styles with sticky dots on or with suede soles.

You may hear noises from your baby that sound like real words, with mum and dad being among the first ones. At this stage, try to encourage your baby to make sounds in general, as well as speaking actual words. If your baby has a dummy, try to reduce their time with it to just naps and bedtime to encourage them to speak more.

10-MONTHS

Your baby's speech will improve month on month now, so encourage and praise them as much as possible. Make sure that you are using the correct full words so that your baby hears what they should sound like. For example, if they say part of a word, repeat back the full form word to them with some positive encouragement.

If you haven't already, it's a good idea to get some stair gates installed as your baby will be very interested in exploring upstairs or downstairs. Whilst they may be able to get up very quickly, they will not be able to make it down again safely.

At this age, your baby will take a keen interest in other babies and children, especially those older than them. They may be able to wave at you or blow you a kiss and have formed good attachments with other caregivers. Whilst your baby will not possess its full range of social skills yet, it's a good idea for them to socialise with other children as much as possible. Try to give them a bit of freedom to express themselves, but step in if there's any undesirable behaviour like biting, hitting, or hair pulling. Make sure that you are firm in expressing that you are not happy with their actions and that their other carers take the same approach too.

11-MONTHS

Following on the theme of discipline, by around 11-months your child will understand the word *'no'*, even if they don't respond in the way you'd like - cue the tantrums! They may also be able to follow simple instructions.

Your child is likely to be showing you more of their character now and becoming more independent. They may push you away if you try to help with a task, so try to be patient and wait for them to ask or signal for help. Keep describing everything you are doing, such as when you are helping your child get dressed. It's a good age to start setting some boundaries, even though it may be a few months before they are really following them.

You can encourage your child to drink from a cup by themselves and start to hold a spoon or fork. They may miss their mouth but stay positive and give them lots of praise.

They also love to throw things at this age, so beware!

12-MONTHS

Wow, you've reached your baby's first birthday! Walking unsupported is just around the corner now, so encourage your baby to keep practising their cruising and walking with your help. It is worth mentioning that babies cannot tell you when they are tired and will fall over a lot more when they are, or make strange movements, which can be very worrying.

To encourage unaided walking, kneel in front of your child. Holding their hands or elbows *(or just be there to catch them)* and allow them to walk towards you whilst you shuffle backwards. Walking behind them with their arms above their head isn't the right way to do it *(how often do you see adults walking with their hands above their head?)*. It also affects their ability to balance by themselves, as well as increasing the risk of joint dislocation, which is common amongst infants. This is also why babies and children of any age should never be lifted or swung around by their outstretched arms - even if they do find it fun.

It may be a few days or weeks before they transition fully away from crawling, but it will come. You will see that their energy levels increase, and they may be sleeping for less time during the day.

At 12-months, your child will be called for their next round of vaccinations. This round includes four different immunisations, containing Hib/MenC vaccine *(single jab containing meningitis C first dose and Hib fourth dose vaccines)*, the first dose of MMR, the third dose of pneumococcal *(PCV)*, as well as the third dose of the meningitis B vaccine. It is possible that these will be given as four separate injections, but your surgery will be able to advise on this in advance.

13 TO 15-MONTHS

As your child moves into their second year, you'll really start to see the difference from them being a baby and becoming a toddler.

Although your child may not be walking confidently by themselves yet, there's plenty of time to help them establish this. Even if they are walking, you can encourage them to walk independently to build their confidence and their leg muscles.

Your child will be becoming much more adventurous in their play now, thanks to their developing fine and gross motor skills. They will be able to pick up and move a toy easily and should be able to understand that it is still the same object that has moved, not a new one - they're finally grasping object permanence!

They will be experimenting more during playtime; bath time and mealtime so be ready for plenty of mess. If you can, head outside and play with water, bubbles, or paint, or get creative with sensory materials like rice, jelly, cooked/uncooked spaghetti, or cotton wool.

Your child's speech is expanding every week, with more words being added to their vocabulary. The words that they are confident with will sound clearer too, although some letter sounds can be tricky to master.

At around 15-months, your child will come to the end of their teething journey;

although it may be later than this if their first teeth came through late. The final teeth to emerge are the molars, which are the big teeth right at the back of the mouth. Unfortunately, due to the size and position of the molars, they do tend to cause painful teething for your child, even if they haven't had any symptoms before.

16 TO 18-MONTHS

By the time your toddler is approaching 18-months, their personality will really be shining through, and you may start to recognise some of your own traits in them too *(good and bad)* - behaviour certainly is taught.!

Some aspects will be less developed still, such as their social skills. Sharing takes a long while for your toddler to understand, particularly as an only child. You can encourage sharing at home by calmly demonstrating what kind sharing looks like. Try to encourage your child to offer you an object and understand that they have done a good deed with praise.

By 18-months, your child will have mastered around twenty words with confidence and will be *'speaking'* much more frequently. You can encourage them to expand their vocabulary with word games or singing familiar songs such as nursery rhymes. It can be useful to sing the same songs at home as your child sings at nursery or childcare. Girls have been seen to develop their speech quicker than boys, so don't be hung up on comparing your baby to others, every child develops at a different rate.

Whilst your child may have taken to weaning well, they are likely to enter a fussy phase at around 18-months. This coincides with them developing more understanding about the world around them and becoming fearful of trying new or unfamiliar things. Try not to bribe or coerce your child into eating foods they are not comfortable with. Instead, it can be helpful to offer a range of foods and let them choose or give them options to make a choice from. In this way, you are reinforcing their independence but also getting them to eat. The fussy eating stage can continue for a good few months or even years, but the majority of children do grow out of it. If you have concerns around your child's weight, or don't think they are getting enough nutrition, speak to your health visitor or GP.

If bedtime is a struggle at this age, now is a good time to start enforcing more of a routine and your child should be falling asleep by themselves. This can be a challenge, for both the child and for you, especially if you are co-sleeping or staying with your child until they fall asleep. There are plenty of approaches to try and your child should be able to understand and respond better to you explaining the situation. If you need help with sleep training, speak to our sleep expert, whose details can be found in *'Our Experts'* on page 12.

SLOW DEVELOPERS

The ages for these milestones are given as a rough guide only, as every child develops at their own pace. Even siblings will reach their milestones at different ages and in different ways.

If you are worried about any aspect of your child's development, both mentally and physically, please consult a medical professional. Dr Carly Fertleman's book *'Your Baby Week-by-Week'* has an in-depth look at what you can expect each week following baby's birth, as well as how to care for them. Details can be found in *'Our Experts'* on page 12.

WEANING

Weaning is the stage in infancy when you start introducing solid foods alongside your baby's milk requirements. The advice is not to start offering solids until your baby is around 6-months old, unless told otherwise by your health visitor or GP. At this age, their usual milk is still a vital part of their nutrition and should continue to until 12-months at least. But like we say, every baby is different, and you need to trust your instincts on when it is right for your little one once they've reached the 6-month mark[52].

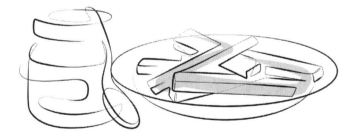

SIGNS TO START

- Can sit up well without support.

- Is developing a *'pincer'* grasp.

- Is keen to participate at mealtimes and are ready or willing to chew.

- Doesn't automatically push solids out of their mouth with their *'tongue-thrust'* reflex.

THINGS YOU'LL NEED

- Highchair - *upright and safely strapped.*

- First cup - *to sip water with their meals from open cups or free-flow cups.*

- Spoons - *rubber or plastic weaning spoons are ideal.*

- Plastic bowls - *you can get them with a suction base to keep them on the table.*

- Ice cube trays - *great for batch cooking small portions.*

- Bibs - *wipeable ones with sleeves are best at keeping baby mess-free.*

- Wipable mat - *for the 'splash zone' around your baby's highchair.*

WHICH METHOD IS BEST?

As you begin your research into this next stage of your baby's development, you'll no doubt come to learn about the different approaches to weaning such as *'baby-led weaning'* (BLW) or *'puréeing',* known as *'traditional weaning'.*

Put simply, a baby-led approach to introducing solids, is where you allow the baby to feed itself with small cuts of food. It means that food needs to be cut into chip-shaped portions so that the baby can hold it, such as cucumber sticks, tortilla, mango slices, or toast soldiers. You can even feed them anything off your own dinner plate to introduce them to a variety of textures, tastes and colours, usually making for less fussy eaters.

A more traditional weaning method is puréeing, which involves spoon-feeding the baby puréed food. This requires more preparation beforehand, such as steaming and mashing softer foods.

Neither is the *'correct'* way of weaning, you can choose either to suit you and your baby's needs. Some families prefer to buy pre-made pots or blend vegetables at home, others prefer to cook one meal for everyone and separate a tiny, cut up portion for their little one for ease. It's a completely personal preference.

HOW TO GET STARTED

It's likely best to start at early dinner time or around lunchtime when baby is not too tired and will likely be less fussy. Weaning can take some time to introduce, so don't rush it - go at a pace that suits you both - after all, it's a whole new skill for baby to learn.

It's worth noting that when you start weaning, most of their food will go on the floor rather than in their mouth, so make sure to put a mat down.

Each food has its own unique flavour and texture that baby will need to get used to, so it can take time for them to settle into weaning. Some days, they might scoff their meal, others, it may end up all on the floor, but don't worry, this is entirely normal and nothing to worry about. Make sure their other feeds *(breast or bottle)* supplement any food they don't eat when weaning and be patient.

Introduce 1 or 2 new foods at a time and pace it, they don't need a full roast dinner on day 1. Pretty soon they'll be eating off your plate!

When cleaning up baby's messy dinner time, be sure not to wipe their face too vigorously as it can make your

baby dribble more. It is best to dab their chin instead, so the reflex that stimulates salivary production isn't triggered. It's messy enough as it is, even without the extra drool!

Want to learn more about weaning? *Let's Talk Birth and Baby* run a *'Weaning Workshop'* with a paediactric dietitian to show you the best ways to wean and how to introduce your baby to a world of new foods and flavours. Details can be found in *'Our Experts'* on page 12.

ALLERGIES IN BABIES

Nearly 5% of children under 5-years old develop food allergies[53]. Most are identified during the weaning stage; others develop them a little later once they've stopped breastfeeding. It's important to keep an eye on your baby, even when they're very young to see if they have developed an intolerance or allergy to something you or they may be eating.

Allergies and intolerances in infants occur when your child's immune system reacts to certain foods. Some allergies can be mild, with stomach upset as one of the symptoms. Some allergic reactions can be severe, with swelling, rashes, vomiting and possibly even anaphylaxis if your child encounters an allergen. In contrast, intolerances are typically mild with symptoms linked to their digestive system *(diarrhoea)*.

When you start introducing solid food to your baby, it's a good idea to start introducing common allergens one at a time, in very small amounts, so that you can spot any reaction and pinpoint what food caused it.

COMMON ALLERGENS

- Wheat
- Cows' milk *(CMPA)*
- Eggs
- Nuts
- Peanuts
- Seeds
- Soya
- Shellfish
- Fish

These allergens can be introduced from around

6-months as part of your baby's weaning diet, just like any other foods. Once introduced and no allergy symptoms are presented, they should then become part of your baby's everyday diet, as to minimise the risk of future allergy or intolerance.

Gluten is also another allergen that you should look out for as it's becoming more and more common. A gluten allergy is often diagnosed as coeliacs disease. This level of sensitivity to gluten *(found within wheat, rye, and barley)* cannot be diagnosed if gluten is not in your baby's system. Therefore, it's worth noting that this shouldn't be excluded from their diet. Children also can develop an intolerance to wheat later.

You should start introducing eggs and peanuts as early in your weaning journey as possible. Delaying their introduction beyond 6 to

12-months could increase the risk of developing an allergy to them.

Some allergies are outgrown (e.g., *milk and eggs*), but peanut allergies are typically lifelong.

ALLERGY SYMPTOMS

- Vomiting & diarrhoea
- Red rash
- Facial swelling
- Wheezing/shortness of breath
- Itchy throat
- Nasal congestion
- Eyes that are red and itchy

In serious cases, foods can cause anaphylaxis and may require epinephrine to counteract the allergy. This can be life-threatening in babies and toddlers. If you believe your child is going into anaphalactic shock, call 999 immediately.

INTRODUCING ALLERGENS

If breastfeeding, two options are available if your baby develops a cow's milk allergy *(CMPA)*. This is an increasingly common allergy amongst babies. This allergy needs to be diagnosed by a doctor, where you will also be supported by a dietitian - whether you are fully and solely breastfeeding or not.

Firstly, you can cut all dairy from your diet so that it doesn't filter through to your breastmilk. Secondly, you can switch to dairy-free formula as either supplement to give them the extra calcium, or instead of breastfeeding. It is worth talking to your GP about which formula will be best so they can prescribe it.

For other allergens:

- Be sure to introduce one allergen at a time. Never give two or more new allergens to your baby in one day.

- Ensure your baby is well and not recovering from illness. If your baby has eczema, aim for the skin to be well managed/under control before starting.

- Start with a small amount and build up gradually e.g., ¼ of a teaspoon, increasing slowly over the next few days.

- Consider offering the food earlier on in the day, such as in the morning, to allow you time to monitor for any signs of a reaction during the day.

- If your baby refuses the food initially, don't despair!

Try again another day or consider mixing it into a food already tolerated and accepted. Do not force feed - allow baby to go at their own pace.

● Consider the best way of supporting your baby to consume the allergenic food - often parents find that a purée or mashed foods initially are easier for guaranteeing consumption of the allergen, compared to baby-led style finger food. This depends on your baby's skills and progress with eating.

● Once you've successfully introduced an allergenic food, it's important to keep giving it to your baby regularly. This may be easier for some foods such as wheat which is in several foods, but for options like egg and peanut, aim to incorporate in baby's diet at least once per week, but ideally up to 2 or 3 times per week.

If you're at all worried about introducing allergens or notice a reaction to food that doesn't quite fit the typical reactions list mentioned, do pay your GP or paediatrician a visit, so that they are able to help guide you through food introduction and help identify what may be causing a reaction - it could

even be unrelated to food, so it's always worth getting a medical opinion.

Keeping a food diary during this time and noting any allergens (*usually highlighted in bold in the ingredients list if using ore-made purées, sachets, or pouches*), when they were consumed, and the type of reaction could be really helpful. This helps doctors identify the causes, type of allergy and can greatly help with any treatment.

TRADITIONAL WEANING RECIPES

If you happen to be struggling for new and interesting ideas to help you with weaning your little one via the traditional purée method, here are our top five tried and tested traditional weaning recipes which you can try yourself without any stress:

CELERIAC, CARROT AND APPLE PURÉE

INGREDIENTS:

- ½ celeriac, peeled and cut up into chunks
- 3 regular carrots, peeled and cut into chunks
- 2 apples *(eating not cooking, e.g., granny smiths, braeburn, gala, pink lady)* peeled, cored, and cut into chunks

METHOD:

Steam the ingredients over water for around 15 minutes or until they become tender *(whichever occurs first).*

Blitz into a purée, adding milk if needed to increase the smoothness of the texture.

APPLE AND BANANA PURÉE

INGREDIENTS:

- 2 apples *(eating not cooking)* peeled, cored, and sliced into chunks
- 1 banana, peeled and cut into chunks

METHOD:

Steam the ingredients for around 8 minutes or until soft.

Blitz until at the desired consistency.

TIP: As your child gets older, try mashing rather than blitzing the ingredients

APPLE AND BLUEBERRY STEW

INGREDIENTS:

- An eating apple peeled, cored, and cut into chunks
- 60g of frozen blueberries
- 150ml water

METHOD:

Put ingredients into a saucepan and add the water.

Cook for around 10 minutes or until the apple and blueberries are completely soft.

Pour the mixture into a bowl, stir, and then wait for it to cool before serving.

COURGETTE AND CAULIFLOWER PURÉE

INGREDIENTS:

- 200g of courgette peeled and chopped

- 100g of cauliflower florets

METHOD:

Cook the cauliflower florets in boiling water for around 12 minutes until they are soft, before draining them and setting them aside.

Steam the chopped courgette for around 8 minutes, before combining the vegetables and blending them until you reach the desired consistency.

Add cheese if you want to add some extra flavour to the dish.

LEEK AND POTATO

INGREDIENTS:

- 1 potato peeled and chopped

- 1 leek washed and diced

- 2 tablespoons of milk

METHOD:

Bring a pan of water to the boil. Add the chopped potatoes for around 10 minutes on a high temperature.

Add the diced leek to the pan before cooking for another 5 minutes.

Once the ingredients are soft, drain and mash the ingredients before letting it cool to serve.

If the mixture is too thick before serving, add the milk.

BABY-LED WEANING IDEAS

Baby-led weaning *(BLW)* can be a difficult balancing act in finding the right foods. Avoiding the pitfalls and worrying about allergies can be a stressful business. On the next page, you'll find a rundown of everything you should know, as well as some great starting foods for trying BLW.

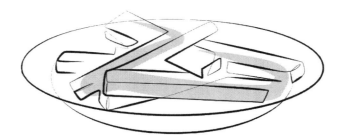

Once you start BLW, you don't need to be quick with introducing solids. Instead, try starting only offering solids once a day and then increase this as your child shows they want or need more.

When it comes to what foods to give them, the firsts foods you choose should be along the lines of fresh fruit, soft, cooked vegetables and healthy carbohydrates and fats. If you can provide a selection, your little one should be naturally capable of choosing the foods that meet their needs.

On the flip side, some of the food types you should avoid include stimulants such as sugar or chocolate, unhealthy or processed food, any food with extra or added table salt or sugar and foods with higher choking risk such as grapes, popcorn, and nuts.

FOODS TO TRY

- Avocados
- Sweet potato
- Pumpkin
- Soft, cooked carrots, apples, and beets
- Banana

Always remember when trying BLW, to always supervise your child and let them be the one to pick up and put the food in their mouths to avoid risks of choking and encourage independence.

MEAL IDEAS

- Apple fritters
- Avocado on toast fingers
- Cucumber and carrot sticks with hummus
- Roasted sweet potato, carrots, and parsnips
- Fruit salad
- Peanut butter on apple slices
- Pancakes with fruit
- Porridge or yoghurt with fruit
- Curried meat with rice
- Macaroni cheese
- Mini quiche
- Flapjacks

BABY'S FIRST WORDS

One of your baby's most important milestones and definitely one you'll want to try and get on camera - your baby's first words are precious. Many parents long to hear the words '*mama*' or '*dada*' come out of their baby's mouth amongst all the other gargles and giggles but sometimes babies come out with the most unexpected words, so careful what you say around them!

Getting your baby to pick up on language starts very early on, recognising your voices and reacting as a small infant, making sounds themselves and finally, when they're able to say a word and understand its meaning. It can take a few months of vocal experimentation until they get the order of vowels and consonants round the right way. This can be seen as early as 8-months old, however, some children don't start talking until they've passed their second birthday. Every child is different. Once they do hit this milestone though, you'll never be able to get them to be quiet!

Some common first words can include 'dada', 'mama', 'bye-bye', 'no', 'hi', 'ball', 'dog' and other one or two syllable, repetitive sounding words.

Much before they're able to say words, they will understand them. The best way to encourage your baby's first words, is simply to speak to them, a lot! Narrate your day, talk to them in simple words and point at objects and people as you say their name. Have conversations as if they are talking back and watch to see if they respond by way of facial expressions, movements, sounds, or even words! When they do make an audible sound, make sure you respond positively, with a smile and show you are listening, this encourages them to try again[54].

Singing songs and reading books is also a great way to get your child picking up on words. Repetition is key. Make sure you listen out for half-words, your baby may not be able to say all the syllables or letters yet, so words they want to say may be shortened or changed slightly until they're able to pick up the full word.

If you think you know what they are saying, repeat the full word back to them. This helps them learn the right way to say it, they may even repeat it back to you.

BABYPROOFING

Once your little one enters your home, it will be sooner than you think before they start crawling and eventually walking their way around your humble abode. To that end, it is essential to make sure that there is nothing they could bump their little body on, causing unnecessary stress for both you and your baby.

A simple way to start this process, is by getting on your hands and knees *(yes you heard us correctly!)* and crawling around your house to find any ground-level risks and hazards to consider, as there is more down there to consider than you may believe.

SAFETY MUST-HAVES:

☐ Smoke and carbon monoxide detectors

☐ Door and cupboard latches and locks

☐ Non-slip pads

☐ Corner bumpers

☐ First aid kit

☐ Safety tassels or cord stops *(for curtains and blinds that use looped cords)*

☐ Baby gates

WAYS TO PREPARE YOUR HOME:

- Move furniture in front of low plug sockets.

- Tuck away or completely hide electrical cables.

- Move wobbly objects *(lamps, TVs, vases, etc.)* out of reach or steady them appropriately *(e.g., floor lamps behind furniture).*

- Keep smaller household items out of baby's reach

(purses, electricals, baby wipes).

- Check that none of your plants are dangerous to small children and potted plants are out of reach.

GOOD LUCK!

BABY'S FIRST STEPS

One of the biggest milestones in early parenthood, is the day you get to see your little bundle of joy take their first steps. This day is something which brings many to ask, *"when will it actually happen?"*

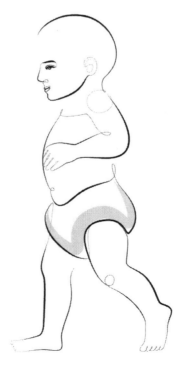

When it comes to your baby walking, there are a few stages they will go through before their big day, these stages being:

- Rolling over
- Crawling
- Standing

These stages will usually occur over their first twelve months in the real world, but they can occur sooner than this as it all depends on how quickly their muscle strength develops. Most infants begin walking at around 12 months[55].

One thing you may begin to see throughout these stages, is your baby begin to try things such as pulling themselves to a standing position and crouching or 'bouncing' in this position. These are signs that your little one is getting ready to take those wonderful first few steps.

If you want to speed this process along a bit, some things you can do which can help with this could be:

- Buy a push along toy/baby walker (e.g., trolleys, carts).
- Make them try reaching for a toy whilst holding onto a nearby piece of furniture.

- Encourage 'cruising' along or between pieces of furniture.

As mentioned before, to encourage unaided walking, do not walk behind them holding their arms above their head, as it affects their ability to balance by themselves, as well as increasing the risk of joint dislocation.

Depending on your baby's development, these steps can result in your little one walking on their own anywhere between 12 and 18-months old, but this can be longer for some babies. This would be nothing to worry about, so get ready. Once they get started, they won't ever seem to stop!

STOPPING BREASTFEEDING

When you want to stop breastfeeding your baby, is totally up to you and your baby however, the World Health Organisation *(WHO)* and UNICEF recommend that babies are exclusively breastfed until at least 6 months old[38] and ideally continued alongside solids until 2 years old or beyond. Whenever you decide is the right time to stop breastfeeding, it is important that doing so is done gradually to allow your body to adapt and reduce the risk of engorgement and/or infection. This will also help your baby with the adjustment.

COMMON REASONS TO STOP:

- You just want to.
- Sore or painful breasts.
- Low milk supply.
- Lifestyle changes *(e.g., going back to work)*.
- Going on holiday.
- Change in childcare situation.
- Illness or medications that can affect milk.

The *'National Breastfeeding Helpline'* can help you if you're unsure of when to stop. You can call them on 0300 100 0212 *(every day, 9.30 am to 9.30 pm)*.

There's no correct way or foolproof method to stop breastfeeding. Stopping breastfeeding should happen gradually, rather than going cold turkey and can take a few weeks or months to stop completely while your baby begins replacing feeds with solid foods.

HOW TO STOP

Babies don't just breastfeed for food, but for comfort too. Phasing out your feeds gently will allow baby time to get used to the idea and will also prevent your breasts from being engorged, as well as prevent mastitis.

Drop 1 feed at a time. It doesn't matter which you drop first, so its whatever fits in best with you whether that's your night feed or dinner that's swapped. Many mothers prefer to keep the night feeds until last, as the tryptophan in breastmilk *(that turns into melatonin)* makes them sleepy and helps them settle.

Once you've dropped one, you can then start thinking about dropping another and another until you've stopped altogether.

Some women choose to transition to formula or alternate/combine both breast and formula feeding at this point. If combining, wait until you've fully established your milk supply. The reduction in feeds may prevent your milk from coming in. If you wish to transition, you can start by combining, or alternating bottle and breastfeeds. This again can be done over time and any changes in your baby's weight should be noted. When replacing breastfeeding with traditional or baby-led weaning, you can replace their feeds with wholesome meals filled with nutrients, carbohydrates, rich proteins, and fats.

STARTING AGAIN AFTER STOPPING

Stopping breastfeeding doesn't have to be permanent. Starting again can take a lot of time however and regaining the same level of milk supply can be hard. How well-established your milk supply was already, can determine your success in bringing it back once you've stopped.

TO START AGAIN

Stimulate your breasts the way you would if hand-expressing *(covered earlier in the book)* and offer your breast to your baby regularly. This will encourage your body to start making milk again. Regular skin-to-skin contact can also promote milk production too.

Whichever way you choose to stop, start, or transition away from breastfeeding, if you run into any issues or aren't sure about the whole process, or your baby just doesn't want to give up the boob, talk to your health visitor or a lactation consultant as they can offer further advice and help guide you along this journey.

POTTY TRAINING

Ah, potty training. Another messy milestone you encounter as a parent. Unfortunately, it's not something with a set timestamp or process. You don't necessarily know when you will start, or how it will go, but what you do know, is that there is a load of things to consider and an impending mess if it goes wrong. So here are some starting points to consider:

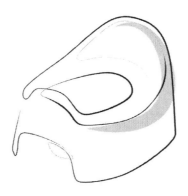

HAVE A STRATEGY

Potty or training seat? Make a list of all the questions you might have about training, get an answer that works for your situation, stick with it, and get everything you need to fulfil it. This can mean different accessories, pull-ups instead of nappies, numerous potties around the house and more, but being equipped means you are ready for anything.

BE PATIENT

Potty training can take time. By waiting until they demonstrate they are ready, the actual training can take less time. If you need to use a slightly longer approach, why not try getting them used to being around a potty or toilet and in a bathroom setting. Make it fun with toys and games to make it seem like less of a daunting or unfamiliar object. You could even get them to sit on the potty next to you when you go to the toilet to show them what to do.

When they are ready, one technique thought to be effective, is going nappy-free. This gets your baby familiar with the idea of needing the toilet, as well as having an accident if they don't make it! The one downside to this, is you need a safe place to do this, ideally somewhere without a carpet, somewhere with hard, moppable flooring for easy clean up.

PREPARE FOR ACCIDENTS

Accidents are an inevitability. As a result, make sure to have several cleaning kits ready for any situation and maybe stash away any nice cushions, rugs, or blankets that may be the unfortunate victims of the puddle, until your little one is a bit more prepared!

Encourage your child to be open about having accidents, make sure they know telling you is okay, as I'm sure you'd rather know, than find yourself unknowingly sat on a pee-soaked surface.

By following this advice, you should have the basic knowledge needed to keep a cool head and hopefully, a clean floor!

CREATE A ROUTINE

If they wake with a dry nappy, sit them straight on the potty, as well as around 45 minutes after having a feed or drink. Only put them on the potty for a few minutes at a time.

NURSERY VS. CHILDCARE

One decision you may not have even considered properly if you're unable to have a parent working from home, is whether you want to be putting your baby into a nursery or whether instead, you would use at-home childcare. To help you make your mind up, here is a quick breakdown of the benefits and drawbacks of each.

NURSERY

One of the guaranteed benefits of a nursery setting for your child is that it is a great social environment for them to be in with other children their own age, and different stimulants to keep them occupied.

Some of the limitations of a nursery setting however, are that they can be an expensive option, especially if you have multiple children. The set opening hours also means there are limitations to the number of hours parents can work in a day. There is a benefit however, to the open hours drawback, as by having this, it gives your little one a clear introduction to the idea of a routine. With the nursery option, also comes several necessary discussions or thoughts, as you will need to consider whether you want the nursery to be close to home, close to you or your partner's place of work or whether you want to be travelling long distances to nursery each day.

CHILDCARE

With childcare or a childminder, the main benefit found, that is the more intimate and unique an experience your child has, the more of a positive impact this has on their ability to create healthy emotional attachments and relationships with people in future. This is something less likely to happen in a nursery setting.

Some of the benefits parents will notice from a childminder, are that they are more than likely to be cheaper, as well as being able to provide a greater amount of flexibility surrounding your working hours and when you would need to drop off or pick up your child or have them work in your own home.

Some parents also find that childminders are much easier to talk to about their child and consequently, are more at ease about their progress and health, as well as the simple fact of leaving their child with someone they have vetted and can trust.

Whichever option you choose, make sure you think about it carefully. Discussing it with your partner ensures you are both comfortable and prepared.

SEPARATION ANXIETY

More often than not, babies and toddlers get very clingy to one parent, or both and will start to cry if separated from them, even for a short time[56]. This is particularly difficult when it comes to leaving your child with family for the day or starting nursery and preschool. As your baby develops, they start recognising faces but don't learn object permanence until around 7-months. Essentially, they don't realise that you still exist if they can't see you. So, leaving the room can feel like you're gone forever until they develop this understanding.

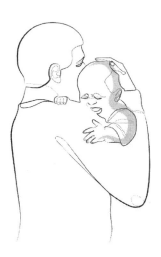

Sometimes, their confusion and anxiety about not being able to see you, or not recognising who they're with, can go on for a few years, but it's incredibly common and is something they usually grow out of.

As babies grow more aware of their surroundings, they will realise they don't feel safe without their *'protectors'* with them and makes them feel upset, resulting in lots of tears. This can include situations where you're with someone new, for example, a preschool teacher, even if you're there. This fear kicks in and so it's important that you're able to make it as positive a situation as possible, so they feel safe and secure either on their own in their cot or leaving them in day-care.

DEALING WITH IT

We know how gut-wrenching it is to hear your child upset and the mothering instincts kick in and you just want to wrap your arms around them and tell them it's okay. There are, however, some simple ways to make sure they will be okay when you're not with them.

Mums can get separation anxiety too! It's completely natural for you to feel anxious without your baby and them without you, so try not to feel guilty. It's a sign of just how well you and your little one has bonded!

The key is to focus on positive reinforcement and helping your baby deal with their feelings and better understand them. They need to learn that they will be perfectly okay if you leave them or leave the room. By leaving your baby with another caregiver regularly, you won't mentally scar them. You'll be helping them learn to cope without you, which is an important step towards independence.

TIPS

1. PRACTISE SEPARATION FOR A SHORT TIME

To start, you can leave them with a family member or friend, someone they know well, for a few minutes while you leave the room. Gradually work towards longer separations. The next step is to start leaving them in less familiar settings, such as a friend's house. Again, starting off with short separations and working up to longer periods.

2. TELL THEM WHAT YOU'LL DO TOGETHER WHEN YOU SEE THEM LATER

Talking about what you'll do together once you're back, is a good way to give them something to look forward to, as well as being given the reassurance that you are, in fact, coming back. For example, you could say: *"When mummy picks you up later, we can go to the park! Doesn't that sound like fun?"*

3. LEAVE THEM WITH THEIR COMFORTER OR SOMETHING OF YOURS

It can be a great comfort to your baby to have something that they associate with you or something that brings them comfort - like something that smells like you, or their favourite toy or blankie. This can help reassure them while you are away.

4. TURN SAYING 'GOODBYE' INTO A POSITIVE

Leaving your baby is hard, even for 5 minutes, but despite what you feel, have a smile on your face, wave and say *'see you later'* in a confident, happy tone. Saying goodbye sometimes has a negative effect, so *'see you later'* can help them understand that you're coming back.

EXTERNAL SUPPORT

Until babies can pick up on object permanence and trust that they will be safe wherever they are, whomever they're with *(excluding stranger danger of course)* it's important not to let their anxiety prevent them from experiencing new things like having a sleepover at auntie's house, or spending a day making friends at nursery. It most certainly shouldn't stop you from getting on with your life either and things you need to do, such as go to work or do a food shop without your baby.

If their separation anxiety doesn't fade and is causing them a lot of distress and they don't just snap out of it a few minutes after you've left, talk to your GP or paediatrician and they can help you with some techniques, or even some therapy to help you both take this important step towards their independence.

WHEN TO ASK FOR HELP

We hope that reading this book has helped you prepare yourself for pregnancy, birth and beyond. We hope some of those nerves you've been feeling in preparation for your big day have begun to settle and you're feeling more confident about the parenting journey that lies ahead of you.

If you still have any questions surrounding conceiving, issues with breastfeeding, what to do and avoid throughout the pregnancy, birth and beyond, or other general queries, then why not get your questions answered. You can submit your questions to our 'Ask the Fans' Facebook postings to get advice from other parents or get an expert's opinion by jumping onto one of our Instagram and Facebook live events or Q&As to give you the most comprehensive answers possible.

Remember to contact your midwifery team throughout your pregnancy, if you experience any of the following symptoms:

- Unusual or severe cramping.

- Unexpected changes in the movement of your baby.

- Difficulty breathing.

- Bleeding.

- Leaking fluid.

- A high temperature.

- Persistent and/or severe vomiting.

- Persistent and/or severe diarrhoea.

- Fainting or dizziness.

Don't forget, we have a team of experts on hand to answer your pregnancy and baby questions. However, if you are worried about your personal health or pregnancy the place to go is your midwife of GP. If you have any questions about any of the topics covered in this book, please contact the relevant experts, whose details can be found in 'Our Experts' on page 12.

If you are unsure as to whether a symptom you or your baby is feeling is serious, contact your doctor, as this will allow early identification of any issues (if there are any) or you will be reassured that everything is OK.

SOURCES

1. Radochova V, Stepan M, Kacerovska Musilova I, Slezak R, Vescicik P, Menon R, et al. Association between periodontal disease and preterm prelabour rupture of membranes. J Clin Periodontol. 2019;46(2):189–96.

2. Weng X, Odouli R, Li D-K. Maternal caffeine consumption during pregnancy and the risk of miscarriage: a prospective cohort study. Am J Obstet Gynecol. 2008;198(3):279.e1-8.

3. Factors affecting fertility [Internet]. Fertilitynetworkuk.org. 2018 [cited 2021 Jul 14]. Available from: https://fertilitynetworkuk.org/fertility-faqs/factors-affecting-fertility/

4. Shettles LB. How to choose the sex of your baby. New York, NY, USA: Bantam Doubleday Dell Publishing Group; 2006.

5. Whelan. Boy or Girl. Pocket Books; 1983.

6. Rooney KL, Domar AD. The relationship between stress and infertility. Dialogues Clin Neurosci. 2018;20(1):41–7.

7. Infertility [Internet]. Nhs.uk. [cited 2021 Jul 14]. Available from: https://www.nhs.uk/conditions/infertility/

8. Pelvic inflammatory disease [Internet]. Nhs.uk. [cited 2021 Jul 14]. Available from: https://www.nhs.uk/conditions/pelvic-inflammatory-disease-pid/

9. Fibroids [Internet]. Nhs.uk. [cited 2021 Jul 14]. Available from: https://www.nhs.uk/conditions/fibroids

10. Zondervan KT, Becker CM, Missmer SA. Endometriosis. N Engl J Med. 2020;382(13):1244–56.

11. Irregular periods and getting pregnant [Internet]. Webmd.com. [cited 2021 Jul 14]. Available from: https://www.webmd.

com/infertility-and-reproduction/irregular-periods-and-getting-pregnant

12. Infertility [Internet]. Org.uk. [cited 2021 Jul 14]. Available from: https://cks.nice.org.uk/topics/infertility/

13. Fertility problems: assessment and treatment | Guidance | NICE. [cited 2021 Jul 14]; Available from: https://www.nice.org.uk/guidance/cg156/chapter/context

14. Murdock C. IVF attrition rate: Why don't all eggs create embryos? [Internet]. Rmact.com. [cited 2021 Jul 14]. Available from: https://www.rmact.com/fertility-blog/ivf-attrition-rate

15. How much does IVF cost in the UK? [Internet]. Abcivf.co.uk. [cited 2021 Jul 14]. Available from: https://www.abcivf.co.uk/how-much-does-ivf-cost-uk

16. Government Digital Service. Surrogacy: legal rights of parents and surrogates [Internet]. Gov.uk. GOV.UK; 2012 [cited 2021 Jul 14]. Available from: http://www.gov.uk/rights-for-surrogate-mothers

17. How much does surrogacy cost? [Internet]. Brilliantbeginnings.co.uk. 2020 [cited 2021 Jul 14]. Available from: https://www.brilliantbeginnings.co.uk/how-much-does-surrogacy-cost/

18. Smith GC. Use of time to event analysis to estimate the normal duration of human pregnancy. Hum Reprod. 2001;16(7):1497–500.

19. Corps D. Births in England and wales - office for national statistics [Internet]. Gov.uk. Office for National Statistics; 2020 [cited 2021 Jul 14].

20. Care Quality Commission. NHS Patient Survey Programme : 2019 survey of women's experiences of maternity care : Statistical release. Qual Eng. 2002;14(4):531–7.

21. Morris JK, Wald NJ, Mutton DE, Alberman E. Comparison of models of maternal age-specific risk for Down syndrome live births. Prenat Diagn. 2003;23(3):252–8.

22. NHS website. What happens if your baby is breech? [Internet]. Nhs.uk. [cited 2021 Jul 14]. Available from: https://www.nhs.uk/pregnancy/labour-and-birth/what-happens/if-your-baby-is-breech

23. Bustos M, Venkataramanan R, Caritis S. Nausea and

vomiting of pregnancy - What's new? Auton Neurosci. 2017;202:62–72.

24. NHS website. Severe vomiting in pregnancy [Internet]. Nhs.uk. [cited 2021 Jul 14]. Available from: https://www.nhs.uk/pregnancy/related-conditions/complications/severe-vomiting/

25. Mitchell-Jones N, Lawson K, Bobdiwala S, Farren JA, Tobias A, Bourne T, et al. Association between hyperemesis gravidarum and psychological symptoms, psychosocial outcomes and infant bonding: a two-point prospective case-control multicentre survey study in an inner city setting. BMJ Open. 2020;10(10):e039715.

26. Healthy eating [Internet]. Nhs.uk. [cited 2021 Jul 14]. Available from: https://www.nhs.uk/start4life/pregnancy/healthy-eating-pregnancy

27. Stacey T, Thompson JMD, Mitchell EA, Ekeroma AJ, Zuccollo JM, McCowan LME. Association between maternal sleep practices and risk of late stillbirth: a case-control study. BMJ. 2011;342(jun14 1):d3403.

28. Littleboy K. Birth characteristics in England and Wales - Office for National Statistics [Internet]. Gov.uk. Office for National Statistics; 2019 [cited 2021 Jul 14].

29. NHS website. Stretch marks in pregnancy [Internet]. Nhs.uk. [cited 2021 Jul 14]. Available from: https://www.nhs.uk/pregnancy/related-conditions/common-symptoms/stretch-marks/

30. Solomons E. Caesarean section. Am J Obstet Gynecol. 1962;84(6):839.

31. Al-Zirqi I, Stray-Pedersen B, Forsén L, Vangen S. Uterine rupture after previous caesarean section: Uterine rupture. BJOG. 2010;117(7):809–20.

32. Jain S, Eedarapalli P, Jamjute P, Sawdy R. Symphysis pubis dysfunction: a practical approach to management. Obstet Gynaecol. 2006;8(3):153–8.

33. Gottesman N, Riley L, Meyers MF. 40 weeks pregnant and beyond: What to do when you're overdue [Internet]. Parents.com. Parents; 2009 [cited 2021 Jul 14]. Available from: https://www.parents.com/pregnancy/giving-birth/preparing-for-labor/when-youre-overdue/

34. Care of women presenting with suspected preterm prelabour rupture of membranes from 24+0 weeks of gestation [Internet]. Org.uk. [cited 2021 Jul 14]. Available from: https://www.rcog.org.uk/en/guidelines-research-services/guidelines/gtg73/

35. Galliers L. i-Size car seat regulations come into force [Internet]. Which? 2015 [cited 2021 Jul 14]. Available from: https://www.which.co.uk/news/2015/04/i-size-car-seat-regulations-come-into-force-399945/

36. What is a rear facing car seat & why are they safer? [Internet]. Incarsafetycentre.co.uk. [cited 2021 Jul 14]. Available from: https://incarsafetycentre.co.uk/safety-centre/what-is-rear-facing

37. The Lullaby Trust. Safer Sleep for Babies Factsheet 9: Car Seat Fact Sheet [Internet]. 2019 [cited 2021 Jul 14]. Available from: https://www.lullabytrust.org.uk/wp-content/uploads/9-car-seat-factsheet-2019-09-09-1.pdf

38. Exclusive breastfeeding for six months best for babies everywhere [Internet]. Who.int. [cited 2021 Jul 14].

Available from: https://www.who.int/news/item/15-01-2011-exclusive-breastfeeding-for-six-months-best-for-babies-everywhere

39. Cutting down on plastic, one nappy at a time [Internet]. Foe.scot. 2018 [cited 2021 Jul 14]. Available from: https://foe.scot/cutting-down-plastic-nappy/

40. Canter L. Nappies: which are best – disposables or reusables? The guardian [Internet]. 2015 Jul 4 [cited 2021 Jul 14]; Available from: http://www.theguardian.com/money/2015/jul/04/nappies-which-best-disposables-reusables-cost-ethics

41. Atkin E. Biodegradable nappies: are they actually better for the environment? [Internet]. Madeformums.com. MadeForMums; 2019 [cited 2021 Jul 14]. Available from: https://www.madeformums.com/reviews/do-biodegradable-nappies-biodegrade/

42. NHS website. Reduce the risk of sudden infant death syndrome (SIDS) [Internet]. Nhs.uk. [cited 2021 Jul 14]. Available from: https://www.nhs.uk/conditions/baby/caring-for-a-

newborn/reduce-the-risk-of-sudden-infant-death-syndrome/

43. Dummies and SIDS [Internet]. Org.uk. [cited 2021 Jul 14]. Available from: https://www.lullabytrust.org.uk/safer-sleep-advice/dummies-and-sids/

44. The Lullaby Trust. How to reduce the risk of SIDS for your baby [Internet]. [cited 2021 Jul 14]. Available from: https://www.lullabytrust.org.uk/safer-sleep-advice/

45. Did you know that #colic is a very common condition affecting 1 in 5 babies? Find out how to soothe a colicky baby [Internet]. Nhs.uk. [cited 2021 Jul 14]. Available from: https://www.nhs.uk/start4life/baby/breastfeeding/breastfeeding-challenges/colic/

46. Hegar B, Dewanti NR, Kadim M, Alatas S, Firmansyah A, Vandenplas Y. Natural evolution of regurgitation in healthy infants. Acta Paediatr. 2009;98(7):1189–93.

47. Dr Lynn Thomas, MStJ, BSc, MBBS, MA, FRCP. Choking baby first aid [Internet]. St. John's Ambulance. 2021 [cited 2021 Jul 14]. Available from: https://www.sja.org.uk/get-advice/first-aid-advice/choking/baby-choking/

48. Overview - Postnatal depression [Internet]. Nhs.uk. [cited 2021 Jul 14]. Available from: https://www.nhs.uk/mental-health/conditions/post-natal-depression/overview/

49. Ramchandani PG, Stein A, O'connor TG, Heron J, Murray L, Evans J. Depression in men in the postnatal period and later child psychopathology: A population cohort study. J Am Acad Child Adolesc Psychiatry. 2008;47(4):390–8.

50. Muentener P, Herrig E, Schulz L. The efficiency of infants' exploratory play is related to longer-term cognitive development. Front Psychol. 2018;9:635.

51. Goodwyn SW, Acredolo LP, Brown CA. Impact of symbolic gesturing on early language development. J Nonverbal Behav. 2000;24(2):81–103.

52. Foote KD, Marriott LD. Weaning of infants. Arch Dis Child. 2003;88(6):488–92

53. Wilbanks S. Food Allergies in Children. J Nurse Pract. 2014;10(9):761.

54. NHS website. Help your baby learn to talk [Internet]. Nhs.uk. [cited 2021 Jul 14]. Available from: https://www.nhs.uk/conditions/baby/babys-development/play-and-learning/help-your-baby-learn-to-talk/

55. Schweizerischer Nationalfonds zur Foerderung der wissenschaftlichen Forschung. Child development: Early walker or late walker of little consequence. Science Daily. 2013 Mar 28 [cited 2021 Jul 14];

56. DC Department of Behavioral Health, Prevention and Early Intervention Programs, Healthy Futures. Understanding Separation Anxiety in Infants and Young Children: OSSE 2016 Infant and Toddler Conference. 2016 May.

WITH THANKS

Your Baby Club is made up of a small team, all striving to help parents and parents-to-be with one of the biggest events in their lives. We pulled together the best offers, discounts, freebies, and competitions, as well as dedicating their days finding and writing tips, tricks, and advice on YourBabyClub.co.uk to ensure no parent is left in the dark with anything conception, pregnancy, or baby related.

Using bloggers, real parents, and experts, we were able to write *Your Baby Bible: The Ultimate Guide to Having a Baby* to make that journey towards parenthood that little bit easier.

Here, we give thanks to those who made this book possible:

Louise Broadbridge & Our Experts

Jasmine Gurney - Head of Content & Social

Raphael Marsh - Creative Director

Robert Dunne - Content Marketing Executive

Laura Driver - Social Media Manager

Eemaan Beardon - Design and Operations Executive

Illustrations by Aleksandra Godlevska

Cover by Anna Claudia Bovi Diamond

THANKS FOR READING

Printed in Great Britain
by Amazon

17086506R00215